THE
EVERYTHING®
Guide to
Personal Finance for Single Mothers

Dear Reader,

After an acrimonious divorce, I raised my daughter and son virtually alone for fifteen years. I have faced the challenges you face, and I conquered most of them. My children and I weathered several financial downturns and learned valuable lessons about personal finance, inventiveness, and frugal living. What I want you to gain from this book—which Robert and I have labored to make highly informative, relevant, and understandable—is that you can be the pilot of your own financial ship. You can master the language and the skills required to navigate what may appear to be choppy financial waters, and you can establish habits that will make it entirely possible for you to build a healthy and wealthy life for yourself and your children. I hold fond hopes and dreams for you, my many soul sisters who strive so very, very hard to raise children under difficult financial circumstances and to whom I say, "Take the reins of your financial fate, educate yourself, act decisively, invest in your future, live long, and prosper."

Susan Reynolds
Robert Bexton, CFA

The EVERYTHING® Series

Editorial

Publisher	Gary M. Krebs
Director of Product Development	Paula Munier
Managing Editor	Laura M. Daly
Associate Copy Chief	Sheila Zwiebel
Acquisitions Editor	Lisa Laing
Development Editor	Jessica LaPointe
Associate Production Editor	Casey Ebert

Production

Director of Manufacturing	Susan Beale
Production Project Manager	Michelle Roy Kelly
Prepress	Erick DaCosta Matt LeBlanc
Design and Layout	Heather Barrett Brewster Brownville Colleen Cunningham Jennifer Oliveira
Cover Design	Erin Alexander Stephanie Chrusz Frank Rivera

THE
EVERYTHING®
GUIDE TO
PERSONAL
FINANCE
FOR
SINGLE
MOTHERS

A step-by-step plan for achieving
financial independence

Susan Reynolds and Robert Bexton, CFA.

Adams Media
Avon, Massachusetts

This book is dedicated to all single mothers who are working diligently to create a brighter future for themselves and their children; also to my former advisor, Jan Berry Kadrie; my sister, Rozanne Reynolds, as well as my soul sisters, Paula Munier, Gale Giorgi, and Wanda Whalen, all of whom raised fabulous children, virtually alone; and my children, Brooke and Brett Aved, who inspired this single mother and made it all worthwhile.

An Everything® Series Book.
Everything® and everything.com® are registered trademarks of F+W Publications, Inc.

Published by Adams Media, an F+W Publications Company
57 Littlefield Street, Avon, MA 02322 U.S.A.
www.adamsmedia.com

ISBN 10: 1-59869-248-8
ISBN 13: 978-1-59869-248-8

Printed in the United States of America.

J   I   H   G   F   E   D   C   B   A

Library of Congress Cataloging-in-Publication Data

Reynolds, Susan.
 The everything guide to personal finance for single mothers / Susan Reynolds and Robert Bexton.
  p. cm. — (An everything series book)
 ISBN-13: 978-1-59869-248-8 (pbk.)
 ISBN-10: 1-59869-248-8 (pbk.)
 1. Finance, Personal—Handbooks, manuals, etc. 2. Women—Finance, Personal—Handbooks, manuals, etc. 3. Single mothers. I. Bexton, Robert. II. Title.
 HG179.R429 2007
 332.0240086'947—dc22   2007001121

This book is available at quantity discounts for bulk purchases.
For information, please call 1-800-289-0963.

Contents

Acknowledgments

We wish to thank Paula Munier, Lisa Laing, and Jessica LaPointe at Adams Media for their professional contributions; Brian Ballerini for his consultation and networking skills; Margie Myers and Kenny Harris for moral support and consultation; the San Francisco Public Library and Borders in Emeryville, California, for the endless cups of coffee and loan of many books.

Top Ten Ways to Improve Your Finances

1. Stop hiding, and own up to your real circumstances. You can't change your financial situation if you don't look your present circumstances straight in the eye.

2. Create a game plan to get your finances in order.

3. Reduce credit card debt and avoid falling back into that black hole.

4. Become and remain financially conscious.

5. Reduce expendable spending and increase savings. Create a solid budget that will meet all of your basic needs.

6. Vastly increase your financial knowledge. When the savings accumulate, it will be time to make investment decisions.

7. Create concrete, realistic goals for your future. Just remember— success will breed success.

8. Invest in yourself and your future. Taking measured risks in the investment business is the only way to build your capital assets and increase your wealth.

9. Protect your assets and investments. Making smart decisions to properly safeguard your wealth and your children's financial security is a huge part of financial genius.

10. Plan for your children's education. If you want to give your children the opportunity to obtain a higher education, you need to activate a serious savings plan now.

Introduction

▶ ACCORDING TO A study by the Women's Legal Defense Fund, custodial parents (primarily women) suffer a 25-percent drop in income at the time of divorce. Noncustodial parents (primarily men) often experience a 35-percent increase in their standard of living after a divorce. A California study revealed worse numbers for aging women, whose standard of living drops 73 percent while their ex-husbands' rises 42 percent. Without question, your earning power is diminished; most likely, it's dropped far more than 50 percent. And you still have to maintain a household, raise your children, and work.

Divorce is a financial disaster for most families and for the economy. Almost half of all divorced fathers fail to meet their child-support payments. Only 25 percent of divorced fathers pay full child support, but even then it is far more likely that the divorced mother's—along with the children's—income has decreased substantially. Average visitation for divorced fathers is around once a month, and divorced women with minor children make up a major segment of Americans living below the poverty line. In addition, single mothers often sacrifice their own welfare—including financial—for the sake of their children.

Like it or not, a divorced, widowed, or never-married mother is a woman on her own—a woman forced to take responsibility for every aspect of her newly single life (kids or no kids). A divorced, widowed, or unpartnered mother has to deal with financial realities and make financial decisions that will affect her and her children for decades. An informed single woman must, indeed, develop the skills and the confidence to make smart decisions and gain control over her financial reality. The only way to squelch fears and insecurities is to deal with your new reality and act accordingly.

This book has been researched and written to steer you through whatever personal financial minefields you are navigating and to help you build an operational vocabulary that will give you a real leg up on handling your personal finances. Together, the chapters cover everything you need to know about the most relevant topics, and each gives you down-and-dirty tactics for making smart money decisions. This book will help you maximize your options—no matter your income—and create a financial game plan that will bolster your net worth and provide you and your children with the future you all richly deserve.

You will find this book an invaluable resource in guiding your way through the money jungle as your family and finances grow and as you meet critical financial turning points in life, like the purchase of a home or helping your children pay for their college education. If you apply this information to your finances, you will be on the way to achieving your financial goals and being able to claim financial independence in the near future, one step at a time.

Chapter 1

Single Mothers and Personal Finance

Over 10 million American women are raising children on their own. For most, anything having to do with finance is a personal subject, and they often would rather avoid the topic altogether. Women often feel embarrassed that they aren't doing enough, and if they get in financial trouble, are likely to be too ashamed to discuss it. Contrary to these common conceptions, it is important to realize that the phrase "personal finance" merely means the amount of money you have coming in and what you do with it.

Everyone Needs a Personal Financial Plan

Personal finance is simply the money that makes your life what it is—how much you earn and how much you save; where you live; what kind of car you drive; how much you spend on clothes or vacations; how much you accumulate in retirement accounts or invest in stocks, bonds, or mutual funds; how you afford college for your children; and whether you prosper or merely limp along.

Developing a personal financial plan means taking the reins, educating yourself, becoming a savvier money handler, and assuming full responsibility for your financial future. Whether it means managing a meager income and budgeting to afford necessities or cleverly investing inherited or expendable income to cement a lucrative lifestyle, personal finance is both very personal and very important to your present and future welfare.

FACT

According to David Bach, author of *Smart Women Finish Rich,* 90 percent of women will have sole responsibility for their finances at some point. Three out of four people living in poverty are women, and seven out of ten women will live in poverty at some point in their lives.

It's really pretty simple: Without a financial plan, you probably won't be going anywhere worth going financially. Dreams and goals create a roadmap that will eventually get you where you want to go. Whether you like it or not, even the small decisions and choices you make today to forego impulsivity and better your finances will have a major impact on the quality of your life in the future.

Peter Sander, author of *The 250 Personal Finance Questions Everyone Should Ask,* pinpoints three characteristics that create financial success: awareness, commitment, and control. In other words, you need to make yourself truly aware of your personal financial reality. Once you've written it down in black and white—income, expenses, assets, and liabilities—you need to create and commit to a plan for bolstering your income and assets and effectively managing your expenses and liabilities. You need to make conscious decisions to stay on course and consistently monitor your progress.

A vital step to gaining control of your personal finances is creating meaningful, achievable, and time-based financial goals. Once you've established your financial priorities, you need to create a comprehensive game plan for achieving them within your timeframe. The hardest part, of course, is sticking to the strictures required to realize long-term goals—keeping your eye on a dream that seems far away and that may look that way for a long time.

Your Feelings about Money

Money is an emotional subject—in every culture, in every family, and in every marriage. Unless you have tons of it, money becomes a grail that you pursue. Whether it's for basic needs, exotic fantasies, or good deeds, money is the commodity by which we all operate. Those who have fat bank accounts either started the game with chips or learned to play it well.

ALERT!

Approximately 47 percent of women over the age of fifty are single. Those unmarried female baby boomers are expected to live fifteen to twenty years longer than men, but only 20 percent will be financially secure in their retirement. An astonishing 58 percent of female baby boomers have less than $20,000 saved for retirement.

It's not uncommon for people to feel anxious, even to the point of nausea, when faced with money decisions. Some dread financial responsibility and evade reality until the last possible moment. Without question, living on the edge of financial disaster makes bill-paying a miserable task. Unfortunately, those who shun financial responsibilities tend to create their worst fears. Money is a form of energy. Although you don't want to become obsessed with it, you do want to embrace it, welcome it, and become comfortable with it. You want to obtain financial mastery. As you educate yourself about money management, you'll become increasingly confident, decisive, and proactive, all of which will attract money rather than repel it.

If anything having to do with money makes you feel anxious or nervous, Stacy Johnson, author of *Life or Debt*, recommends keeping the following in mind:

- It's not having enough money that sets us free; it's having no debt. The people who have more money than they'll ever need and the people who don't owe anyone anything are the only ones free to do what they want.
- The decisions you make about borrowing and spending have a far-reaching, inclusive effect on your quality of life. Living life without debt means you are free to pursue your passion.
- If you're in a job that works against your grain or doesn't fulfill your fondest images of yourself, you won't be happy no matter how much money you're earning.
- The more things you buy, the more tied down you become. Some people become prisoners of their possessions instead of the other way around.
- Anyone you owe money to owns you.

Give serious thought to what money means to you. Do you require lots of it to feel secure or happy? Are you obsessed with watching every penny you spend? Do you live above or below your means? Do you prefer that someone else handle your finances, or do you love the feel of money in your hands? Do you feel qualified to understand and employ risky investments, or do you prefer to keep your money in low-risk accounts?

Surrender the Fairy Tale

Now that you've given some thought to how you view money, it's time to debunk some long-held myths and fairy tales about women and money. Even if you've been lucky enough to escape them, these underground beliefs are probably hiding in the dark corners of your mind. Their dusty tendrils can garble the truth and have more influence than you can imagine on how you—and others—think about women and money. These supposedly innocuous stories were whispered in your ears late at night, when you were nodding off to sleep, and they crept into your consciousness whether you liked it or not.

Like most American girls, you probably fell in love with fairy-tale princesses and the gallant white knights who rescued them. However, one drawback to believing in fairy tales and princesses is that many people interpret them literally. The real "gold" your dream princess acquires lies in the symbolic meanings. The gold coin is not a gold coin. It's the shining quality within the princess: her talent, her wisdom, and her ability to act decisively. The prince is not literally a prince, but the internal masculine qualities that a princess must "marry" in order to become whole.

Cinderella, for example, the premier mythological fantasy princess, had to work to earn her golden slippers. Disney truncated the original fairy tale, turning those gold slippers into glass. Although the original included magical "birds" that helped Cinderella complete her tasks, there was no fairy godmother who showed up and bestowed riches. In fact, in the original fairy tale, Cinderella had very important psychological tasks to perform: to reconnect with the spirit of her dead mother, discern the value in hard work, sort out good from bad, reorder her universe, and know her own personal worth—from within—before she was rewarded with golden slippers. Cinderella had to consciously remove her feet from the wooden shoes of her past in order to purposefully don the golden slippers of her future. The prince was just icing on the cake. He also had to see Cinderella in her degraded state and value her inner beauty and inherent value before he could take her as his rightful bride.

FACT

Unfortunately, many wives tend to assign financial planning to their husbands. Even more unfortunately, as a result of their husband's poor planning, one out of every four widows depletes her husband's death benefits within two months. Approximately 80 percent of all widows living in poverty were not living that way when their husbands were alive.

Between these two interpretations of the same fairy tale, there are small—yet essential—differences. The prince was not the answer to all of Cinderella's problems; he was her reward and her future partner in life. "Happily ever after" did not mean that the heroine was going to live a passive life. Indeed, she was not going to fade into oblivion; she was entering into a fully empowered (self-empowered) partnership. Cinderella's happiness came from knowing her own self-worth and acting decisively in her own best interests, and that is the potent lesson of the original story. Rather than waiting for a "prince" to make your dreams come true, take control your own future, sort out your finances, and learn to make money decisions that propel your life forward.

How Money Myths Affect You

Particularly in American culture, people tend to measure their self-worth by their earning potential, how much money their parents had, how much money they have, the size of their houses or cars, the expensive clothing they can afford (or go deep into debt to acquire), or their bank balances. For many formerly married women, these measurements were applied to their husbands, even though it's a skewed way of measuring value. The myths about women and money are worse—primarily that they don't understand it, that they can't manage it, and that they'll never earn enough to become rich. In fact, women have been trampling those myths for generations. Nevertheless, don't assume you're free and clear of cultural subterfuge. It's important for you to sift through the cultural and personal myths that may be undermining your own feelings of self-worth and how they are intertwined with money.

Take time to write down any myths that your culture—and especially your family—perpetuated, and then revaluate the message. Does it match with your experience? Do you know it to be completely false? Does it fashion a positive image that serves you? Here are a few common misrepresentations to get you started thinking about the myths that may be negatively influencing your ability to handle complicated financial matters:

- Women aren't very bright.
- Women aren't good at math.
- Women don't have a head for business.

- Men don't like women who make a lot of money.
- Men like dumb women they can dominate.
- Men are better at earning, managing, and investing money.
- A rich husband will take good care of you.
- Money is too dirty for women to worry their pretty little heads about.
- Money doesn't make you happy.
- Women are compulsive shoppers.
- Women have champagne tastes on a beer budget.

With the advent of credit cards in the 1970s, Americans embraced immediate gratification, a cultural attitude their grandparents didn't have. People of that earlier generation bought what they needed only when they had cash to pay for it, and they rarely indulged in buying things they didn't need. Since those days, people have all been led to believe that they can afford to use credit cards or borrow money to get what they want, and advertisers have become very rich by preying upon their insecurities.

ALERT!

The Employee Benefit Research Institute (EBRI) publishes research on the economic security of American workers. They found that Americans are not saving: In 2005, the national savings rate was zero. Europeans save 10 percent and Italians 16 percent of their household income. And credit card usage has skyrocketed. People are going deeply into debt for things that they once paid for in cash.

Many people fear that they're not measuring up. Overspending then becomes an addiction that staves off the fear of being "less than." On some level, many people have come to believe that they are not full, complete, worthy human beings without the appearance of a certain status in terms of looks, money, or possessions. Unfortunately, they end up trading their hard-won money for a few minutes of pleasure or a boatload of unnecessary goods or services. Contemporary culture sells the belief that owning certain "stuff" will guarantee social acceptance. Ironically, when you go into debt to obtain those lifestyle markers, you are simultaneously lowering the chances that you'll ever actually be rich. Don't trade tomorrow's financial independence on a feeble, completely unnecessary attempt to keep up with your neighbors.

Even fears about death can affect the way you manage money. When those pesky fears arise, you might be tempted to slap a piece of plastic on the table to obtain something that you think will enrich your life. What you're really doing is buying the "buy now, feel better" philosophy that—in reality—rings false. People often run around like hamsters on a treadmill, acquiring stuff that eventually ends up in the garage, gathering dust. If you want true financial freedom, you need to realize that all that stuff is never, ever going to make you happy. Embracing who you are and seeking ways to nourish your soul creates the only wealth worth pursuing.

How Your Past Shapes Your Future

Transformation begins with self-knowledge, going back into your past to sort out where your thoughts, feelings, actions, and reactions to money began. *Everyone* is a product of her environment, as these three financial scenarios illustrate:

- If your parents were loaded, you may have enjoyed luxury, but you may not have a clue how to make smart investments or become financially independent. You may have a gold belt in shopping, but if you don't know how to generate income streams, funds could dry up quicker than an Iowa prairie in August.
- If you grew up in a middle-class family, your parents may have given you the impression they were better off than they were. You may have reasonable expectations but no idea of how to bump yourself up to the next level.
- If you grew up impoverished, you may have deeply ingrained fears about losing money or have a tendency to let any money you do earn slip right out of your fingers. A poverty mindset may cause you to lie awake in anguish every time you spend money or to suffer massive anxieties over money worries. You may believe that you

will never have enough—even that you don't deserve it, effectively imprisoning yourself in poverty.

Without question money talks in families—speaking volumes about your ability to create goals and achieve them, save or spend money wisely, feel grounded and secure or like the rug is always being pulled out from under you. Use the following series of questions to rediscover and rethink your cultural and familial myths:

- How much money did your grandparents have? How about your parents?
- How was money discussed in your home?
- Did your grandparents or parents have excessive spending habits?
- Did they make solid investments and build toward financial wealth?
- Did they live in fear of being poor and scrimp on basic necessities?
- Did they impose any attitudes or beliefs on your ideas about money?
- Did they teach you how to handle money, invest money, or increase wealth?
- Did they accept that they would never have money and do nothing to alter their fate?
- When they talked about money was it in worried whispers, shouting matches, or while twisting a paper napkin?
- Did they have a laissez-faire attitude about money, and were they justified in doing so?
- Did they display measured decision-making and planning skills?
- Did they spend lavishly or only spend when absolutely necessary?
- Did they budget money, or were they constantly bouncing checks?
- Did your father handle the money matters and take care of your mother?
- Did your mother handle everything and belittle your father for not doing so?
- What underlying feelings and beliefs established your attitudes about money?

Write a short but well-thought-out financial biography that paints a portrait of your cultural and your familial climate as you grew up. Focus on how the presence of, absence of, obsession with, or disregard for money affected you socially, physically, emotionally, and spiritually, and answer the following questions:

- Did you live in the land of milk and honey, or was your family constantly living on the brink of financial disaster?
- What effects did a middle-class background have on your financial undercurrents?
- Did you feel financially secure, wealthy, or poor?
- Did you vow to be richer, smarter, more adventurous, or more conservative than your parents?
- Did you feel guilty, remorseful, or afraid when you spend large amounts of money?
- Did you feel a rush of adrenaline when you drop large amounts of money on clothing or shoes?
- Did you consistently spend more than you could afford?

The goal here is to probe into your past so that you can write a future based on self-examination, self-knowledge, and choice.

Divorcing Your Marital Habits

When you are freshly out of a bitter, acrimonious divorce, your perspective on everything is skewed. You are well on the way to separating your thoughts and beliefs from those of your ex-husband. It's time to rethink—and think outside the box—when it comes to money and all of its inherent, cultural, familial, subjective, and very personal meanings. Rather than falling sway to cultural biases, or to the limitations or unreasonable expectations of your parents or your former partner, it's time for you to sort out what you really believe—or what you want to work toward believing.

Now that you've filtered through your family's mythology, unearthing beliefs that subliminally affected your ideas about money and how to handle it, it's time to take a hard look at your most recent financial partnership.

First, you'll want to explore your singular financial history—how you were doing before you coupled. Then you'll want to take a discerning look at the ways in which your husband or partner impacted your thoughts about money, solvency, and investments, and how you handled money in general. Use the following questions about how you and your partner handled money as a starting point:

- Were you financially sound prior to marriage?
- What were your personal financial habits prior to marriage?
- Were you happy with your financial situation?
- Were you happier spending or saving?
- What really made you happy?
- After marriage, did you let him take the financial reins?
- Did you truly feel that he was trustworthy?
- Did he make good financial decisions?
- Did you want what he wanted?
- Where did you differ?
- What drove you crazy?
- What did you learn from his/your mistakes?
- What would you have done differently?
- What did you learn from your successes?

This rethinking process is a critical step in reordering your financial universe. When you've cleared the decks of negative beliefs or limitations imposed by others, you create opportunities for new thoughts and beliefs to form. These new beliefs will become the cornerstone of your new financial philosophy, which will set things in motion and lead to a concrete action plan. You have taken the first true steps to being and becoming financially independent—in control of your financial decisions and experiencing the joy that follows a job well done! Repeat this as your new financial mantra: I am reordering my financial universe, and I *will* soon reap the rewards.

Chapter 2

On Your Own . . . Again

While there can be many, many benefits to being single, being a single mother presents an enormous challenge. Even if you came out of the death, divorce, or separation with a safe cushion of money and assets, you will now be fully responsible for all the financial decisions that will directly affect you and your children for decades to come. If you are not money-savvy, this could cause massive anxiety or lead to impulsive decisions that undermine your long-term security. Time to gather yourself and begin again.

Making Smart, Necessary, Immediate Decisions

First, you have to accept that absolutely everything has changed. You cannot go forward with a solid base if you don't get a firm grip on what your situation is now and from this point forward. You have to think for yourself, and think smart. The first precept might simply be "Do no harm." If you are uncertain what to do, keep the status quo until you feel more confident about your course of action. Focus on what requires your immediate attention: paying down debt or creating an emergency fund, for example. The first—and very important—task is to discover and record all aspects of your financial situation, as follows:

- Create a list of all your income.
- Create a list of all credit card and loan balances, including car loans, student loans, personal loans, mortgages, home equity or line of credit, and any taxes owed.
- Create a list of all retirement and savings accounts. Including health savings accounts, certificates of deposit (CDs), education accounts, and investments.
- Create a thorough list of all monthly expenditures, such as utilities, groceries, clothing, automobile gas and upkeep, education expenses, child care expenses, entertainment, and so on.
- Create a temporary livable budget that reflects your new circumstances.
- List and review insurance policies.
- If needed, name your children as beneficiaries on insurance policies, CDs, bank accounts, and retirement plans.
- Select guardians for your children.
- Create a rudimentary will and a living will until you can more properly create a lasting one. (See Chapter 13.)

Other than fulfilling the necessary, immediate tasks—establishing how much money you really have to live on, how it will be dispensed, and what you have to work with—it's advisable to wait at least six to twelve months before making major, or any long-term, decisions related to money. Even if you feel pressured, allow yourself time to steady your emotions and learn as much as you can about financial management before making major changes.

Establishing Your Bottom Line

It's important at this stage to determine the quality of life you want to create for yourself and your children. No matter where you set your goals on the money continuum, it's important to define what's most important. Begin by making a list of what really matters in terms of lifestyle, needs, and dreams, and then prioritize the list. Keep refining the list until you feel it reflects who you are, where you're going, and what you'll find when you get there. For instance, owning a home may be extremely important for some, while returning to school to obtain an advanced degree may be the primary goal for others.

ALERT!

Studies have shown that only 41 percent of Americans are better savers than spenders. Savers develop positive habits like budgeting, tracking expenses, balancing checkbooks, paying bills as they come in, and living within or below their means. Nine out of ten savers reported that they feel very confident, maintain their ideal weight, and feel good about how they look. Spenders reported consistently feeling frustrated and unhappy with their circumstances.

What you are seeking is absolute clarity on who you are and how you want to live your life. Now that you are a single mother, you're the one steering the ship. Will you set your sails on a particular destination, charting and navigating through all the twists, turns, and setbacks likely to occur to reach it? Or will you relinquish your fate to the open sea, sailing in uncharted waters that may, or may not, have a good outcome? The longer someone remains directionless, the longer they don't get anywhere. It's an undeniable fact that single mothers have a mother lode of daily child care responsibilities that make it difficult, at best, to find time to focus on what they want for themselves. But it is important to realize that a single mother who doesn't focus on herself—and what she wants for herself in the long term—is likely to end up far poorer than she would have if she had taken the time to establish her bottom line and create concrete goals that get the ball rolling.

Making Long-Term, Calculated Decisions

After the dust has settled and your grief is subsiding, it's time to contemplate your long-term goals and to make decisions that will help you accomplish them. Sit yourself down and make a list of things you want to create for the future and what you need to address now to make them happen. Examples include the following:

- Can you afford to stay in your current home?
- If not, where do you want to live? What can you afford?
- How can you move up at work or increase your income?
- What are your long-term financial goals, and do how you plan to achieve them?
- Do you need, or desire, additional education?
- How will you fund college or additional training for yourself or your children?
- How will you increase your savings and fund a retirement plan?

What you're seeking is generic ideas about what you want to create for the future and whether you need to weigh them in making decisions that deal with your immediate, pressing needs. Chapter 3 discusses financial goals in depth, as well as how you can create concrete action plans to achieve them. For now, let's move on to preliminary—and ongoing—financial responsibilities and how you can meet them.

Assuming Fiscal Responsibility

For many people, learning about personal finance at the level required to truly prosper feels intimidating. It's as if we feel handicapped in that arena, when, in fact, we haven't exerted the energy necessary to learn and follow basic principles—earn more, hold onto more, spend less, manage debt, and invest for maximum return. Where you put your energy is where you blossom, and learning about personal finance is a very worthwhile expenditure of your time and energy.

Some immediate tasks that you need to undertake are as follows:

- Create a household inventory for insurance purposes.
- Copy and store important documents like birth certificates, passports, deeds, loan documents, insurance policies, divorce decree, wills, and car titles in a fire safe and at a relative's or friend's house. Make sure others know where they can find this information in an emergency.
- Set up a system to manage bills.
- Balance your checkbook monthly. If you need help with this, ask your local banker to help you reconcile a statement. Computer programs can also do this for you if you simply input the information.
- Check all credit card statements to make sure the charges belong to you, and match up corresponding receipts. Set up a file for each credit card so you can access each statement easily if a problem arises.
- File deductible receipts in a tax file, and file warranty receipts in a warranty file.
- Check tax returns, and establish a file for each of the last five years. Unless you bought or sold a house or large assets, such as stock, you can toss returns more than five years old.

Learning financial concepts frequently feels like studying rocket science, so give yourself a little leeway to feel jumbled, stymied, and even childlike. Learning how to organize and take responsibility for financial matters on your own—all while balancing parental responsibilities—may present a sharp learning curve. But if you simply read along and do the work step by step, one day everything will begin to drop into place.

Get Organized

One of the first tasks you face is organizing all of your financial records and maintaining them. It may be a drag to do this, but apparently there are differences between those who get their lives truly organized and those who procrastinate, or simply fail to do so. According to Jean Chatzky in *The Ten Commandments of Financial Happiness*, the differences are striking.

Characteristic	Organized	Not Organized
Financially secure	72 percent	23 percent
Worried about finances	56 percent	86 percent
Knowledgeable investors	24 percent	7 percent
Good money managers	61 percent	28 percent
In control of finances	73 percent	42 percent

Set Up a System

The best way to take responsibility for money management is to set up a system that works. Select a drawer, a file holder, or a basket where you place monthly bills. Open all mail when it arrives. Discard junk mail, and immediately shred all those endless credit card offers. Then, put all your bills into the designated, easily accessible drawer, file, or basket. Create a monthly payment schedule to remind you when bills are due. You can opt to have most bills arrive the first of the month, the middle of the month, or the end of the month. If you have sufficient funds in your checking account, pay bills when they arrive. Alternately, set up automatic payments from your checking account, or select at least two days a month when you pay bills.

It's prudent to buy and use an accounting program, which is very easy to use and helpful in simplifying and expediting your bill paying. The savvier you become, the more you can create reports that show you how you are doing on credit card debt, budgeting, saving, and managing your finances in general. Remember, a single mother needs to accept responsibility for her financial fate, particularly if she hopes to avert disaster and bolster her chances of amassing wealth.

Keeping the Ex-Husband Accountable

According to the government, more than half—*half!*—of all fathers who owe child support do not pay it. The Child Support Recovery Act of 1992 enacted laws that make it a federal crime for fathers to default on court-ordered child support due children living in another state. Your local Child Support Enforcement Office can assist you in taking measures to force payment. (You can also find help online, at *www.singleparentcentral.com*.) If you report the father's failure to pay to the IRS, for example, they will divert any refunds he earns to you.

FACT

Nearly 50 percent of all first marriages and 60 percent of all second marriages end in divorce, so you, my dear, are far from alone. In fact, the next time you're in line at a movie, look at the person in front of and behind you. Of you three, two of you will have gone through a divorce.

If your former husband or partner fails to pay child support, it is imperative that you act immediately by filing a motion for contempt of court. Although it's wise to use an attorney, this is something you can file and present to a judge. But don't wait, because it will take weeks before you have a court date. On that date, the alleged violator must appear in court to explain why he has not complied and why he should not be held in contempt. If the person is found guilty of contempt, the judge can seize his assets, levy fines, and even send him to jail.

As of 1998, federal law requires employers to turn in the names, addresses, dates of birth, and Social Security numbers of all new hires, which means that even if the father has crossed a state line, it's easier to find him today than it was in the past. Some of your options for tracking down a deadbeat dad include searching these routes:

- **Motor vehicle records:** You can call the state bureau with his name, Social Security number, and date of birth to find out what vehicles he has registered and to obtain his current address.

- **County tax records:** Your county clerk of courts can provide you with deeds, taxation information, and property assessments.
- **The IRS:** The IRS will intercept a delinquent payer's income tax refund. Ask your local child support agency to verify the amount due and submit it to the IRS.
- **Social workers:** Ask your city or county social workers to obtain information from his bank, his mortgage provider, or other financial institutions to determine his assets. You can then attach liens on real estate or personal property and attach bank accounts to collect past-due support.

Although it can be difficult and frustrating, holding the father financially accountable is important to your children's future. They deserve to have their father's fiscal and emotional support, and the law agrees. Ideally, two parents create the best financial circumstances they can afford and work together to provide for their children. If that's not realistic—or even imaginable—in your situation, make every effort to deal with his financial lapses in a measured, responsible way. It's not your job to browbeat a deadbeat father, but it is your responsibility to make sure your children have the advantages that he can afford and that they so richly deserve.

A Healthy Foundation for New Relationships

When a new relationship becomes increasingly serious, you'll probably fear, and still absolutely have to broach, the difficult subjects—sex and money. This is particularly important because you have children. You're older, wiser, and fiscally responsible, so just as you would safeguard your children from other dangers, take steps to safeguard your children's financial future.

Lay It All on the Table

If you're at the move-in stage, ask for a meeting in which you will share credit reports, FICO scores, credit card and loan balances, and net worth statements. This will be your opportunity to find out his true situation and to find out how he handles his financial responsibilities. It would also be a good idea to ask to see the last three years of income tax reports, as well as records of child or spousal support and payroll stubs. You are entitled to know the absolute truth about his financial situation. A man who balks at openly sharing may well have something to hide—even if it's only a tendency to control all financial decisions.

Good credit is sexy! Fair Isaac, a renowned credit-scoring company, commissioned a survey that revealed that financial responsibility was the third most-desirable trait in a romantic partner. Around 50 percent of the 1,000 subjects chose faithfulness and honesty as the most important traits; 22 percent ranked financial responsibility.

You'll also want to create common financial goals and make commitments to fulfill them. For smooth sailing, set the parameters for how much each will bring into the household, who will pay for what expenses, and how you will negotiate disagreements or problems as they arise. If you have varying philosophies about spending and saving, now is the time to define your expectations, limitations, and boundaries. If it makes you feel insecure that he likes to play online poker as a hobby, perhaps you can establish a poker fund that he can feel free to use, as long as he doesn't dip into other household funds. If you like buying new shoes every month and can afford them, perhaps you'll want to list new shoes as a line item in your combined budget.

In the beginning, particularly if you aren't buying a house together or otherwise mingling debts, it makes sense to keep the majority of your finances separate. You can establish a common household account, and then, as the relationship grows, you can begin to merge your financial assets and debts. It's always wise to have some money that remains yours to control, whether it's a clothing budget or mad money. People feel more secure when they have money that they control and that they don't have to answer to someone else as to how they spend it. Also, you'll want to have credit cards and other debt accounts remain in your name so that you maintain a healthy credit rating.

It's also important to discuss behavioral expectations. If you want to sit down together every month to pay joint expenses, balance the checkbooks, and create new goals, make sure he understands how important this is to you. If you agree to turn everything over to him but are uncomfortable not being on top of things, ask for a monthly meeting in which you review all the finances. Maybe you want joint meetings before any major purchases, or you'd like to establish joint savings that build toward the purchase of a new car. Whatever you require to make you feel secure, knowledgeable, and powerful within the relationship is, and will remain, important. It's the failure to talk about finances clearly that creates problems that can quickly become—or at least feel—insurmountable.

Set Ground Rules

Instead of counting on your romantic feelings to pacify all problems, take the time to write out a very concrete "cohabitation agreement" that will specify the financial agreement you have worked out together—your mutual rights and obligations with respect to joint and separate property from now on. Define both partners' expectations and how they will be met, or worked toward. Without a written cohabitation agreement, your right to receive support, share in assets acquired during the length of the relationship, make medical decisions on his behalf, or claim an inheritance will be difficult at best to obtain.

FACT

The American Bar Association reported that 90 percent of all divorces in the last decade originated in arguments about money. Some marriage experts estimate that 75 percent of all divorces result from constant arguments about finances.

It's not wise to rush into co-ownership of houses, so if he is moving into your house, you may want him to pay rent for a period of one year, at which time you will renegotiate. If you decide to purchase property together, consult with a lawyer or financial consultant to determine the best way to structure ownership. "Joint tenant" means that the survivor owns the property in the event of the other's death, while "tenants in common" means that the property goes to the deceased's estate, so that heirs end up owning the property. If you're paying down 60 percent to his 40 percent on a new house, state that clearly, and specify how you want that to be handled in the event of a sale.

You also want to protect your assets. Make a list of everything you own, including investments, furniture, and heirlooms. Co-ownership from the point of cohabitation can be negotiated, but what's yours prior to the relationship should remain yours. Also, to fully protect your children, leave them listed as your beneficiaries on bank accounts, insurance policies, investments, or wills. If you decide to marry, by all means renegotiate the financial agreement, keeping in mind that once you marry, each person will become mutually responsible for both parties' financial management.

Chapter 3

Where You Want to Be: Setting Your Goals

Creating personal financial goals is extremely important and worthy of your complete attention. James Cash, the founder of J. C. Penney, said it in a more succinct and poster-worthy way (as in, paste it onto your bathroom mirror so you can live it as a credo): "Give me a stock clerk with a goal, and I'll give you a woman who will make history. Give me a woman with no goals, and I'll give you a stock clerk."

3

Why Goals Are Important

If you live without setting goals, you will probably always wonder what you could have done if you'd only focused your energy and really tried. Even if you bump along in life without strong direction, in most cases, you and your children will be fine. You may have a mediocre, stressful job; you may never travel to Europe because you can't afford a plane ticket; you may live your life worrying whether you can afford next month's rent; and your children may forego college—but living without goals in America is possible. The problem is that you will live well below your potential on every level, and neither you nor your children will create the lives you deserve.

Creating goals is a means to an end. Goals provide a roadmap. They give you a point on the horizon to focus on and then help you harness the energy to get there step by step. Long-term goals are really the formulation and clear statement of your dreams—what you want to accomplish in your lifetime. Short-term goals are the blueprint for achieving those dreams. Only by illuminating the stepping-stones along the path are you able to take potent steps that lead you forward. Pablo Picasso, one of the greatest and most productive artists of all time, believed in goals and stated so clearly: "Our goals can only be reached through a vehicle of a plan, in which we must fervently believe, and upon which we must vigorously act. There is no other route to success."

FACT

According to Thomas J. Stanley Ph.D., author of *Millionaire Women Next Door,* two thirds of self-made millionaire women set clearly defined goals. In fact, most regularly set daily, weekly, monthly, annual, and life-time goals. These women also reported a history of being able to plan and achieve their goals. Of the one-third who said they didn't create a defined set of goals, one-half had already achieved their goals, and the other half created broad-ranging goals, such as becoming financially independent.

You need goals to keep your attention and your focus on what's important. It's so easy to become overwhelmed by everyday life that you can lose sight of what you're working toward. Suddenly you're standing in Macy's feeling the siren call of a silk blouse and a cashmere sweater, and the lack of real goals that can drown out the siren calls lead to a financial downturn. We need achievable goals and a viable game plan to achieve them so that we make constructive decisions. Once you get into the habit of checking your impulses against your goals, you'll turn the tide on your financial fortunes. It's a matter of decision making, even when temptation arises. Without a goal-oriented compass, you'll end up racking up thousands of dollars on credit cards instead of saving up for a down payment on a house. Stay focused, and you'll come out a winner.

What to Do First

You can't set goals if you don't have dreams to fulfill. The first step is to contemplate what is most important to you and to establish a list of values. Values are your spiritual bottom line—what will ultimately bring you meaningful pleasure. Of course you value your children, but what is your intention toward them? Perhaps it's building a secure future, which could entail establishing educational funds and providing a stable home in a safe neighborhood. Perhaps it's having more time to spend with them while they are young, or creating a business that will support all of you for the next ten years *and* build resources for your retirement, so you won't be a burden on them.

What you need is a mission statement for your life, something that conveys who you are, what you value, and what you want to accomplish— in one simple phrase. Simple doesn't mean easy; it means clear, concise, memorable, motivational, and purpose-driven. Esoteric statements lead nowhere. Search your heart and soul for what matters most to you and give it a grounded spin. Saving the world cannot be done, but using your organizational skills to establish a nonprofit business that brings musical education into the local school system *can* be done. You want your dreams to be fanciful, yet achievable—in this lifetime.

Dream Big

Creating goals is not about lowering expectations, nor is it about taking jobs just to meet financial goals. It's about soul-searching to figure out who you are meant to be in this world and then envisioning new opportunities for yourself. All adults all have to support themselves—and single mothers have to support their children and their long-term goals—but you don't want to surrender your dreams. You want to plot and plan ways to incorporate your dreams into your livelihood. If you set goals to move toward your dreams, you can eventually create a life that is far more in sync with who you are and what you want for yourself.

Po Bronson, an author who tapped into a national obsession with his bestselling book, *What Should I Do With My Life?*, believes that business success in the future starts with just that question: What should I do with my life? "People don't succeed by migrating to a 'hot industry' or by adopting a particular career-guiding mantra. . . . They thrive by focusing on the questions of who they really are—and connecting that to work that they truly love, and in so doing unleashing a productive and creative power that they never imagined."

FACT

Researchers have found that single female raccoons and bears that receive no help from a male in caring for their children seem to develop larger brains than those with coparenting or communal support. They credit the difference to the higher cognitive and perceptual abilities that a solo mother needs to keep her child safe, fed, and warm.

Create an Emergency Fund

This needs to be short-term goal number *one*! Every financial advisor/ writer in the world stresses this point, and every struggling woman moans. Of course it's hard to accumulate a single month's expenses—let alone the recommended three—to cover emergencies. It's the reason insurance was invented, but emergencies arise that are beyond insurance. Cars break down, children break legs (requiring a babysitter while they recover), roofs leak, hot-water tanks fizzle, landscaping fries, and sometimes a woman needs a break.

Fat emergency-fund accounts accumulate interest and allow you to sleep soundly. Make your first short-term goal to be opening an emergency savings account of at least two month's salary. This cash pillow is requisite before you start investing.

Embrace Your New Reality

You are now on your own. Even if you receive spousal or child support or have a safety net from insurance payouts, every financial decision you make from this point forward is on your shoulders. They all need to be tailored to fit the reality of your new status. It's up to you to become an informed investor and a sound financial planner. As you ponder your goals, keep this very much in the forefront of your thoughts and then generate genuine ideas to bolster your financial status and to live your dream.

How to Create Long-Term Goals

Long-term goals are dreams that are in alignment with your values and that fulfill your heart's desire. Long-term goals often require you to work toward them by fulfilling a series of short-term goals over a long period of time. The long-term goals are really your dreams—the circumstances you want to create that will bring you inner happiness—but they require a belief that you'll get there eventually. They also require an ability to sustain belief and expend energy.

To create these kinds of goals, you need to look deeper than the task at hand. If your heart's desire is to build a foundation of security for yourself and your children, that's a laudable and valid lifetime goal, but you will need to break it down into a series of achievable goals.

Buy a Home in Three Years

Buying a home is both a major commitment and a multistep goal that requires extensive planning and careful execution. First, to make it a concrete goal, you might want to shop around to determine your ideal, affordable neighborhood. Assume you see a house that fits the bill and costs $170,000. You will need to add 12 percent to the price to account for price increases in real estate between now and when you buy. Your down payment will need to be at least $9,500 (5 percent of $190,000), and your payments will be $1,452 per month with a thirty-year fixed-rate mortgage charging 9 percent interest. (You can look up what monthly payments would be for your loan using online mortgage payment calculators.)

If you're a first-time buyer, an FHA loan will usually allow you to borrow an amount that, together with property taxes (assume 1 percent of the home's value) and payments on your other debts, consumes up to 41 percent of your gross (pretax) income. In this scenario, you would need an income of at least $51,000 per year to get the mortgage on this home, assuming that you have another $100 per month in interest payments on other debts.

To build your $9,500 nest egg, you will need to save $243 per month and grow it at a rate of 6 percent per year. Also, since you want to secure your down payment, you may choose to minimize risk on your savings by investing conservatively—choosing high-quality bonds, rather than volatile stocks, for example.

Save $30,000 Over the Next Ten Years

To reach this goal, you would need to deposit $227 per month into a checking account paying 2 percent interest over the next 10 years. On the other hand, if you invest the funds for a return of 7 percent, you can lower your monthly nut to $175. Depending upon your level of comfort, you could also opt for a money market fund that would fall somewhere in the middle. The point is that you need to create the goal, determine how much you need to save to reach it, and then investigate the best way to maximize returns on investment. The table on page 35 shows how much you would need to save if you earned 7 percent on your investments.

Open My Own Business in Seven Years

Many of us hold this dream, and it's a valid, achievable one. In terms of creating financial goals, ask yourself these questions:

- What kind of business will I open?
- Do I need more training or certification to be able to run my own firm?
- What will be my initial cash outlays to create the business?
- How much cash will I need to cover personal expenses before the business makes money?

Once you define what you want, why you want it, when you want it, and how to get it, write specific, measurable, and achievable goals. Create target dates and a list of tasks required. Then place a list of your goals in prominent places—your bedroom, your home office, and your refrigerator—so that the daily reminder will spur you on to success.

Generally, you need to save $100 per month for every $10,000 you want in cash at the end of seven years. You also need to invest those savings in higher-return investments, including riskier assets like stock during the first few years. As the target date approaches, you could reduce risk and switch your investment to high-quality bonds.

If you can start yo ur business part-time while working for someone else, adjust the goals accordingly—based on how quickly you estimate that the business will be solidly profitable, allowing you to safely fly solo.

Pay Off My Mortgage

If you have the disposable income and no higher-interest debts, paying off your mortgage ahead of time is a fabulous long-term goal. If you've just purchased a home using a thirty-year mortgage charging 9 percent interest, you can end your loan in twenty-two years by paying 8.5 percent more than the minimum payment. You can pay your fifteen-year mortgage off in twelve years by paying an extra 13 percent over the minimum. If that's too high, adjust your goal to what is achievable.

How to Create Short-Term Goals

Short-term goals break down your long-term goals into manageable bites. Each time you achieve a short-term goal, you are moving closer to the ultimate, long-term goal behind it. Some believe in doing something daily that works toward fulfillment of your short-term, manageable goals. As long as you create them and set a viable deadline for achieving them, you're on the right track. Short-term goals should be all of the following:

- **Specific:** You should be able to state the goal in positive language and break it down to its smallest denominator.
- **Measurable:** The goal should provide quantifiable, visible results within a certain time frame.
- **Attainable:** Attaining the goal should be a bit of stretch, but definitely within your reach.
- **Valuable:** Achieving of this end should align with your core values.
- **Progressive:** Achieving this goal should also be a step toward a long-term goal.
- **Primary:** Your identified goal should be a top priority that will motivate you to get going.

People often confuse short-term goals with tasks, and it's important to distinguish between them. Tasks are a series of to-do items that you need to address to move you closer to achieving a short-term goal. A short-term goal is a bar you set for yourself that achieves something of value. When you complete a task, you feel relieved that you can finally strike it off the list, but you don't feel the enthusiasm and excitement that comes when you achieve a true goal.

Your goal may be to get your finances organized, and that might include the following tasks:

1. Buy filing folders.
2. Separate all your bills, bank statements, loan statements, investment statements, tax returns, and so on.
3. File the physical copies in clearly marked folders.
4. Research and buy a financial and budget tracking software program.

5. Enter all the pertinent data that will allow you to stay on top of your monthly finances.

That's a series of five tasks that are needed to reach your short-term goal. You're relieved as each task is done, but when you have all five tasks completed, you feel elated because you are more in control of what's happening, and you feel motivated to reach for the next short-term goal—learning how to invest.

Accentuate the positive. The whole point of making goals is that you are creating a positive vision of your future. If goals are conceived as punishment, you won't feel inspired to achieve them. Instead of writing, "I won't spend any money on luxuries for six months," write "I am choosing to pay down my credit card debt to zero." It's not deprivation; it's empowerment!

Pay Down Credit Card Debt by 25 Percent over the Next Six Months

Credit card debt can be a financial killer—unless you've resorted to payday loans (which you should avoid at all costs!), it's probably the most expensive debt you can have. Most people would rather pay the minimum every month, incurring interest on their credit balance, than go without new clothes, shoes, or gadgets for the children.

If you have $2,000 in credit card debt, you can meet this goal by paying about $115 per month over the next six months, provided you also cease charging anything else. Your choices are pretty simple: Earn more, or spend less. If you can find a second job that pays $10 per hour for an extra three hours every week, for the next six months, you would meet your goal. If you choose to pare down spending, your first task would be to review your budget and find extra funds that can be allocated to the debt. The next task might be to literally deposit cash into a piggy bank until the payment date arrives.

Also, once you've made your selections, it's important to keep your promise to yourself. If you've chosen to eliminate video rentals and movies, for example, the next time you find yourself standing outside a theater, you can remember your goal and feel good about your choice—and then quickly redirect your energy. Also, another part of the same goal will be to avoid charging new merchandise. Once you've met your initial goal of reducing your credit card debt by 25 percent, you may want to adjust your goal to paying it down completely, or only charging what you can pay when the bill arrives, or at least charging no more than 30 percent of your available credit limit (to improve your FICO score) and then paying triple the minimum payment until it's paid down.

Establish a Money Market Account

This is a quickly achievable, and highly desirable, short-term goal. The tasks involved in meeting it might go as follows:

1. Research money market accounts. (See Chapter 5 for online resources.)
2. Determine the one best suited to your circumstances and needs.
3. If you need to amass additional funds to meet minimum deposit requirements, develop and implement a short-term savings campaign.
4. Then, when ready, make an appointment and go in to set up the account.

Create a Workable Savings Budget and Open an Account

Creating and sticking to a savings budget is a choice that will pay dividends for life. It's also an exercise that requires you to check your ego at the door so you're open to lifestyle changes. To create a workable savings budget, you must estimate how much you spend every month in elective categories like gourmet food, eating in restaurants, buying fast food, or splurging on things like impulse or trendy clothing, vacations you can't really afford, health club memberships, cable television, video rentals, nights out with the girls, movie dates with the kids, or manicures. You can then determine what and how much can be trimmed or eliminated to invest in a savings account.

Set goals for how much you'll save per month based on how much you want to save over time (see the table that follows). For instance, if you are thirty years old and want to have $342,283 at age sixty-five, plan on saving $200 each month, starting today. Make sure to maximize the return on your investments—if you save $200 every month for thirty-five years and only earn 4 percent each year, you'll have approximately half of what you'd end up with if you achieved a 7 percent per year return. Thanks to the magic of compounding, when your savings grow at 7 percent instead of 4 percent, you almost double the total amount saved at the end of thirty-five years.

Savings Given Monthly Contributions

Years to spending date	$100	$200	$400	$500	$1,000
1	$1,238	$2,476	$4,952	$6,190	$12,380
5	$7,120	$14,239	$28,478	$35,598	$71,196
10	$17,105	$34,210	$68,421	$85,526	$171,052
15	$31,110	$62,221	$124,442	$155,552	$311,105
20	$50,754	$101,507	$203,015	$253,768	$507,536
25	$78,304	$156,608	$313,217	$391,521	$783,042
30	$116,945	$233,891	$467,781	$584,726	$1,169,453
35	$171,141	$342,283	$684,565	$855,707	$1,711,414
40	$247,154	$494,308	$988,617	$1,235,771	$2,471,542
45	$353,766	$707,532	$1,415,065	$1,768,831	$3,537,661
50	$503,295	$1,006,590	$2,013,180	$2,516,474	$5,032,949

Assumes 7 percent per year gains on investments after taxes.

If you start out short of the required minimum for investment vehicles with higher rates of return (CDs, mutual funds, bonds, and so on), make it your goal to accumulate the minimum as quickly as possible, and then switch the funds to investments that will grow at 7 percent or higher. You can spend the months required researching investment options. (See Chapters 5 and 12.)

Slash Entertainment Costs 50 Percent over the Next Six Months

Dinner and drinks out, movie outings, concerts, and cable television may seem essential, but what's essential about paying $4.50 for a drink, $6 for a tub of popcorn, or $600 every year for movie channels you seldom watch? Your entertainment spending may be the easiest part of your budget to cut. Achieving this uncomplicated short-term goal will make you feel great and perhaps motivate you to extend the cutback and allocate the savings to your retirement plan.

How to Monitor Your Progress

If you've created visionary long-term goals, you've already faced hurdles in achieving the short-term goals necessary to materialize those dreams. You may feel like you failed, but the beauty of failing to reach short-term goals when working toward your long-term goals, is that even if you only accomplish a fraction of the goal, you're in a better place than you would have been without the goal in place. Failure in this context is normal, and in reality it's a mark of success—you are still moving in the right direction and benefiting from the effort. Learning how to better structure short-term goals is progress, as is being more conscious of your financial realities. Taking financial responsibility is a huge success, and it's quite possible you set your initial goals too high.

It's advisable to review your progress toward short-term goals at least every three months. Some questions to ask include the following:

- Are your short-term goals effectively working toward your long-term goals? If not, what needs to be changed?
- Are you making the returns on your investments that you need to meet your long-term goals? If returns have been falling short, you

either need to save more, or find a higher-return investment to meet your goals.

- What caused the missteps? Did you miss your savings hurdle because of unexpected one-time expenses, or because you fell off the budget wagon? What do you need to do to get back on course?

After you have analyzed your goals, make any adjustments to existing goals—extending or shortening the completion date, adjusting the tasks, raising or lowering the financial reach, or whatever is required. If your long-term goals still reflect the dreams you want to manifest, and you have reached some, or all, of your short-term goals, create a new set of logically ordered, short-term goals that will maintain the momentum.

ALERT!

Prioritize your goals. If you have massive credit card debt, or delinquent accounts, addressing these crisis situations needs to be a top priority. The cost of carrying high-interest debt or allowing delinquencies to affect your FICO score, will defeat goals before you get them off the ground. Once you've fought the debt dragon, you can refocus your goals on savings and wealth creation.

The review process helps you—and your children, if they are participating—recognize your progress. And by all means, celebrate the milestones, no matter how small. Anything worth accomplishing is only achieved by envisioning, recording, and mastering a series of tasks, goals, and dreams. If you have taken the reins by creating goals and working to achieve them, you are on your way to financial health and, quite possibly, wealth.

Chapter 4

Becoming Financially Literate

It's true that financial planners, brokers, and investors often use terms that are foreign to the rest of us. Although it's undeniably challenging, if you want to be able to differentiate between a good investment portfolio and a mediocre or inadequate one, you need to learn the vocabulary and gain at least a basic understanding of the concepts. This way, you will acquire a financial vocabulary that will help you whenever you talk with a financial advisor or tax consultant.

Learning the Lingo

While financial lingo sounds exclusionary, few of the concepts are difficult. When you talk with a broker, or read through a book like this, and you come across a term that you don't know, take heart. Your author or financial advisor also didn't know what the term meant at one point. If you can read and understand this sentence, you can understand investment concepts.

ALERT!

Experts estimate that some 42 million Americans live paycheck to paycheck. In surveys, 60 percent of Americans revealed that a one-week delay in receiving their paycheck would result in failure to pay an essential bill, such as mortgage, rent, or car payments. If you're similarly living on the edge, it's time to pare back expenses or generate more income.

Utilizing Resources

The fact of the matter is that merely reading about financial matters will vastly increase your understanding and comfort level, which will in turn lead you to make smarter and proactive decisions about your money. Rather than tackling books, start with magazines, newspapers, and the Internet. Try some of the following publications:

- *Kiplinger's Personal Finance* magazine
- *Fortune* magazine
- *Forbes* magazine
- *Money* magazine
- *SmartMoney* magazine
- *BusinessWeek* magazine
- The *Wall Street Journal*
- *The New York Times*
- The business section of your local newspaper
- Marketwatch.com (*www.marketwatch.com*)
- MSN Money (*http://moneycentral.msn.com*)
- Yahoo! Finance (*http://finance.yahoo.com*)

Your local library may offer free access to many of these resources. Many of the listed magazines and newspapers also offer access to their publications online.

Finding the Time

If you going to take full responsibility for your financial future, you need to find the time to become more knowledgeable so that you can make beneficial choices that will directly affect your future. Set a reasonable goal, such as to read one article a day, or one book a month. Take notes when you read and put your notes in files according to topic so that you can review them when you need to make a decision relevant to that topic. It will take a while, but you will begin to put all the pieces together.

Creating a Workable Budget

One of the first things you need to gain control over your own finances is an honest assessment of your current financial flows. Every single mother needs to know how much money is coming in, how much money is going out, and how much she owes to credit cards, banks, or other creditors. You cannot build a financial future without a clear picture of what you owe, what you earn, and where your money is going.

Stay on top of your budget. If you have fallen short for two straight months, write down every cent you spend and track the source of excess. Sticking your head in the sand will only make the situation worse. Get the matter in hand and trim where necessary. You'll feel better and get back on top sooner.

A budget worksheet is a great way to organize your finances to make sure you're not spending more than you have can afford and to keep yourself on target to reach your financial goals. While it is almost impossible to hit your budget figures exactly during the first few months, use your shortcomings as the roadmap for crafting a truly refined, workable budget. Basically, to create a workable budget, you need to assemble the following information:

- **After-tax income:** This is the amount you receive in a check after your employer withholds income taxes. To raise your standard of living, find a way to raise your income.
- **Savings:** Paying yourself first every month means building a financial cushion and a lucrative future. The more you can increase your savings, the better.
- **Required expenses:** These are your unavoidable, necessary costs. Trim where you can, and if you are living beyond your means, lower your expectations and your spending budget.
- **Expendable expenses:** These are the things you may enjoy but that you don't need to live, such as alcohol, jewelry, expensive groceries, fancy coffees, dining out, movie rentals, or cable television service. You can seriously pare down or eliminate these budget items.

It's important to figure out every conceivable expense that weighs down your true-life spending pattern. Use the following list as a guideline for creating the in-depth list of expenses you will need to create a thorough, realistic, functional budget:

- Rent or mortgage
- Personal and residential taxes
- Medical insurance, dental insurance, glasses or contact lenses, medicine, co-pays
- Car insurance, gas and car maintenance, parking expenses, tolls
- Home or renter's insurance
- Utilities (electricity, water, gas), Internet, cable, telephone, cell phone
- Groceries, eating out, entertaining at home
- Loans or credit card payments
- Savings
- Tuition or student loans
- Grooming expenses (haircuts, cosmetics)
- Clothing and clothing maintenance, shoes, coats

- Entertainment (movies, concerts, book purchases, coffee, night out with the girls)
- Special occasions (birthdays, weddings, Christmas)
- Emergencies
- Professional associations, conferences, classes
- Gym or club memberships
- Vacations, getaways
- Veterinary bills
- Children (school activities, tuition, child care, medicine, lessons)

If you've made your budget and you can't figure out how you will be able to save money given your current income and circumstances, first consider reducing some of your expendable expenses, and then reduce required expenses until you can bolster your income. If you can raise your income and still keep your budget costs level, you can plow the overflow into savings or investments. Whatever you do, avoid spending more than you earn. Here's a sample budget reflecting narrow margins and a budget that restrains spending:

Sample Budget for One Month

Income	
Salaries, wages, tips, etc., as well as interest on checking account, after taxes	$3,000
Savings	
Savings to build two- to five-month emergency cash balance	$50
Savings for down payment	$100
Savings for retirement	$150
Savings for children's education	$10
Savings for vacations	$50
Savings subtotal	$360

(continued)

Required expenses	
Mortgage or rent payment, including homeowner's or renter's insurance	$850
Utilities—electric, garbage, water, heat	$80
Food, excluding fancy nights out and alcohol	$550
Medical and other insurance premiums	$30
Clothing, including cleaning	$100
Car payments, insurance, maintenance, public transit	$300
Telephone and Internet	$45
Credit card and other debt	$25
Child care	$100
Other required expenses	$250
Required expenses subtotal	$2,330
Expendable expenses	
Food eaten out, alcohol, other nonrequired food expenses	$40
Movie rentals and theater visits, including snacks	$15
Vacation expenses	$40
Cable and nonessential Internet and telephone	$50
Gifts and donations	$10
Other expendable expenses	$50
Expendable expenses subtotal	$205
Subtract savings and all expenses from income; this is your budget buffer	$105

If you can manage it, it's very wise to save the amount of your budget buffer. If your buffer is negative, you need to cut expenses and/or increase your income.

Review your budget regularly and make adjustments to reflect changes. If your salary bumps up slightly, make sure you know exactly how much extra cash is actually coming in. Before you rush out to buy a fancier car, allocate a healthy portion to paying down your credit card debt or to upping your monthly savings.

Calculating Your Net Worth

Planning your financial life without knowing your net worth is like trying to navigate a remote, unknown territory with a map but no idea of where you are on the map. You might take purposeful steps in one direction, but if you don't know where you are, you won't end up where you want to be.

Calculating your net worth shows you exactly where you stand financially. Your net worth is the total value of your liquid assets minus your debts. Assets include cash, stock, bonds; the equity in your home; and any personal property you could sell relatively fast, like extra cars or jewelry. Debts include car loans, mortgages, home equity loans, furniture loans, student loans, and credit card debt.

FACT

Some 19 million middle-class Americans are suffering from "affluent attitude," acting as if they have incomes in the top 1 percent when they clearly do not. An additional 20 percent think they will someday join the elite, but 99 percent will never make it. Unfortunately, many Americans inappropriately mirror the expectations, aspirations, and spending habits of the very wealthy.

You might automatically put your car down as a valuable asset, but unless you're in the process of selling the car and won't buy a replacement, you'll never see that value as cash. A car is a depreciating asset. The same can be said for jewelry and other personal property that you aren't in the process of selling. Even if you could part with valuable jewelry, you would probably only achieve 50 to 80 percent of its retail value. Some financial advisors include the cash value of life insurance policies in the assets column, but unless you are in the process of redeeming them for cash, they may skew your net worth calculation.

Calculating Your Net Worth

Assets (add)	Liabilities (subtract)
Home (appraised value)	Mortgage
Car	Loan balance
Jewelry	Equity loan
Antiques	Credit card balances
Bonds	Student loans
Total assets	Total liabilities
Net worth = total assets minus total liabilities	

Once you have a clear picture of what you really have and what you really owe, you will see where improvements need to happen. If one of your long-term goals is to buy a home, you'll need to accumulate a down payment. If you want to travel, you're going to need a couple thousand dollars to see Europe. The point is that many of your goals require cold, hard cash that will be paid out of your net worth, so to reach your goals, you'll want to increase your assets and diminish your liabilities. By knowing your net worth at the outset and staying on top of it, you'll be able to track your progress.

Consulting a Financial Advisor

After you have computed your net worth, established a budget, outlined your debts, and devised a plan to conquer them, it's time to sit down with a financial advisor. This professional can help you better understand your true situation, refine your goals, and advise you how to best invest whatever money you do have. Also, if you are ready to purchase a home, an hour spent with a financial advisor can be very beneficial. Get all your financial ducks in a row, and have pointed, prepared questions. To stay focused on the information, you need to become increasingly savvy about investments, the house you want to buy, or your budgeting needs.

When and Why You Need to Hire a Financial Advisor

If you've accumulated somewhere close to $100,000, it can be a good idea to consult with a financial advisor. A financial advisor will look at the investments you've already made, the level of risk you can and want to take, and the return you require. He or she will consider your future wants and needs and what you might need to change to be able to afford them.

You can get free or lower-cost financial advice through discount brokers like Charles Schwab, but if you have enough money saved—usually $250,000 or more—and are worried about managing taxes efficiently and setting up trusts for your children or taking other complex financial steps, consider using a fee-only financial advisor.

If you've just started accumulating savings, it's best to focus on the first steps in the process: Save more money and invest it.

Finding the Right Broker or Financial Advisor

A financial advisor is a professional trained to create a financial plan that will maximize your chances of being able to afford the things you want in life. He or she will usually create a written financial plan for you that you can later consult to check your progress. Ask around among friends and coworkers, call your Better Business Bureau, or ask your banker for references. Once you've selected three potential advisors, ask them if they are willing to meet with you briefly to see if they are the right fit for you. You may be able to assess this over the telephone, but it's always helpful to see the person before you make a final decision.

Know Who Is Paying Them

Many financial advisors are paid on commission. They receive large payments for selling load mutual funds, annuities, or other investments to you. There is an obvious conflict of interest when you deal with financial advisors who profit by generating activity in your portfolio that may leave you less well off financially. If you have enough money, use a fee-only financial advisor, who may have a professional designation like CFP or CFA after their name. Fee-only financial advisors are paid based on the amount of assets they manage, so the more money they make for you, the better off they are.

As a result, fee-only advisors are more likely to work for your benefit when considering investments.

Know Where Their Loyalties Lie

You definitely want to know how your prospective financial advisor makes her money. If she is compensated based on product sales, it's likely that you will be sold those products, regardless of whether there are better options for you. If you firmly believe that your advisor won't do the wrong thing—if, say, she's a close friend you trust with your life—this may not be an issue.

Go In Fully Prepared

If you are going to see a financial advisor, put together a financial plan that you think could work. Also consider the risk you are willing to take and all the large expenses that you need to make over your lifetime (paying for your children's education, buying a home, taking care of your parents in their old age, and so on). Your advisor will appreciate that you are prepared, especially if you arrive with an open mind, ready to listen to and take the advisor's suggestions.

QUESTION?

What would be a reasonable fee range?
Many fee-only advisors charge fees for advice—from a couple hundred dollars for a financial plan to thousands of dollars for a family financial plan including estate work (wealth transfer to kids and grandkids, accounts used to minimize taxes, and related legal and tax consultation). Most fee-only financial advisors also charge 0.75 percent to 1.5 percent of assets per year.

Determine Your Risk Quotient

Be ready to tell the advisor what level of risks you are willing to take. Keep in mind that investing involves measured risks you must take to achieve your financial goals. It usually takes some time to get used to the volatility in your portfolio, but without taking risks you won't achieve much in the way of return.

How to Evaluate a Financial Advisor

The National Association of Personal Financial Advisers (online at *www .napf.org*) provides a financial advisor checklist that will help you determine whether you've found the right advisor for your needs, as follows:

- Did she spend at least two hours at your initial meeting getting to know you, your financial situation, your goals, and your concerns?
- Did she fully answer your questions?
- Does she represent others within your income bracket range?
- Did she help you develop a strategy for improving your financial situation, establishing savings and retirement funds, and developing wealth?
- Did she provide you with supplemental materials that addressed your concerns or helped you learn?
- Did she fully explain any costs involved in the consultation or follow-up?
- Were her costs reasonable?
- Does she have a solid reputation?
- Did she help you create a workable strategy?

Establishing Your Values and Trusting Your Instincts

Do your research thoroughly, and then trust your instincts. If you feel uneasy about an investment, probe deeper before sinking large amounts of cash into it. If you feel that a brokerage firm is pushing you in a direction that leaves you doubting their intentions, trust that instinct and express your concerns. While it's wise to listen to information from a savvy investment counselor, you are the one who has to live with the consequences, and you have the right to make all of your financial decisions.

If your conscience flares when investing in companies that pollute the atmosphere or use animals for cosmetic testing, you have a multitude of choices that will align with your principles.

You can, for example, purchase shares in socially responsible mutual funds. Each socially responsible fund has its own investing mandate that instructs its managers not to invest in banned companies and industries—for instance, those that adversely affect the environment, sell products like guns or cigarettes, or make money, directly or indirectly, on gambling. The investing mandates of socially responsible funds vary. One fund might be allowed to invest in companies that support the distribution and use of condoms, while others explicitly oppose the practice. Mandates are usually spelled out in the fund's prospectus or clearly stated on the fund management firm's Web site. Any time you make smart investments that also align with your heart, you'll sleep better at night.

FACT

According to the Bureau of Labor Statistics, mothers who work full-time contribute a total of $476 billion a year to household incomes. Working mothers make a vast contribution to the U.S. economy. According to Mediamark Research, in 2005, working mothers spent $94.8 billion on new cars, $16.5 billion on clothing, and more than $26 billion on vacations.

Investment Clubs Versus Investing Solo

Investment clubs offer you the opportunity to meet people at various stages in their investing career—beginning to seasoned—with common goals and a passion for investing. Since most clubs pool funds, they frequently form committees to research stocks and develop a communal process for stock selection. This offers you a chance to learn a lot about stocks in a short amount of time.

FACT

NAIC (National Association of Investors Corporation), a nonprofit, tax-exempt organization that offers investment information and education, has reported that all-women investment-club stock accounts often out-perform all-men club accounts. In 1999, women's clubs scored 24 percent in gains versus the 19 percent earned by the men.

Investment clubs offer a chance to learn how to invest in individual stocks from others who may have more experience than you. Interaction with other investors will open your eyes to new investment styles and ideas you wouldn't have considered on your own.

The only major negative of being part of an investment club is the time commitment. You will be expected to attend some meetings, and you may also be asked to collect information about companies in the group's stock portfolio or to make stock recommendations to the group. Whatever method you choose to explore, take any and every opportunity to learn about financial management and investing. Remember, knowledge is power!

Chapter 5

Banking and Short-Term Investing

Most banks no longer actively solicit customers by offering deposit gifts, but you can win definite advantages—such as lowered minimum deposit requirements, competitive interest rates, or free checks—that make shopping for a bank worthwhile. The same holds true for short-term investing. This can seem like a lot of comparison-shopping for a small benefit, and yet shopping around raises earning potential that adds up in the long run. Avoiding hidden fees, utilizing higher-yielding bank products, and discovering lucrative short-term investments are simple financial steps that will help you maximize your savings.

What You Need to Know about Banking

Some banks have options that can benefit you, and others charge excessive fees. Rather than selecting a bank for proximity, family tradition, or effective advertising, you can save money by knowing your banking options, how banks function, what practices will incur unnecessary expense, and what practices will help you save money. Your choices boil down to the following:

- **Local banks:** These offer the advantage of letting you build a relationship with your banker. They may charge higher fees, but they may also be quicker to handle mistakes or to acquire loans.
- **National banks:** Fees, including ATM charges, may be lower, but these banks may also make more mistakes that require excessive effort on your part to sort them out.
- **Savings and loans:** These may offer higher interest rates and loan accessibility, but they may not be as flexible on checking services.
- **Credit unions:** Membership usually requires an affiliation with other credit union members (such as a Chevron credit union for Chevron employees). Credit unions are owned and controlled by the people who use them, as nonprofit organizations. You can find credit unions at *www.creditunion.com*. Because they're nonprofit groups, credit unions can offer rates and loan terms more favorable than those offered through other banks.

The types of accounts available include the following:

- **Basic checking:** This type of account is used only for bill paying and daily expenses (earns no interest).
- **Interest-bearing checking:** If you can stash and maintain a $1,000 balance, this might be a better option. These accounts pay interest but usually require a minimum balance to offset charges.
- **Basic savings:** Shop for competitive rates and services such as overdraft protection or automatic deposits.
- **Money market:** This type of account combines checking, savings, and investment funds. They usually require a healthy deposit to open, but they may also provide free checks and pay interest.

- **Express:** These accounts can be useful if you use ATM, Internet, or phone for access or to pay bills.
- **Lifeline:** These accounts usually have restricted check writing and are aimed for the low-income customer.

Rather than choosing a bank because you recognize the name and think thousands of branches throughout the country (and world) give them more credence, or because it's where your family has always banked, a savvy woman will shop for banking services with the same diligence she uses when shopping for clothing and shoes.

Selecting a Bank

Bank branches are seemingly everywhere—store fronts with little differentiation, which makes some people willing to walk to the closest corner branch and open an account, despite the bad service and without regard for the interest, fees, and loan availability offered by that bank. As a financially savvy woman, you can do better! Make sure you understand the following points in order to make an informed decision when choosing a bank.

Questions You Need to Ask

As you shop for the best banking opportunities, ask the bank representative the following questions:

- What are the service charges?
- How long does it take for a check to clear? Banks typically limit the amount of money you can readily access from deposited checks. To avoid overdrafts, ask your bank how much is available for immediate withdrawal, and how many days will it be before the entire amount is available.
- What is your overdraft policy?
- What is the interest rate on savings accounts?
- What are the advantages of having a checking or savings account there?

Automatic Bill Payments

This is an arrangement you make with your mortgage company, credit cards, insurance companies, and other debtors to withdraw funds from your checking account. Funds are extracted on a set date each month, unless and until you cancel the arrangement. Make sure you notify credit cards when terminating automatic withdrawals or they will clip you for returned check fees when their bank hits up your bank for the funds. Also make sure you mail credit card payments—at least the minimum amount due—by the due date. Make sure you keep abreast of all the amounts being withdrawn and that you have adequate funds to cover them. When you cancel or alter the arrangements, make sure you check the statements for three months to verify that automatic payments have been cancelled or altered per your instructions.

Scheduled Transfers

Money is transferred from one account to another, per your instructions. You can opt to have a portion of your direct deposit sent to your savings account, or to have 20 percent of your balance transferred to your savings account on a set date each month.

Overdrafts

When you don't have sufficient funds to cover a withdrawal or a check, the bank may pay the amount and charge you a penalty. You need to know their overdraft policy, whether you have overdraft protection, and what they will charge you for overdrafts. You may be able to use your savings as overdraft protection, but—obviously—it's far better to avoid the problem altogether. Overdrafts also mean charges from the bank—and the credit card company or landlord or your doctor—and can affect your credit rating.

Controlling Your Finances

How you watch your money will be as important as how much money you earn. When you receive your bank statements (whether by snail mail or e-mail), it's vitally important that you scour it for errors and validate any charges. If you find errors, you may only have sixty to ninety days to catch and correct them, so it's best to call the bank, and then write a verifying letter so that you have a record for your files.

ALERT!

Most employers offer direct deposits for your paychecks. Make sure you know the actual date that the funds will land in your account so that you can make sure any automatic deductions or expenses can be fully funded by the due date. Give yourself at least three days' leeway to account for glitches.

Also, it's imperative that you balance your checking account monthly. It may seem daunting, but if you stay on top of it, it's merely a matter of checking all credits against your withdrawal receipts, checks, automatic withdrawals, or charges; checking the debits against your deposit slips or direct deposit paycheck stubs, or interest earned; and then subtracting any not-yet-recorded items from the bank balance.

The Virtues of Short-Term Liquidity

Short-term liquidity means that your cash remains easily accessible. While ideally you are working toward long-term investments, you always want a certain amount of cash available for minor emergencies or blips on the financial radar screen. The smart investor maximizes returns on her cash by choosing money market accounts, or purchasing certificates of deposit or T-bills that earn a higher interest rate than traditional checking or savings accounts.

Assessing Your Account Options

As soon as you accumulate more than $500 in your savings, it's time to deposit the money into an account that will earn competitive interest rates and yet remain liquid (accessible). Many people assume their local banks pay competitive interest rates on savings or checking, and they opt for the comfort of keeping it all under one umbrella. In fact, savings and checking accounts often pay little to no interest, and many have monthly charges that eat away at your savings. Instead, you can house your savings in a money market account that will pay higher, competitive interest and that frequently offers other benefits.

The Federal Deposit Insurance Corporation (FDIC) insures up to $100,000 per person per FDIC-insured bank (you can check online, at *www .fdic.gov*, to see if your bank is insured). The FDIC also insures up to $250,000 per person, per insured institution for individual retirement accounts (IRAs), as long as the individual owner directs the investment. When a management firm ("plan administrator") controls the investment of employees' IRA assets—as is the case with most company profit-sharing and defined-benefit retirement plan assets—the accounts are not FDIC-insured.

FDIC Coverage

Insured	Not Insured
Checking*	Mutual funds, including money market funds
Savings*	Annuity funds
Trusts*	Life insurance policies
Certificates of deposit (CDs)	Stocks
Treasury bills	Corporate bonds
Treasury notes	Municipal bonds***
IRA accounts**	U.S. Treasury securities ****

*Up to $100,000 (per insured bank) **Up to $250,000 (per individual, per insured bank) ***Usually covered by private insurance **** U.S. Treasury securities (bills, notes, and bonds) are backed by the full faith and credit of the U.S. government

Taking the time to make an extra 1 to 2 percent per year may seem pointless, but even a slightly higher return on your cash assets can make a big difference over a few years' time. Once you learn the best places to stash your cash and make the minimal effort required to buy T-bills or deposit your funds in money market accounts, you will share in the windfall that your bank and brokerage firms have been earning on funds most people park in zero or low-return accounts.

A money market account is a mutual fund that invests in short-term securities, like U.S. Treasury debt obligations, short-term bonds backed by homeowners' mortgage payments, CDs, and short-term funds lent to large corporations. Many large brokerage firms, banks, and credit unions offer money market accounts that include unlimited check writing and an ATM card. Most require a minimum balance of $2,000, but you can find institutions that will open an account with a minimum balance of $500 or even less. Shop around for the best interest rates and perks. The only downside to money market accounts is that they are not federally insured, but they are still among the safest options. Money market funds invested in short-term treasury bonds currently yield about 3.3 percent on average, according to the Web site *www.bankrate.com*, but yields on any short-term cash investment like a money market or CD will vary over time.

Current interest rates for banking institutions fluctuate, so it's always prudent to check the rates, which is published daily in your local newspaper in the financial or business section. You can also go online to *www.bankrate.com* to find out which institution is paying the highest rates.

Money Market Accounts

Money market accounts have been around for eons, but in past decades you had to deposit a minimum of $10,000. Today, they're far more accessible to everyone. Some firms that offer these accounts include Fidelity Investments (minimum investment $2,500), Merrill-Lynch ($2,000), Charles Schwab ($2,500), Morgan Stanley ($2,000), and Edward Jones ($1,000).

Certificates of Deposit (CDs)

Certificates of deposit (CDs) are bank-issued securities that pay a fixed rate of return for a specified period of time, ranging from one month to ten years. The rates may be higher than money market account rates. One

advantage CDs have over money market accounts is that they are federally insured up to $100,000; however, the major disadvantage is that you
can rarely withdraw or cash in the CDs before they are due without paying a penalty that cuts severely into your interest earnings. Money market
accounts are always liquid, and you are not penalized if you need to withdraw the funds. Therefore, if you find a money market account that pays
equal or higher interest rates to comparable CDs, you should choose the
money market account.

ALERT!

Although CDs are federally insured up to $100,000, they are only as safe
as the bank that sells them. To check whether your bank's deposits are
safe by virtue of federal government-backed Federal Deposit Insurance Corporation (FDIC) insurance, visit the official Web site of the FDIC
online at ✍ *www.fdic.gov.*

To find the best rates, you rarely need to go further than the Internet. Sites
that provide valuable information include *www.bauerfinancial.com*, *www*
.banked.com, and *www.bankrate.com*. CDs can also be purchased through brokerage firms, and brokerage firms are more likely to offer liquidity—you may be
able to cash in your CDs before the date of maturity by paying a small commission that will be less than the clipping you'll take from traditional banks.

Treasury Bills (T-Bills)

Treasury bills (T-bills) are fixed-income securities that can be purchased
from the U.S. Treasury Department (*www.publicdebt.treas.gov*) or through a
bank or brokerage firm. They are typically issued in $1,000 increments and
mature in a year or less. Unlike CDs, T-bills do not pay interest. Instead, they
are issued at a discount and are paid in full upon maturity. Thus, you might
purchase a $10,000 T-bill for $9,500 and receive $10,000 when you cash it in
a year later.

T-bills are fully insured by the U. S. government and thus are logically
the safest investment. If you buy them through a broker, you can usually sell
them or only a small commission and collect your money within three days.

The Virtues of Mid-Term Liquidity

If you are confident you won't need to tap your funds for two to five years, you can afford to take slightly higher risks. Investing in bonds or treasury notes are a couple of ways to reap higher returns. If you want to make your money grow, let's talk options!

Bonds

High-quality government agency bonds are only slightly riskier than money market accounts, CDs, or T-bills. Agency bonds are a loan you make to government agencies (Fannie Mae, Freddie Mac) that write mortgages. The bond serves as an IOU, and it clearly spells out how much you are lending, when the note will mature, and how much interest you will receive. Interest is typically paid in semiannual installments.

FACT

Treasury bills ("T-Bills") are among the safest investments you can buy. Moreover, gains on T-Bills are not subject to state or local taxes. This tax break makes T-bills, which pay relatively low rates of interest, a more palatable investment; an equivalent but fully taxable interest-paying bond would have to offer a higher rate of interest to provide you with the same gains after taxes.

Bonds are available in $1,000, $5,000, or $10,000 increments, and they can mature in any time range from one to up to thirty years. Shorter maturities mean lowered risk and lower interest rates. Government bonds are assumed to be the safest in the bond universe. On the opposite end of the bond spectrum, "junk" bonds issued by corporations are much riskier but also pay more interest.

Treasury Notes

Treasury notes are bonds issued by the U.S. government in increments of $1,000. Maturity dates range from two years to ten years. Notes can bought directly from the government or through brokerage firms. Buying through a brokerage firm will involve paying a commission, but once again, doing so keeps the funds more liquid and outweighs the small price you pay.

Treasury note interest payments are exempt from state and local taxes. If you sell the note prior to maturation, any gain you incur is taxable at the federal, state, and local level, as a long-term gain if held more than one year and a short-term gain if held less than one year. Long-term capital gains are taxable at 20 percent. Short-term gains are taxed as ordinary income, so the rate depends on your tax bracket, most likely 25 to 28 percent at the federal level.

ALERT!

Money market accounts typically offer a higher interest rate than traditional checking or savings accounts, with no hidden charges. Shopping for the highest rate can pay off—some money market accounts pay four times the rate of traditional bank accounts and still offer free checking and ATM cards.

Corporate Bonds

Rather than the U.S. Government, individual corporations sell corporate bonds, and thus the government does not secure, or guarantee, these bonds. Corporate bonds will be as solid as the company that offers them, so it's imperative that you check the company's credit rating. Your broker will be able to tell you what the major credit rating companies say about the rating of the bonds you are considering buying. Ratings from Standard & Poor's, a major bond-rating company, start at AAA (highest credit rating) and descend: AAA-, AA+, AA, AA-, A, and so on. If a company's bond has a rating below BBB-, that bond is considered relatively speculative and not "investment grade." If you are buying individual bonds on your own, stay above a BBB rating.

If you have a portfolio with less than $1 million in assets, buying individual corporate bonds will probably expose you to more risk than necessary. In this case, it's better to buy into a diversified bond mutual fund or bond market-tracking exchange-traded fund.

Municipal Bonds

State or local governments issue municipal bonds to pay for public improvements, such as bridges, roads, or schools, or to cover nonspecific short-term government funding shortfalls. Because interest is not subject to federal taxes, or home state taxes when the bond funds a government in your state, investors in high tax brackets benefit most by holding municipal bonds. Gains on municipal bonds, if any, are subject to federal and state taxes. Since they are generally backed by private insurance, municipal bonds are very safe investments. However, highly rated municipal bonds generally offer moderately low rates of interest. They can be useful as a safety valve in balancing higher risk investments and rounding out your portfolio.

FACT

A bond will repay the owner a certain amount, known interchangeably as the "face value" or "par." A bond trading at par trades at the value you will receive when the bond matures. In the case of otherwise nontaxable municipal securities issued by your own state and treasury securities, buying at par value when possible will let you avoid larger capital gains taxes as long as you hold the bond to maturity or sell earlier at par.

Municipal bond yields may be higher than they seem. If you buy a fully taxable bond yielding 7.14 percent and have a 30 percent marginal tax rate, you will keep 5 percent after taxes (7.14 multiplied by 1–30 percent). This means that a municipal bond yielding 5 percent will give you the same after-tax interest as a 7.14 percent fully taxable bond. Thus, a lower-yielding municipal bond may do more for your net worth than a taxable bond with a higher yield. Individuals with high incomes, and high marginal tax rates, benefit most from nontaxable bonds. You don't pay taxes on gains and income in IRAs and other tax-deferred retirement accounts. Municipal bonds, whose benefit is the tax shelter, should therefore not be purchased for your IRA and similar tax-advantaged accounts.

When you invest in bonds, you earn interest as well as the difference between the price you pay for the bond and the principal you collect at the bond's maturity. The total return you receive per year from the bond, including regard for both sources of return, is quoted as its yield to maturity (YTM) or yield to call (YTC). Yield to maturity is the total return earned when you hold the bond to maturity. Callable bonds offer the issuer the opportunity to repurchase the bonds before the maturity date. This usually happens when rates fall, and the issuer can save money by repurchasing its existing bonds at the call price and then reissuing them at a lower rate. Callable bonds specify a call date that determines the first date an issuer can call the bonds. YTC is the annualized total return you will earn on the bond if it is repurchased at the first call date. Generally, it's proper to expect to earn the lower of a bond's YTM or YTC (if it has one).

Chapter 6

Assessing and Conquering Your Debt

Not only has the federal government been overspending, throwing the entire society into a deficit economy, but individuals and families have grossly overspent—and grossly overcharged their purchases onto high-interest credit cards. Americans owe $1.7 trillion dollars in personal debt, and one-third of that is credit card debt. If you stacked a pile of $100 bills, a million would reach just over six feet. A billion would be a mile high, and a trillion would skyrocket 350 miles into the stratosphere.

A Maxed-Out Economy

Statistics show that most Americans are staggering under the weight of exceptional credit card debt. Indeed, taken on a national basis, the amount of the debt creates a bleak reality; taken on an individual basis, it's catastrophic. Maxed-out credit cards can easily become a downward spiral that all too quickly becomes a fiscal death spiral for many.

FACT

The total volume of consumer loans—credit cards, auto loans, and other nonmortgage debt—more than doubled between 1990 and 2000, to $1.7 trillion. The average American carries approximately $8,400 in credit card debt.

Many enter their thirties with five-figure debt, which leads to a sense of powerlessness and hopelessness about any ability to become solvent, much less save money or build a retirement. Once caught in its wicked web, high-interest credit card debt is a monster that will haunt your waking and sleeping dreams.

Good Debt Versus Bad Debt

Most financial advisors advocate that consumers have no more than 36 percent of their total gross income allocated to debt repayment—including house payments, car payments, insurance payments, medical payments, credit cards, and student loans. It is important to make smart money decisions by differentiating between good and bad debts—maximizing one and minimizing the other.

Basically, when a debt vastly increases the actual amount to be paid for a product that doesn't increase in value, it's a bad debt. When debt is used purposefully and intelligently to build wealth, such as to invest in a solid business venture, it's a good debt. Some examples include the following:

- When you buy a product on a credit card or by acquiring a loan, and that product immediately goes down in value, or loses any potential to gain in value, that's a bad debt.
- When you borrow to buy something that will result in increased value—by taking out student loans, real-estate loans, home mortgages, and business loans, for example—that's a good debt.
- When you have debts that are tax-deductible or that will produce more wealth in the long run, they are also good debts, provided you repay them as soon as possible.

Taking a second mortgage to pay down credit card debt can turn bad debt into good debt, particularly if you obtain a home-equity loan with a tax-deductible, 6 percent interest rate to pay down credit card balances logging 20 to 30 percent interest—provided you pay it off as soon as possible and don't max out your credit cards again. In general, buying a home or refinancing to vastly reduce excessively high interest rates is usually good debt, as is generating limited debt to buy investments that are virtually guaranteed to meet expectations within a short period of time. (Note that stocks can be unexpectedly volatile and rarely justify a home equity loan.)

Credit cards generally create bad debt. If you paid off your balances in full every month, prior to the grace period, you wouldn't pay any interest and would thus avoid generating bad debt. Unfortunately, few of us are able to pay the balances in full each month. In fact, the vast majority of people overcharge and end up paying the minimum amount due, which immediately generates bad debt. And once you're under the elephant that maxed-out, high-interest credit card debt quickly becomes, it's exceedingly hard to dig your way out—and it's very, very costly.

Pros and Cons of Credit Cards

Actually, there are few pros to having credit cards. Created as a convenience, they have, in fact, become a nightmare. Even if you open an account with the intent of paying the balance in full each month, it's incredibly easy to rack up balances so high that it will take years to pay them down. Pretty much everyone is guilty of adding to, rather than diminishing, credit card balances.

Credit Card Pros

Other than convenience, and perhaps minimal protection, the biggest pro to having credit cards is that successful management of three bank cards and two department store accounts can, indeed, bolster your credit rating. However, lenders blanch when they see excessive credit cards, maximization of credit limits, slow payments, late payments, chronic delinquencies, or other worrisome debt repayment habits.

FACT

Americans both love and abuse their credit cards. Reportedly, the amount of outstanding personal credit card debt more than tripled between 1990 and 2002, from $173 billion to a whopping $661 billion.

Credit Card Cons

The cons frequently far outweigh the pros. Credit card issuers are constantly seeking customers who charge beyond their means and make minimum payments carrying 18 to 30 percent interest for long periods of time. Often the interest charges will double, or even triple, the amount originally charged, making you poor and the credit card company rich. Also, credit cards now charge $25 to $30 in late charges, or for going over your credit limit, and both offenses may boost your interest rate. (The average late fee for credit cards was $27.46 in mid-2005.)

Every month that you make a partial payment on your credit account, you are charged exorbitant interest, and the disposable or durable item you purchased not only continues to lose value, the amount you paid for it continues to increase. Clothing, for example, usually drops 50 percent in value the minute you wear it. This loss in value doesn't even take into account what that debt could potentially do to your credit rating.

When you apply for a loan or seek a new credit card, potential lenders will acquire your credit report and review your debt-to-income ratio. If you have used well beyond 30 percent of the available credit on your credit cards, they may charge you high interest rates, decline your loan, or refuse additional credit.

Even when you have racked up large balances, credit card companies continue to barrage you with offers, and they all sound tempting, particularly when they offer a low-interest introductory rate. However, be aware that all credit card companies source your credit rating or FICO score to determine your credit worthiness, and all inquiries are registered and may penalize you in the long run. Also, those fabulous offers almost always come with caveats:

- The rate can triple within months.
- They will raise your rates if you miss one payment.
- They keep raising your credit limit and urging you to spend more money.

If you charged $3,000 on your credit card and made minimum payments of $148.50 over the next two years, you would pay an extra $559, adding 18.6 percent to the total cost. With one late fee, your interest and fees could leap to 28 percent, raising your required monthly minimum to $159, and increasing the extra costs to $691, adding 23 percent to the total cost.

You have to read the small print—word for word. And you'll have to monitor all of your statements to watch for hidden charges or elevations in your interest rate. Despite ten years of outstanding credit and always paying her bills on time, one month a friend didn't mail the payment in time to reach the company on the due date, and they raised her interest rate to 30 percent—and she didn't even notice for a year!

Avoid Department-Store Credit Cards

Department stores are always trying to entice you to open an account. The sales clerks are trained to push these offers, which usually include 10 to 20 percent off your current purchase. "It's easy," they say, cajoling you into what is ultimately not a good idea. Department stores are notorious for charging high interest rates on their credit cards.

ALERT!

If you think your government is protecting you, think again. In 1996, the U.S. Supreme Court lifted restrictions on credit card companies, allowing them to ding you whatever they want as a late fee (around $29 presently). Also, if you default on any credit account, universal default now permits any credit card company to brand you a high risk and raise your interest rates accordingly.

Any time you opt to apply for a credit card to save 10 to 20 percent on your current purchase, you are setting yourself up for exorbitant interest rates that will soon result in your paying more than you saved. What the stores don't tell you is that they may boost your interest rate 15 to 25 percent within months, which means any balances will cost you far, far more than you saved initially. Plus, an excess of department store credit cards on your credit report may diminish your credit worthiness.

Only opt to hold credit cards at stores you frequent often, and limit your choices to two or three at most. If you cannot pay cash or use your debit card, you're better off paying with a bank credit card. Remember: Just say no to department store credit card offers.

Create a Game Plan to Reduce Debt

Transferring balances to another card and opening new cards gives you the very false illusion that you can get your debt under control. This is a very bad idea. There is no way to address the problem but to tackle it head on and to cease all credit card spending. In the past, you could declare bankruptcy and wipe the slate relatively clean (never 100 percent) and rebuild your credit score over the course of seven years. However, the government rewrote the bankruptcy laws recently, which means most people have far more limited options to make debt go away. Many more people will have to face the consequences of a series of bad decisions made over the course of many years, and you don't want to ever find yourself in that position.

Write It All Down

The first thing you have to do is assess your real situation. You cannot tackle the debt unless and until you are ready to make a completely honest appraisal. You need to pull out all your credit card statements; education, car, home, and home equity loan statements; utility bills; insurance bills; and anything else that documents how much you owe. It's time to record the cold, hard reality of each. Below is a sample table to help you start the process of tracking your debts.

Credit Assessment

Creditor	Amount Owed	Minimum Payment	Interest Rate	Credit Limit	Due Date	What I can pay
First home	$45,000	$500	7.95%	n/a	2nd	$500
Cigna Medical	$750	$89	6.7%	n/a	15th	$89
Bank of America	$6,200	$120	18.95%	$8,000	25th	$120
Macy's	$859	$45.00	24%	$600	16th	$45

Read the Fine Print

Compiling the list of accounts also means that it's time for you to get out a magnifying glass and read the fine print. You're looking for the following:

- **Interest rates (APR):** This is the annual percentage you pay for the privilege of using the credit card. Even if you opened the card at 9 percent, if you missed any payments, racked up one or more late payments, or surpassed your credit limit, the issuer may have added a stiff interest hike (unannounced). Make sure you monitor what your finance charges are per month.

- **Periodic rate:** This is the interest rate you are charged on your purchases or balance each month. You can calculate this by dividing your APR by 12 (months).
- **Finance charge:** This is the monthly fee added to your balance based on the monthly interest rate. Compute it by dividing your APR by 12 and multiplying it by your balance.
- **Grace period:** The amount of time (25 to 28 days) that lapses between when you make the purchase and when you have to pay those charges to avoid interest charges. If you are only making minimum payments on existing balances, you lost the advantage of paying within the grace period. Some cards now eliminate grace periods, but they can be useful, so opt for cards that still offer them.
- **Fixed versus variable rate:** Most credit cards have variable rates, and the very bad news is that most of them state in the small print on the back of your bill that they can raise your rates at any time, for any reason. You need to monitor this rate so that you can catch hikes in time to minimize damage.
- **Annual fees:** This can include a $40 to $80 fee for the privilege of using the card. Try to find a card that doesn't charge an annual fee—easiest to do when you have good credit.
- **Hidden fees:** If you read the small print, these extra charges are not really hidden. Charges can include balance transfer fees, cash advance fees, special services, and over-your-limit fees, all of which can be excessive.
- **Credit limit:** Remember your target is to get the balance down so that 70 percent of your credit limit is available (but not used!).
- **Consequences:** If you don't pay the bill on time, will you lose your house, your car, or your account? How much will your interest rates increase if you falter—go over your credit limit, slow pay, miss one month, pay less than the minimum, or fail to pay?

This information will help you know what needs to be paid first and to construct a viable game plan for paying down your debt. Congratulations! Knowledge is always better than denial, and you've just learned an important step in mastering your debt and becoming a savvy consumer.

Phone Calls That Can Change Your Life

Once you have the credit card accounts ordered, it's time to call each credit card company (or department store) and request a reduction in your interest rate. If you have been a long-term, responsible customer, they may automatically reduce the rate. If the first person you speak with says that they are not authorized to lower the rate, ask to speak to a supervisor. It's wise to maintain a professional, polite tone and calmly ask for what you want. If you still don't get what you want, ask to go another step up the ladder. Persist, and you will often succeed.

If you are going through a rough patch financially that you expect to smooth out, don't be afraid to share this information and to ask the supervisor if she will allow you to make interest-only payments for six months, or if she will assist you in setting up a long-term payment plan. The issuer may freeze your account for the time being, but that will help you get your finances back in line, and you can reopen it when times are better.

Get Ready, Get Set, Pay Down!

Okay, now it's time to create an action plan to pay down your debt. Using the assessment table that you created, you need to rate the urgency. For example, things like house payments, car payments, utility bills, and insurance payments take priority over credit card debt. Order your essential (hopefully good) debts so that you will pay the most important bills first. Once again, using the chart you created, allocate funds to pay minimum balances on all the accounts, and then subtract them from your income. Using this figure, deduct your budgeted living expenses to calculate the real amount of income remaining to pay down credit card debt.

Generally, you'll want to pay down the cards with the highest rate of interest first. However, if all of your cards are maxed out, and all the interest rates are in the same range, you may want to distribute funds to bring them all down to a more manageable balance. Ideally, 70 percent of your credit limit should be available. Once you have reduced interest rates, or agreed to a payment plan with the creditor, it's important that you meet your commitments to the creditor and commit to your own plan for maximizing payments to pay off, or at least pay down, the accounts.

Develop a Cash Mentality

Now you've read about the difference between good debt and bad debt, and you've been warned about incurring further credit card debt. Hereafter, any time you are tempted to whip out a credit card to purchase something that will not increase in value, you can do yourself a big favor: Ask yourself if you could pay cash for it. If you cannot afford to pay for it in cash, then you're better off not buying it.

ALERT!

Federal interest-rate hikes have increased punitive interest rates (things like late payment fees, over-your-limit fees, returned check fees, or missed payments) 25 to 30 percent in recent years. Also, over-the-limit fees shot up 17 percent from 2001 to 2004 (around $33.50), and grace periods are shrinking (from 28 days to 23 days, or zip on some cards).

Ideally, it's best to truly use your credit cards sparingly—almost strictly as an emergency safety net. If you are using your credit cards and paying off the balances in full, then fine. But if you are racking up credit charges, maxing out your cards, and paying minimum balances, you are endangering your long-term stability and decreasing your ability to obtain low-interest loans. It's vitally important that you reduce any bad debt that is dragging you down. When things are back in line, keep in mind that good debt creates wealth while bad debt saps wealth.

Chapter 7

Repairing Credit and Improving FICO Scores

Like it or not, your credit history is submitted to three credit reporting agencies, each of which computes a FICO score—a Fair and Isaacs Company formula that has been widely used to assess credit worthiness. This credit rating is used to determine whether you are worthy of the lowest interest rates or whether you are only eligible for secured or high-rate credit. One of your ultimate financial goals will be to boost and safeguard your FICO scores.

Credit Reports Defined

Your credit report is a document that offers potential lenders—or employers, or insurance companies—a report card on your ability to handle debt. It is created as soon as you establish a bank account, begin work, save money, or acquire credit. The information accumulates from day one and can sit there forever. Three credit reporting agencies—Equifax, Experian, and TransUnion—gather and dispense your credit information. Your credit report contains personal information, credit information, public information, and inquiry information, as follows:

- **Personal information:** Your name, age, Social Security number, where you've lived, and where you've worked (and for how long)
- **Credit information:** Accounts you've opened, cosigners, your credit limits, current balances, late payments, and delinquencies (accounts not paid)
- **Public information:** Information gleaned from public agencies, such as bankruptcy filings, tax liens, judgments, arrests, and occasionally child-support payments
- **Inquiry information:** A list of everyone who purchased your credit report over the last two years

A 2003 survey by the American Institute of Certified Public Accountants revealed that approximately 30 percent of women describe themselves as "confident" or a "risk taker" when it comes to managing money. Time to dust off the mirror and see yourself as you truly are—empowered, educated, energetic, and extremely capable!

Although there are smaller companies that collect credit data, one—or all three—of the major credit reporting agencies will have 90 percent of your credit information on file. If you've been turned down for a loan, you can obtain a copy of the report that generated negative information that impacted the lender's decision free of charge. You are also entitled to one free report a year. Go online to *www.annualcreditreport.com* to request one free report from each of the three agencies.

The Fair Credit Reporting Act (FCRA) was put in place to protect your privacy and establish rules for the collecting, reporting, and altering of information in your credit file. The law basically requires the credit reporting agencies to respond to your inquiries within thirty days of receipt of your complaint. They are required to investigate the matter free of charge and record the current status of the disputed item or to delete the item from your credit report. Typically, they will mail a letter to the creditor to verify that the information is correct. If the creditor cannot validate the charges, the credit reporting agencies are required to delete the item from your report and notify other agencies.

They are also required to remove any information that pertains to someone else, correct any inaccurate information, and remove duplicate information. It is, therefore, extremely important that you comb through the reports with a fine-toothed comb and ferret out items that need to be removed or corrected. If you have brought a formerly delinquent account up to date, you can have that positive information inserted.

Credit Report Errors

A relatively reasonable 30 to a whopping 90 percent of credit reports are said to have some inaccuracies. If you find substantial errors on one report, it's important to obtain, check, and clear all three reports individually. To clean up your credit reports, do the following:

- Write a letter to each of the three credit reporting agencies listing the errors.
- Attach copies of supporting documentation (cancelled checks, statements).
- Send the letter via certified mail, return receipt requested.
- Keep a copy for your files, and attach the receipt confirmation when it arrives.

- Follow up with telephone calls, if needed. Write down their name, the date, time, and gist of the conversation and put that documentation in your file.

Keep in mind that you're dealing with a bureaucracy that isn't in the business of correcting reports. You will need to follow up religiously and hound them until the corrections have been made. Once the corrections have been made, the credit reporting agencies are required to send you a copy of your corrected report free of charge. If you request it, they are also required to send the updated report to anyone who received it in the last six months, or, if the requester was an employer, the last two years.

ALERT!

Be wary of companies offering to lower your FICO score or clean up your credit report. No one has a magic wand they can wave over your credit history. They would have to go through the same steps you would—and easily can—do for free.

Once a disputed item has been removed, the credit agencies are not permitted to put it back on your report without sending you written notification and alerting you to the name, address, and telephone number of the creditor submitting the item. You are always free to write directly to the creditor to dispute the information. You can place a copy of this letter in your credit file. Once you have written to the creditor, they are also required to include a notice of dispute if they submit the information again. If the disputed item was not verified, the creditor is not permitted to submit the item again.

If They Are Your Debts

As far as legitimate items that reflect badly on your credit worthiness, you can make efforts to improve them. Bankruptcies will sit on your report for ten years; missteps like late payments will stay for seven years. Criminal convictions may remain in place for decades, as will applications for jobs that pay over $75,000 (which may require a background and credit check by the employer) or applications for credit or life insurance over $150,000.

Even if you were guilty of late payments, overdrafts, or long-running delinquencies, you can still write to the credit agencies requesting that they verify the negative posting. In some cases, the entries may be so old that the creditor may not verify the entry, which means they will remove the item from your credit report.

Pleading Your Case

Creditors are not required by law to report everything pertaining to your account. You can certainly write to the department store, utility company, or credit card company to plead your case. Perhaps you were unemployed for three months back in 2002 and ran late on your accounts. If you write to the creditors noting that you have been an excellent customer—who has paid $1,200 in interest payments, and who rectified that situation and has kept the account current for the past three years—they may opt to remove the negative report.

If your initial inquiry elicits a negative response, write to the president of the company expressing dismay that they have refused to help and again noting how much interest you have paid and the overall health of your account and your paying habits. All you are asking for is for them to write a letter to the credit reporting agencies, and it's not an unreasonable request.

If you are still a customer, don't hesitate to play upon that advantage, noting perhaps that you receive credit card offers constantly and may consider closing your account if they are unwilling to help you restore your good credit standing. Always begin by being very polite, yet straightforward. You'd be surprised how many times the creditors will do what you request.

Should You Settle Old Accounts?

If you have a long-standing unpaid bill, and you are applying for home financing, you may want to offer a settlement in return for a clean slate.

Creditors often leap at offers to pay half of the original amount, particularly if it's been hanging out there a long time. If you do this, however, it is vitally important that you request a letter from the creditor agreeing to the terms of the settlement in return for wiping the slate clean. Don't pay them until you have a written record that they are accepting this payment as final payment on monies due. You want them to report that you are "paying the account in full." If they fail to clear your credit report, you will need this letter to clear it.

Also, if you have a lot of old debts, it may be wise to hire a lawyer to negotiate repayment. In some cases, the old debts may disappear seven years after the last payment, and inquiries may reopen them. Lawyers will know how to negotiate settlements without stirring up the dust, which could save you hundreds, or thousands, of dollars and prevent negative items from reappearing.

If All Your Efforts Fail

If singing your sad (but true) songs fail to motivate the creditors to assist you, the Fair Credit Reporting Act allows consumers to write a short explanation disputing or explaining the history to the credit reporting agencies, who are required to place it in your file. Keep it simple and no longer than 100 words. Sample notations might read as follows: "Late payment was due to move and subsequent lost mail"; "Laid off from work for six months, caught up all accounts upon returning to work"; "Emergency occurred while out of the country, tripled payments upon return."

You can also write positive notes that the agencies are required to send to all inquiries. Samples would include things like these: "I received a $10,000 raise in 2005," or "I earned an extra $7,000 in sales commissions in the first quarter of 2006."

FICO Scores Defined

The three crediting reporting agencies collect and compile information about your credit history and submit it to formulas—which can vary wildly—that will create your FICO score. In a 2005 survey by the Consumer Federation of America, approximately 49 percent of consumers polled were not aware that FICO, the most widely used credit-score formula, calculates their credit score to measure their credit risk.

In fact, mortgage lenders have used FICO scores for years as a predictor of consumers' future bill-paying performance, which determines whether they grant loans and at what interest rate. Today, insurance companies, cell-phone providers, utilities, landlords, and even prospective employers may use your FICO score as an indicator of your stability, trustworthiness, and ability to pay your bills on time.

QUESTION?

What is a good FICO score?

FICO scores typically range from a high of 850 to a low of 300. Seventy percent of consumers have scores above 600. Average scores hover around 720. Borrowers with scores above 740 generally receive the best rates.

FICO collects twenty-two pieces of data from each of the three credit bureaus to tabulate an individual's score. The final number is a composite of individual ratings in five categories:

1. Payment history (35 percent)
2. Amount of outstanding debt (30 percent)
3. Length of credit history (15 percent)
4. Amount of newly acquired credit (10 percent)
5. Types of credit used (10 percent)

Surprisingly, your annual income doesn't even weigh into the equation. Someone could have a very high income and rarely pay her bills on time; conversely, someone could earn an average income but possess a long, stellar payment record. What they are looking for is a long, stable, responsible, well-managed history with credit.

Since these bureaus collect data at different times of the month, it's not uncommon to have a thirty- to fifty-point differential between the individual ratings. The higher your FICO score, the lower the risk you appear to a creditor, which translates into lower interest rates for your loan.

Why is this important? If you score in the 740 to 850 range, lenders might offer you a $350,000, thirty-year fixed mortgage at 6.24 percent in interest, which would result in a mortgage of $2,153 a month. However, if you score between 620 to 674, the lender would charge closer to 8.05 percent, raising your monthly mortgage to $2,581. You would pay an additional $150,000 over the life of the loan.

Each of the three major agencies computes an individual FICO score for you, and because they don't share information, it's crucial that you obtain and monitor all three scores. Seventy-five percent of mortgage companies will request all three scores when determining your credit worthiness, and each may have their own scoring formulas that they use to determine your credit worthiness.

What's Your Score?

Each of the three reporting agencies is required to give you one free credit report annually, and all three will offer to calculate a credit score for a slight fee. Even though their individual scores will not truly represent your FICO score, they will give you a real idea of how lenders will assess your score. To obtain the most realistic picture of your FICO standing, click on "credit education" at *www.myfico.com*, and order all three scores. Lenders often create their own formula, but if not, they typically average these three scores or take the middle one.

QUESTION?

Why should I order my FICO scores?
When you order a report from the credit reporting agencies or ✐*www .myfico.com*, the report provides a list of positive and negative elements that have affected your score. If your score is particularly low, these lists will provide valuable information for improving it.

When you write to request your credit report, make sure you also ask for their FICO or NextGen (a newer formula gaining wide acceptance) score, as follows:

- Equifax calls its FICO score "Beacon."
- Experian calls its FICO score "Experian or Fair Isaac Model."
- TransUnion calls its FICO score "Empirica."

It's a great idea to check your FICO scores once a year; and if you're in the market for a mortgage, order them at least four months ahead so you can clean up any loose ends.

Even though negative history—late payments, delinquencies, liens, and judgments against you—will adversely affect your FICO score for up to seven years, most lenders scrutinize the past two years, minimizing the effect of one thirty-day late payment.

ALERT!

Be wary of companies that offer free FICO scores. These offers usually lead to long-term credit monitoring that isn't free. Also, never send your personal information to an unknown company over the Internet. If you need to order your report more than once a year, be safe and pay the $12.95 per report on *www.myfico.com.*

Obviously, you want to maximize positive history. If your FICO score is on the low end, you'll want to create a plan to address the problems and reverse the trend. However, it behooves every consumer to do everything possible to boost her FICO score.

FICO scores are used for many purposes, such as these:

- Predicting your credit paying habits
- Predicting the likelihood that you will default on loans
- Predicting which accounts you would be likely to pay first (utility, insurance, home, auto, credit cards)
- Predicting whether you will file insurance claims

- Detecting fraud in insurance or credit applications
- Calculating how much profit a credit company will earn from you
- Noting whether you are likely to respond to credit offers via mail

There is no truly reliable means to assess any of the above, but lenders, insurance companies, and even employers will often acquire and review your FICO score to make judgments about you, your credit worthiness, or your long-term reliability.

What Damages My FICO Score?

Although FICO scores and how creditors evaluate or use them in their full assessment can vary widely, there are definite actions that will negatively affect your FICO score. The following may create red flags or drop your FICO score:

- **Moving around a lot (residences and jobs):** Creditors like stability, knowing where you are, how long you've been there, and that you have a steady, reliable income.
- **Slow payment or missing payments:** Creditors don't want people who drag their feet. The two most important factors in your score are whether you pay your bills on time and how much of your available credit you actually use.
- **Minimum credit history:** Creditors don't know how you'll handle debt. It takes six months to establish a credit report, and activity in the last six months to keep it alive. If you're not carrying any installment debt, it could work against you.
- **Too many outstanding balances:** They might worry that you're using your cards to fund your daily living expenses, or that you are maxing out.
- **Too much available credit:** If you have $50,000 available in credit limits or lines of credit and an average or below-average income, they may fear that you'll run up those accounts, which would then end up competing with their company for regular payments.
- **Too many inquiries:** They might assume you're constantly searching for new credit.

A negative or low FICO score can affect your ability to obtain credit cards, personal loans, lines of credit, cell phone contracts, mortgages, car leases, rental agreements, insurance, or anything that requires a credit check. Some banks will refuse to issue ATM cards to people with perpetually low FICO scores.

How to Improve Your FICO Score

Rest assured, you can definitely improve upon and bolster a flagging FICO score. Revitalizing your FICO score is as easy as taking these steps:

- **Paying all of your bills on time:** This is probably the single most important factor in the FICO calculation. You simply cannot make a habit of slow-paying any bills. If you consistently run thirty days overdue, your score can drop 100 points. Get a handle on the bill-paying process, and, if possible, arrange for automatic withdrawals or pay your bills when they arrive (via mail or e-mail). This includes insurance and household bills such as utilities and telephone.

- **Keeping your balances low:** The FICO score evaluates your credit utilization—how much you owe in relation to your available credit. Maxed-out credit cards can lower your score. If possible, limit spending to no more than 30 percent of your credit limit and spread out your spending among several cards.

- **Establishing a positive history:** If you have no credit history, applying for one or two credit cards, charging small amounts, and paying promptly will create a favorable history.

- **Minimizing credit card or loan applications:** Too much availability of credit may indicate that you're spreading yourself too thin. Every time you fill out an application for a credit card or loan, the inquiry is noted on your FICO score, whether or not you open the account or accept a loan. This is another good reason to just say no to all credit card offers. Be very selective and save your credit worthiness for big-ticket purchases like houses or cars.

- **Not consolidating to take advantage of lower interest rates:** While you may think you're beating the system, the credit reporting agencies take a dim view of juggling balances and opening a series of new cards. That's not to say that you shouldn't do it once or twice, but whatever you do, don't run up all your cards again, and don't open a string of new accounts.

- **Not charging new debt:** While you do want some activity on your accounts, paying down balances only to charge them up again will deflate a high score.
- **Thinking twice before closing accounts:** Maintaining older accounts that you have managed well over the years will boost your score. Also, if you close five or six accounts within a short time, lenders may wonder why you're tightening the belt. They judge your ratio of credit available to credit being used, which means having extensive (unused) credit could boost your score, as long as you have the income to afford payments.
- **Paying off small balances:** Any time you can strike off a debt, you're ahead. However, don't let your credit sit idle for long periods of time. Remember, most lenders are likely to review the past two years, so you'll want positive history visible.

Follow these guidelines, and you will have a sparkling FICO score that would make the best money-manager proud!

When and How to Take Drastic Measures

If you cannot meet your monthly expenses, it's time to severely tighten your belt. First, you'll need to review your budget in light of your expenditures. If your income is falling short, you'll need to adjust spending radically and immediately. If you absolutely cannot squeeze your expenses sufficiently to cover all of your debts, you may want to work with a credit management company who would tailor a payment program to your needs.

Finding a Credit Management Company

If you need help resolving debt, credit management agencies will work directly with your creditors to establish a payment plan. Many will consolidate your payments, collect the money from you, and pay your bills. It's crucial that you do some preliminary research to make sure you find a reputable agency. Contact the National Foundation for Consumer Credit, online at *www.nfcc.org,* for more information specific to credit management.

ALERT!

Beware of signing on too quickly for debt management programs initiated by credit agencies. Most will report the debt management program to the credit reporting agencies, meaning it will show up on your credit history. If you have substantial debt, the benefit may outweigh the risk, but ask your counselor if reporting can be avoided.

Look for one that tailors a solution to *your* problems, rather than one that takes the easiest or most profitable solution—one that would benefit the agency and the creditors. If they have more than 50 percent of their clients on debt management programs, they're not trying hard enough to find individualized solutions. You also want one that has debt management training programs that will help you establish healthy financial habits. Also, shop around for an accredited agency with trained and certified counselors. If you feel strong-armed, or unheard, trust your instincts. Your credit history is an asset you need to protect.

Avoid High-Risk Borrowing

You've all seen the commercials on television suggesting that it's easy for anyone who suffers a calamity to call a phone number to acquire a quick $10,000 to cover her escalating bills. Anyone in this situation is already in over her credit head, i.e., a high-risk borrower who has had trouble paying her debts and will most likely continue to default on future payments. The lenders who offer loans to high-risk borrowers charge them exorbitant interest rates and steep penalties for late payment. The effective annual interest rate on high-risk loans is usually over 100 percent per year, e.g., $15 to borrow $200 for two weeks (the typical length of a payday loan) equates to an annual interest rate of 459 percent! Sure, they may throw money your way, but it's a lifeboat full of holes. Here are three very important reasons to avoid high-risk borrowing:

1. The lenders charge exorbitant interest rates. You'll rack up interest charges that will quickly double, or even triple your debt.
2. They have you over a barrel, and they determine the terms: variable rates versus fixed rates on mortgages; the highest interest rates on credit cards.
3. They frequently charge hefty upfront charges.

Increasing Income

If you've cut expenses down to the bone and still cannot meet your debts, it's time to look for a second job. Use your creativity to come up with a list of part-time jobs you could seek (or create) to supplement your income—bartending, babysitting, dog walking, freelance typing, interior decorating, personal shopping, cleaning, gardening, garage sale organization, or plain old errand running. Do whatever it takes to pay down your debt and maintain a solid credit rating. Everyone falls on hard times, but it's up to you how you navigate the territory. Keep in mind the long-term effects, and choose the high road.

If you've done all of your homework, your credit card debt will be paid down, your credit reports will be clean, your FICO score will be at its peak, and you'll be well on your way to regaining control of your finances and building a brighter future for yourself and your children.

Chapter 8
Avoiding Identity Theft

Identity theft has become an American scourge—it's the number-one consumer complaint. Although always a problem, it has surged in recent years, largely due to electronic commerce. All a thief needs is your Social Security number, your address, your birth date, and a little family information to open credit cards in your name. Unfortunately, avoiding identity theft is not as easy as safeguarding your Social Security number—although it's essential to do so. Today, you need consciousness and diligence to protect your credit identity, credit history, and FICO score.

Identity Theft Defined

Identity theft occurs when someone takes your private information—Social Security number, driver's license number, credit card numbers, bank account numbers, place of employment, and even family information, such as your mother's maiden name—and uses that information to pillage your bank and credit card accounts or to open new accounts using your information. According to the Federal Trade Commission, in 2004, consumers between the ages of twenty-five and forty-four were most likely to become victims of identity theft. Thanks to the electronic age of buying online, paying online, and banking online, identity thieves have become adept at finding just what they need—your personal identity information, your bank account numbers, or your credit card numbers.

According to Liz Pulliam Weston, author of *Your Credit Score,* identity theft affects more than 10 million people a year. The Federal Trade Commission survey found that 27.3 million Americans had become victims of identity theft in the past five years. This results in $48 billion in annual losses for business and institutions; $5 billion in out-of-pocket expenses for consumers; and 300 million hours spent by consumers trying to cope with its consequences. It's wise to take precautions and stay vigilant about protecting your personal and financial identity.

How Does It Occur?

Identity theft has become prevalent in the United States and around the world, and there is, in reality, very little you can do to stop it. The most common ways that information is stolen are as follows:

- Someone you typically trust (a waiter at a restaurant, a salesperson in a retail store, or a secretary in an insurance business) scans your credit card into a handheld device called a "skimmer" and uses or sells the information to open bogus accounts.
- Someone confiscates, or finds, your applications for credit, an apartment, insurance, or employment and sells it to identity thieves. Dumpster divers know where to look for such applications.

- Hackers break into databases where your information is stored. You hear about this occurring to hospitals, large corporations, and government agencies. In 2003, 8 million credit card numbers were stolen from one company.
- Bogus companies pose as lenders and call or e-mail you (and often the credit reporting agencies), requesting your credit information.

Once they have your pertinent information, they may call your bank and credit card companies and change the mailing address, allowing them to rack up charges or withdraw funds before you realize that you're not receiving your statements. They can also apply for new credit, in which case you may not discover the fraud until a collection agency calls about unpaid bills you didn't even know existed. Frequently, these thieves will attempt to completely deplete your resources before moving on to another victim. Often the thieves are not rank amateurs but people who have mastered this particular brand of thievery and know far more than you do about maximizing their loot.

ALERT!

The most important information to safeguard includes your mother's maiden name, your Social Security number, PINs, credit card numbers, and preapproved credit card offers. Also, never choose an obvious password, such as your name or your birth date. Instead, choose something obscure—your dog's name, your favorite flower, or your preferred coffee blend, for example.

How to Protect Yourself

Although there's no way to completely eliminate the risk, you definitely want to take steps to protect your identity. First and foremost, purchase an inexpensive shredder. Shred all statements, unsolicited credit offerings or blank checks, and anything that contains your credit card numbers or Social Security number. Ditto for old tax returns and medical records.

Printed Matter

When you have checks printed, don't include your address, your driver's license number, or your Social Security number. Since identity thieves can hijack payment envelopes, or see checks floating around a payment center, anything printed or handwritten on your check can be stolen. Long gone are the days when anyone should ask you for those numbers to verify a check.

Put a lock on your mailbox. Don't leave envelopes containing bank statements, checks, or payment stubs in plain view. Drop your bill payments off at the post office, or better yet, when encryption is in place to protect your information (as it is with most large banking institutions), pay bills online. If you don't receive your monthly credit card bills or bank statements within a week of their expected arrival, check with the post office to make sure no one has filed a "change of address" form.

Just say "no" to unsolicited telephone, e-mail, or snail mail credit offers. Call (888)5OPT-OUT (provided by the credit reporting agencies) to remove your name from any lists sold to credit card companies. You'll probably still receive offers, but far fewer than usual. When you do, shred the letter and any unsolicited "checks" or "preapproved" offers.

Never leave behind or throw away credit card receipts. Take them home, and when your bill arrives, use them to make sure all charges are legitimate. Then shred them.

Keep all of your important records under lock and key. Financial documents, such as credit applications, credit card numbers, medical records, and tax returns; and identification documents, such as birth certificates, passports, and Social Security cards should be kept in a locked file where prying eyes cannot easily access them.

Watch Your Numbers

Be extremely selective about giving anyone your Social Security number. The only entities entitled to it are your employer, financial institutions (your bank or brokerage firm when you open an account, for instance), the Department of Motor Vehicles, some governmental agencies, and a small number of other institutions. When anyone asks for your Social Security number, always question whether they need the entire number, or if they can identify you with only the last four numbers, which has become a common practice with credit card companies. *Do not* give it to supermarket, retailer, or restaurant cashiers, and *never* give it to anyone inquiring over the telephone or on the Internet unless you are absolutely certain they are reputable. In fact, it's always better to hang up or log off and call the banking or credit institution to make sure you're speaking to a real company representative.

Plastic Money

Use one credit card for all online purchases and arrange it so that you can view the account online at any time. Check the balance and all charges once a week to make sure you are the only one using the account.

Call credit card companies the moment you notice a card missing. Federal law prevents you from being held responsible for charges beyond the first $50 (sometimes you will have to fork over the first $50, and sometimes you will owe nothing), but you'll still have a mess to sort out. It is imperative that you act quickly to make sure the thief loses access to your credit.

Guard your ATM card with your life. Thieves can use them to wipe out your checking or savings accounts in seconds. Generally, it's better to use your credit cards more often than your ATM or debit cards, and minimize use of either for small purchases, particularly in fast food restaurants, gas stations, or other businesses where employees may succumb to the temptation to steal information.

Who Wants to Know?

Never provide your financial information to unknown callers. Never presume it's really your bank or credit card company calling. If they say they are reporting a problem, hang up, pull out your statement, and call them directly. And be discreet when supplying your financial information to known sources via cell phone. You never know who's listening.

Identity thieves using fake Web sites' fraudulent e-mails to solicit financial information has become so prevalent they are called "phishing" scams. Don't provide your financial information to unsolicited requests on the Internet. If you initiate the request and know the institution is legitimate, you're probably safe, but keep in mind that technology allows wily criminals to create "look-alike" Web sites that are virtually identical to your real bank or credit card provider's site. If you receive an e-mail request for any information or account changes from a bank or online retailer that you trust, go directly to that company's Web site (not by the link sent in the e-mail) to log into your account and then look for any notices requesting that you provide more information. You can also call, using the number on your statement (not the number on what may be a fake Web site) to call your bank or credit card provider.

Review Your Credit Report

Monitor your credit reports carefully. Stagger the free reports you are entitled to from each of the three credit reporting agencies, and review them for any errors. Credit monitoring businesses are an option, but they are usually costly; you can monitor your own credit for a fraction of the cost. Be sure to check the section of your report titled "Inquiries" to see if a flurry of inquiries regarding opening new credit card accounts has been occurring.

In Cyberspace

Safeguard your computer. Regularly upgrade virus software and install a firewall program to protect personal information stored on your computer. Only download files or click on hyperlinks sent by people you know. Stick to secure browsers that use an encryption code—look for the "lock" icon on the browser's status bar. Also, if you store information on your laptop, use a "log-in" feature that requires a user name and password. When you dispose of your computers, delete all files with a "wipe" utility program that overwrites the hard drive.

If Your Identity Has Been Stolen

If you discover that your identity has been stolen, you must take immediate action. Get ready to make a series of telephone calls and to keep meticulous records of every conversation you have. You will relay this same information when you follow up with letters—which you will send certified mail, return receipt requested. Also, keep track of the hours you spend in case the thief is caught and forced to pay retribution (including paying for your time). Begin by contacting the Federal Trade Commission at *www.con sumer.gov/idtheft.com* to obtain free information on what you need to do.

ALERT!

In 2004, Internet "phishing" scams skyrocketed 1,000 percent in one year. According to the Anti-Phishing Working Group (APWG), somewhere between 3 and 5 percent of victims are hooked by a "phishing" look-alike Web site or telephone or e-mail inquiry. If you are at all suspicious, don't click open any links, and call your credit card or banking institution immediately to verify the communication.

First, make sure you call all of your credit card providers, banks, savings, and investment companies as soon as possible to alert them, and then follow up with letters stating when you called and whom you spoke with and listing all fraudulent charges. It's also helpful to obtain a fraud affidavit on the FTC Web site to include with your letters. You may want to change account numbers on all your accounts, and definitely change PIN numbers and passwords.

Then, call at least one of the credit reporting agencies to report the fraud. They are required to notify the other two agencies and to send you a free credit report. Make sure they put a "fraud alert" on your report, and ask them if they can "freeze" any applications for credit until you request otherwise (some states have laws requiring credit agencies to accommodate your request, and some don't).

The next call you make is to your local police to report the theft—identity theft is a federal crime—and ask to file a report listing all the accounts affected and illegitimate charges. An official report will be invaluable if creditors contest charges at a later date, so if they balk at what can be a tedious and complicated task, offer to provide them with a typewritten list, plus copies of any and all documentation, and be politely persistent. If necessary, ask to speak with the city or county fraud unit or white-collar crime unit.

FACT

The National Do Not Call Registry, activated in 2003, limits the amount of marketing telephone calls you receive. You can list three lines by logging onto ✍*www.donotcall.gov.* If you only have one number, you can also call (888) 382-1222, but make sure you call from the line you are registering.

When you receive your credit report, call all the creditors or banks that are affected and ask them to promptly close all the phony accounts, making a notation that the account was fraudulent and that you were the victim of fraud. Also be sure to ask the banks to stop payment on any checks and notify check verification companies. (The FTC Web site, at *www.consumer.gov*, provides those names and phone numbers.)

The minute you receive collection notices, contact the collection agencies to notify them of all fraudulent debts. Since they tend to be suspicious of delinquent customers' claims of fraudulent debts, it's best to send them letters, including copies of the police reports, and all other documentation.

Once you have taken all the measures possible, if any problems persist, hire a lawyer, and don't surrender any ground. You are a victim of a crime, not the offender, and you deserve the respect and support of the creditors. Collection agencies have strict guidelines on how they are permitted to seek payment. If a collector becomes threatening or abusive, let her know that she is breaking the law.

Chapter 9

Starting Your Own Business

Women are fast becoming the primary owners of small businesses in the United States—and why not? They are visionaries and builders—adept at generating ideas, figuring out how they would work, understanding what's going on in the world and how their ideas fit into it, and developing long-term plans. Women can maximize flexible schedules. They are masters of multitasking and are fully capable of self-motivating and self-monitoring. It's a marriage made in financial heaven—proven by the growing numbers of women who take the leap . . . and succeed.

Time to Start Your Own Business

Most people spend half of their waking hours working; yet more than half of all Americans say they aren't happy in their present work. Approximately 80 percent of Americans working for large companies say they are not using their true skills or talents in their line of work; over 70 percent of working Americans reported feeling "disengaged" at their present job. Studies have also shown that more than 56 percent of all Americans long to start their own business.

The Small Business Administration (SBA) reported that the number of small businesses operating in America has, in fact, grown 49 percent since 1982. Seventy-five percent of all new employment between 1999 and 2000 came at the hands of entrepreneurs, and 2.5 million of the 3.4 million jobs created occurred in small businesses. So many people are creating their own businesses, there's a hip term for the trend: SOHO, for "small office/ home office." The country's 22 million SOHO businesses employ half of the private-sector workforce.

FACT

Women are definitely on a roll, between 1992 and 1997, the number of women-owned businesses increased by 300 percent, from 2.4 million in 1992 to over 8.5 million in 1997. Sales from women-owned businesses topped $8.5 trillion in 1997!

According to the National Women's Business Council, women start 424 new enterprises every day, more than twice the rate for all U.S. firms. Statistics also show that women open two out of three new businesses and employ 25 percent of America's workforce and that 75 percent of these women are still in business three years later, compared to 67 percent of male entrepreneurs. Over the fifteen-year period from 1983 to 1997, women working for themselves—as entrepreneurs, freelancers, contract workers, or other forms of self-employment—accounted for 83 percent of the self-employed.

The National Foundation of Women Business Owners said women become entrepreneurs for four primary reasons:

- They wanted greater flexibility.
- They weren't happy or comfortable in their present job.
- They were bored or working below their capacity.
- They couldn't break through the glass ceiling.

Those are all valid reasons, but other reasons to start your own business include these:

- **You can do it on a shoestring these days.** Consulting, coaching, organizational skills, personal shopper, online auctions, educational tutoring, and a multitude of other businesses can be launched with minimal funds.
- **You can save money.** Particularly when businesses are run from one's home, owners are able to write off a lot of ordinary expenses, such as computers, telephones, printers, travel, and even some entertainment. You may also be able to write off portions of your car and the cost of office space in your home.
- **You can create the rules.** You can set up your business to function according to your rhythms, your needs, and your lifestyle. When emergencies arise, you don't have to call someone else, and you can schedule paperwork for post bedtime or naptime.
- **You can do what you love.** Instead of slogging your way through the day at a job you abhor, you can find a way to do what you love and make money doing it. This requires stamina and determination, of course, but the payoff can be sublime.
- **You can make a lot of money.** It's up to you how hard you work at any given time, which means the harder you are willing to work, the more you can money you can make. You can also generate cost-saving practices, innovation, and new market penetration, all of which will improve your bottom line.
- **You can determine your own future.** The days of job security are long gone. No one works for the same company for thirty years any more, and those who do are likely to watch their retirement funds and pensions dissolve well before they reach the finish line. You need to create your own security, and what better way than to be at the helm?

- **You have amazing resources.** The wealth of information literally at your fingertips means that you can find out anything and everything you need to know to launch a business. Between books and the Internet, someone has done it all and recorded their trials and tribulations.
- **You can join the wave of the future.** The days of dominant powerhouse corporations are fading. Today, niche markets and targeted promotion have leveled the playing field. In fact, today's consumer prefers specialization, uniqueness, and quality, and small businesses that offer personalized service or exceptional, specialized products are the wave of the future.

If you are feeling empowered and desirous of starting your own business, it's time to start delving into how one goes about it. To begin, create your own list of reasons for spinning your fantasies into reality.

Assessing Your Motives

Banish any thoughts that starting your own business will be easy. It will be the hardest task you've ever taken on, and the risks involved often overshadow the rewards. You'll work harder than you ever have, shoulder all the responsibility, stretch your limitations, expose your weaknesses, risk your job security, probably lose your health insurance, and face many sleepless nights. You have to first decide that you have an idea that you can believe in 100 percent, that you have the stamina, drive, determination, persistence, and flexibility required, that you are willing to take the very real risks involved, and that you can, in actuality, afford to do this. If you are going to launch a small business, you need to foster your dreams and look reality in the eye.

You also want to weigh the risk, requirements, and rewards to determine whether you are not only willing but eager to take on the challenge. Creating your own business requires dedication, perseverance, energy, determination, and discipline. It's not a job for sissies, and you will be taking a huge risk. But some of your real rewards could include things like using your real skills and talents, engaging your passions, determining your own future, achieving financial success, and enjoying the freedom that comes with being the boss.

According to Arnold Goldstein, author of *Starting on a Shoestring*, before launching a new business, there are four essential questions you need to answer. "Can you *enjoy* the business? Can you *manage* the business? Can you *earn* from the business? Can you *afford* the business?" If the answers are all affirmative, move on to the planning stages.

QUESTION?

Do business owners really get rich?
Of all the high-income vocations in America, self-employed business owners have the highest probability of becoming financially independent. In fact, according to government statistics, those who are self-employed have about five times as much accumulated net worth as those who work for others.

Assessing Your Skills and Talents

Now that you're psyched about launching your own business, the next challenge is to select the type of business. The litmus test for this decision should be based on what you do best and what gives you juice. You want to create a business that takes advantage of your best skills and talents. Business writers call this "core competence," which they define as a grouping of skills that offer potential customers a particular, quantified benefit—what you have a mastery of that someone else is willing to pay for. Your marketable skills and talents need to be valuable, expandable, and unique in its market. Bruce Judson, author of *Go It Alone!*, recommends focusing on "what you do brilliantly and from which you achieve extraordinary results."

To begin your assessment, ask yourself the following questions:

- Given the option, what do I most enjoy doing?
- What gives me unlimited energy and doesn't feel like work?
- What would my five best friends say are my most marketable talents?

- Do I have leadership skills? Can I develop them?
- What are my core business strengths?
- What are my business weaknesses? Can I overcome them?
- What will be my primary challenge as an owner?
- Do I have the energy and chutzpah required?
- How much do I know about the business?
- How much do I know about running a business?
- Am I willing to make financial sacrifices?
- Am I strong enough to endure setbacks? Downturns?
- Am I a resourceful person?

Keep in mind that an entrepreneur has to play many roles in a start-up business. Some of the hats you will wear, at least temporarily, include these:

- Boss/operations manager/human resources
- Product developer
- Bookkeeper/accountant
- Sales/marketing/publicity
- Visionary planner
- Collections officer
- Receptionist/secretary

To launch and run your own business, you will need exceptional organizational skills, salesmanship, decision-making skills, creativity, adaptability, and fortitude.

What would you be doing even if you never earned a dime from it? How do you love spending your time? What matters most to you in the world? What contribution do you want to make to the world? How can you improve the world? What people do you admire most, and what are they doing that makes them so admirable?

Spotting Global and Regional Trends

Reading newspapers and business magazines—both national and international—are a great resource for discovering trends and ideas. Newspapers and magazines are always looking for feature stories on businesses that reflect trends or unusual success stories, and they pride themselves on being on the cutting edge, so take full advantage of their staff's search for the newest and brightest trends. Don't bog yourself down, but skim *The Wall Street Journal* and *The New York Times* business section regularly and look for trends that interest you, support your idea, or offer concrete knowledge. Money magazines, business magazines, and even hobby magazines are also good resources for deciphering trends or finding a niche. As your idea solidifies, spend three hours a week in your library reading all types of magazines. An idea can as easily spring from *Vogue* as from any other publication.

When looking for a business idea, seek trends and avoid fads. Trends are long-term patterns of change that have a major, lasting impact on large populations or societies. Fads are short-term phenomena that have little to no lasting impact. Some trends include outsourcing, downsizing, and organic food. Fads include wearing Ugg boots in summer, Pet Rocks, and Beanie Babies.

Peruse the business section in your local bookstore and notice which categories are growing—eBay start-ups and Web-site marketing of goods and services, for example. Also, vast quantities of specialized small business guides are available to provide an indication of what's catching on. Look for evidence that the business you are targeting is expanding, diversifying, retooling, or declining. You also need to know if your idea is saturated or whether it's a fresh take on a solid trend, and whether supportive industries are available and stable.

Use your government resources. The federal government conducts amazingly focused studies on virtually every industry you can imagine. Once you find the specialist you need—only a few phone calls away—she will likely have more free information than you could possibly need.

Once you target a business, look for trade associations (almost all industries have one) and call them for information and show dates. Go to regional shows and informally interview as many people as possible—

wholesalers, distributors, buyers, department store managers, and whomever you can get to talk to you. Find out as much as you can about the industry's history, current status, and emerging markets or trends. These people are experts at your disposal. Talk to excited buyers toward the end of the day on the first few days, and then go very early on the last day of the show to talk to exhibitors.

Creating a Business Plan

Even for a small home business, a business plan is not only a good idea; it's essential. A business plan grounds the vision that spawned the idea and provides a concrete roadmap to guide your business through start-up and the first six to twelve months of operation. It will also contain long-range planning—projections for five to ten years—to keep you on course. Not only does your business plan serve as a researched roadmap for your desired progress, it will provide a necessary and impressive way to solicit investors, to seek loans, and to have absolute clarity on what needs to be done and what you can achieve. The business plan comes before everything else.

FACT

At a 1994 Canadian Bankers Association conference, a speaker reported that companies with a written business plan earned, on average, ten times more than companies without a written plan. When assessing potential investments, bankers and financiers look for extensive and viable market research, solid and comprehensive planning, financial savvy and realistic expectations, and relevant qualifications and commitment of the founder.

Research every topic you can imagine related to your idea, and then keep on researching until you drop. You want to know how others have succeeded or failed, what the pitfalls were, and how successful entrepreneurs overcame their obstacles. The more you are armed with knowledge, the more likely you are to structure your business for success. While deciding what business to start involves dreaming, this task involves accessing reality. To get underway, answer the following questions:

- What is your product or service?
- What is your target market?
- Who are your customers?
- Who is your competition?
- What will make you stand out?
- What resources will you need to make this dream come alive?
- What are the first steps you need to take to set it in motion?
- How much start-up capital do you need?
- Who will be your suppliers?
- How will you market your business?

Your Marketable Idea

Just as screenwriters pitch movie ideas in short, staccato sentences that create a clear, engaging, spellbinding, and marketable story, you need to sharply define your idea. Write it out long, if you must, but then whittle it down to a two-minute "pitch" that captures its essence, builds enthusiasm, and proves its viability. Ideas don't have to be huge, but original, innovative, or niche-fulfilling ideas are good ways to begin. Ideally, you will choose something that makes you feel passionately about it, as if you are finally taking on your life's mission.

In creating a niche business—by focusing on a narrowly defined, previously ignored market within a larger market to which you offer a unique service or product—you position yourself as a bigger fish in an already established smaller pond. This brings improved marketability, stability, pricing capability, profitability, and loyal customers. Starbucks, Chico's, and Papa Murphy's Pizza all snagged lucrative niche markets.

Your Business Name

The selection of a business name plays an important role in visibility and identity. You want a name that catches your customer's attention and builds brand identity. Give a lot of thought to this. If you can't come up with something, consult with a marketing professional for ideas and commission that person to create an icon or logo that you will use on stationery and advertising to establish brand identity.

Your Purposes and Goals

This aspect needs serious contemplation. Knowing the purpose of your business speaks to motivation, determination, and vision. You, and your investors, need to feel inspired enough to fork over the time, energy, and money required to meet your goals. Your goals need to be sharply defined and include both short-term and long-term progressions. Goals should be realistic, concrete, and time based.

Partners and Advisors

If you will have professional advisors involved, by all means list them. Ideally, you will have a financial consultant, a tax consultant, and a lawyer to turn to for advice. If you need a partner, brainstorm on the best candidates. If you will need to hire five employees, list the job description and probable costs.

Your Start-Up Capital

This section needs to be thoroughly researched and flushed out as minutely as possible. Don't delude yourself or your potential investors. Write down each and every cost you can imagine, and you'll avoid nasty surprises and impress your investors or financiers.

When establishing any business, no matter how small, it's imperative that you keep meticulous financial records. Since many business expenses are deductible, the IRS will be your friend, particularly in the formative years, but you must have accurate records. Visit the IRS Web site (at *www.irs.gov*) to request the IRS booklet *Starting Your Own Business and Keeping*

Records, or take a bookkeeping class at your local Small Business Development Center (SBDC) or community college.

Your Location

If you will begin in your home, you still have to account for the space, equipment, and costs. If you plan to move into an office space or store-front soon thereafter, include research into rental expense. Keep in mind the your local or state governments may have "urban renewal zones" that may offer cheap rents and affordable labor. Also, the SBA may have "incubator" spaces in which other small start-ups share office space and equipment. Shop around for low-cost opportunities and plan for future growth.

FACT

Arnold Goldstein, author of *Starting on a Shoestring,* defined a "one-tenth financing principle" (a term coined by Jerome Goldstein, no relation to the author) as the ability to start a business on one-tenth of what you think you will need to finance it, or less, as long as you work ten times as hard to make it succeed.

Business Plan Format

When you are constructing a formal business plan, find a book that illustrates an in-depth business plan or consult with your local Small Business Administration (SBA) or Small Business Development Center (SBDC). In general, an official business plan includes the following:

1. **Cover page:** This provides the name of your future business, as well as your full and complete contact information. Minimize copy, but if you have a logo, by all means use it.
2. **Introduction:** Brevity and absolute clarity reign supreme here. Remember the pitch mentality and write sparkling prose—one or two paragraphs maximum—that will entice investors to believe in your idea.

3. **Mission statement:** Brevity, passion, and clarity also apply here. If you don't believe solidly in your mission, no one else will. Tell readers why your new business will be unique in its market, why you're the one to run it, why you're embarking on this adventure, and how much it means to you—and to your future customers. And whittle it down to one or two persuasive, very tightly written sentences.

4. **Overview:** Be specific, but not wordy. Succinctly describe the type of business you want to create, what the product or service will be, what the target market is, who the competitors are, and why your business will succeed.

5. **Economic analysis:** Discuss the market in general—what is happening in your field, why it's an ideal time to launch this business, how you will fit within the industry, and how you will compete successfully. Talk about relevant trends that support your idea.

6. **Financial analysis:** Create multiple spreadsheets illustrating how much capital you have, how much you need, how funds will be spent, projected sales, projected cash flow, and projected annual budget (include fixed costs, overhead costs, employment costs, rental costs, taxes, and so on). You'll also need a balance sheet that shows your company's net worth (assets minus liabilities, and equity, if any), and a feasibility report that plots your costs versus your profits. This report also establishes a "break-even" point to help your investors understand the viability of the business.

7. **Market analysis:** Discuss the product or service market specific to your business—who your competitors are, how they operate their businesses, how your business will fare against them, as well as your advertising and promotional ideas. Emphasize the strategies you will employ to build the business. Demographics, trends affecting the industry, the industry's major players, and supporting materials (such as articles or statistics) round out the picture.

8. **Operational plans:** This is the nitty-gritty breakdown of how your business will operate, including location, number and skill level of employees, management structure, timetables, and plans for growth. Goals or objectives need to be specific, quantifiable, and time-based.

9. **Summary:** Condense the most salient points, highlighting the decision-making aspects: name, location, owners, staff, market, financing, and start-up time requirements.
10. **Appendices:** Charts, graphs, tables, or anything that supports, clarifies, or answers questions should be attached.

Prospective financiers will require an in-depth business plan, and once the business is up and running, revisiting the plan regularly helps assess how you are doing in terms of achieving your goals, as well as pinpointing where and when they need updating. It will also serve as a barometer and roadmap for your continued success.

Creating an Action Plan

An action plan will arise from the goals you set for the first six to twelve months of operation. It generates very specific, time-based steps needed to achieve your goals. If your action plan is "to get your business up and running in the next year," sample start-up tasks would include the following:

- **Establish credibility:** This is important so customers can count on your reputation of excellence.
- **Create a branded image:** Make sure the name of your business and its logo are immediately identifiable and motivational.
- **Amplify visibility:** Get your name out and make your product or services known.
- **Create time-based objectives:** Make these specific. For instance, you might determine to sell $5,000 worth of handmade earrings in the first quarter; to increase sales 20 percent over the next two quarters; to expand your customer base 25 percent in three months; or to expand your product line 30 percent over the next six months.
- **Create marketing strategies:** Outline and implement actions you need to take in the next six months to achieve your predetermined marketing objectives.
- **Create a budget:** Define the parameters of how you will spend money to best achieve your goals.

Creating an action plan focuses your attention on necessary tasks. Creating the plan, reviewing it regularly, completing the tasks within the prescribed time, and then expanding or adjusting the plan to meet new challenges will keep your business flowing in the right direction.

Financing Your Business

Every launch requires start-up capital to get it underway and to keep it afloat until profits can be achieved. If you did your homework and followed the business plan guidelines, you have a realistic idea of the financial needs. To bolster your chances of obtaining financing, or of being able to finance startup yourself, do the following:

- **Cut back on personal spending.** Even if you have outside financing, you'll face emergencies or unexpected setbacks. Vacations or new cars probably won't be affordable for quite a long time, and you (and your children) may have to go without luxuries for a year or more.
- **Clean up and manage your personal debt.** You don't want to float two boats, so pay off all debts, or at least clean up your credit report so you can acquire loans, and manage your debt so you can sleep at night.
- **Don't be afraid to borrow.** If you've got a solid business plan, you will likely find investors or banks willing to loan you money. While you don't want to overburden your business or surrender ownership, borrowed money can work in your favor. Creditors can be more lenient toward owners carrying substantial loans; you can save your money for backup loans (and deduct the interest from your taxes); and you will probably make more objective decisions.
- **Borrow only what you need to get underway.** Ideally, you are funding the business solo, but if not, limit borrowing to start-up costs and minimize those costs wherever feasible. Once you have profitability, leverage it for loans.
- **Hold onto your present job until the last minute.** Expenses will escalate rapidly the minute you resign, and you'll most likely lose health benefits. Even though it's tempting, hold onto your current job until you absolutely have to quit.

Outside sources of financing include these:

- **Friends/relatives:** To maintain long-term relationships, address every conceivable concern and spell out the terms, conditions, and all repayment expectations in a written contract, including the amount, interest rate, payment expectations, lender's ownership or management expectations, what happens if a downturn prevents immediate payment, how long the loan can be extended, and what happens if the lender or loan recipient dies.
- **Banks/lending institutions:** These institutions are always in search of business propositions, but lenders require polished, professional, and complete business plans. They typically want a guarantee—such as your home—or a personal guarantor who can cover your loan if you default. They rarely offer more than 50 percent of the capital required, and you will have to jump through hoops to acquire the loan.
- **Government loans or grants:** Federal, state, and local governments may provide loans or other support, such as employee financing, rent-free locations, research or technology loans, free training, or grants. The Small Business Administration (SBA) is the prime place to research options (although they have stringent restrictions on financial assistance), but also explore government grants that may support women-owned businesses.
- **Private investors:** Typically private investors buy "stock" in your company, which means they purchase ownership equal to their investment.
- **Venture capitalists:** These investors prefer loans well above $50,000. Find them through accountants, banks, or local businesses development organizations (like the SBA). They will require extensive planning and typically require huge market potential, outstanding growth potential, proven management teams, and exit strategies. Between legal fees and management costs, you may end up paying 10 percent of the investment costs.
- **Trade bartering:** Sometimes you can convince suppliers to extend your payment requirements from thirty days to forty-five or even sixty days without incurring additional costs. If you balance this

"free" credit with an incentive to have your customers pay in ten days, you may be able to bridge the gap and fund your business on their coattails.

- **Seller financing:** If you need equipment, you may be able to buy the equipment with no money down and no interest for the first year, which amounts to eleven months of free equipment. (You have to pay in the twelfth month to avoid interest charges.) Or you may be able to ask suppliers who will benefit from your business to finance equipment. Or better yet, buy used equipment and barter for financing.

According to *The Unofficial Guide for Starting Your Small Business,* the most common financing mistakes include the following:

- Starting off with insufficient funds
- Overestimating potential sales
- Not protecting your assets
- Taking on too much interest
- Failing to plan for growth
- Not preparing for temporary downturns
- Misunderstanding cash flow requirements
- Thinking that all you need is a lot of money

To make the most of government support, write to the U.S. Government Printing Office for a copy of the *Catalog of Federal Domestic Assistance.* (You can find their address in the front of your local telephone book.) It describes the types of loans available from various governmental agencies that support small businesses. It also includes the requirements for applying and what you can reasonably expect.

The Pros and Cons of Franchises

Another way to enter the entrepreneurial world is to consider franchise opportunities of profitable businesses. A franchise agreement basically means that you purchase the right to use a parent company's name, product, or service, and that you participate in their collective advertising. You typically pay a licensing fee, an annual fee, and a percentage of your profits, all of which can vary widely. The U.S. Department of Commerce offers a booklet titled *The Franchise Opportunities Handbook* that lists an array of options and guidelines that will help you decide if owing a franchise is really something you want to do. According to their figures, franchises account for 33 percent of American retail businesses.

The pros of franchises include these:

- You adopt a proven idea or product.
- Your business has instant identificati1on.
- You participate in national advertising that builds brand identity.
- The parent company assists you in store development—finding locations, negotiating a lease, designing the store, and purchasing the equipment.
- The parent company may help you fund the business.
- The parent company supplies you with professionally developed promotional materials.
- The parent company offers training and set-up assistance.
- You join a network of franchise owners who can offer valuable support.

The cons of franchises include these:

- The business is someone else's idea and may feel constrictive.
- The costs may be steep, including pricey legal and regulatory fees.
- You start on a larger scale and will most likely require additional employees.
- The parent company rules may be stringent and feel limiting.
- You feel pressured to perform right out of the gate.
- The parent company sales' expectations may be hard to meet.
- The parent company receives high fees and requires a large percentage of profits.
- Complicated management may necessitate legal, tax, and financial advisors.

Franchises can be extremely successful, and some offer generous returns, but it's prudent to research them thoroughly so that you know exactly what you are getting into. Keep in mind that any franchiser is reporting the most positive aspects while downplaying the negatives. Make use of governmental agencies to establish legitimacy and to question the information being provided. Before you invest serious money, be sure to talk to other franchisers under the same umbrella for their assessment. Before you invest in a franchise, abide by the U.S. Department of Commerce suggestions, as follows:

- Look realistically at the risks involved.
- Know the real time and energy required and whether you can provide it.
- Act like a private investigator and find out everything you can.
- Evaluate their "disclosures" by discussing them with existing franchise operators.
- Question their "earnings" claims.
- Seek professional guidance—governmental, local bankers, lawyers, and accountants.
- Know your legal rights before you negotiate.

Also, be wary of advertisements in newspapers and magazines offering "work from home" opportunities. It's better to create your own business than align your time, energy, or finances with a firm that may or may not be legitimate.

Chapter 10

Budgeting for Wealth

Although many people will actually earn a million dollars in their lifetimes, few will be able to transmute it into a fortune. Cornered by debt, many Americans are now forced to work harder just to keep afloat. Largely due to mass over-consumption and irresponsible financial management, we have turned what was once a blissful, hopeful, conceivable American dream into a nation of citizens who are "just getting by." Clearly, if you want to develop wealth, you have to buck the trend and map out your own path to financial health, wealth, and happiness.

Mapping Out Your Real Situation

If you want to build true wealth, you have to start at the beginning—by splashing your face with the cold water that is your financial reality. You cannot improve your situation if you don't first assess what you have to work with and what is working against you. It's essential to know exactly how much is coming in and how much is going out. Money coming in means what you bring home after taxes, not your gross salary. Everyone likes to quote the higher before-tax number as income, but that's not realistic. "Money in" means money that you have to pay for your living expenses, to spend on luxuries, to fund your dreams, and to save.

Once you know what you really have to work with, it's important to create a household budget that will accurately reflect your monthly expenses, making sure that you have covered all of the following:

- Fixed expenses
- Flexible expenses
- Expendable purchases or expenses
- Seasonal fluctuations
- Hidden costs (mini-vacations, gifts, car licensing)

Then take it a step further and literally keep an expense log. For one month, religiously write down absolutely everything your spend money on, right down a cup of plain coffee at Starbucks, popcorn at the movies, the lollipops you bought for the kids at the mall, and the bottle of nail polish you rushed to buy before your last date. You want to know exactly how much money is flowing out of your pocket so that you can plug up the drains. Here are your goals:

- Identify absolute necessities.
- Identify disposable excess.
- Identify unconscious or reflexive spending.

Write all of this down in cold, hard, unforgiving black and white. Even if the numbers look oppressive, by the time you've worked through this chapter, you'll see opportunities for vast improvement. You *can* build wealth,

and we're going to show you the basic steps ι
underway.

FACT

The majority of American millionaires are self-made. In
than 8.9 million millionaires, around 2 percent inherit.
and fewer than 20 percent inherited only a small portion ι
Holding onto wealth is also a learned skill—studies have si
percent of people who win the lottery are bankrupt within ι

Living Within Your Means

First and foremost, you have to live within your means. According to
Stacy Johnson, author of *Life or Debt,* becoming wealthy has nothing what-
soever to do with income or investment knowledge. Accumulating wealth
comes from avoiding debt, living below your means, and investing sensibly
and consistently. Indeed, says Johnson, "becoming financially independent
isn't really a function of how much money you make; it's far more often a
function of how little money you spend."

Contrary to what you might imagine, most millionaires don't live an opu-
lent lifestyle. They don't wear flashy clothes or buy flashy cars. Those who
chase the image of status are usually people who try to sell things to rich
people but aren't rich themselves. In fact, consider these interesting, and
perhaps eye opening, statistics on American millionaires taken from Richard Paul Evans's book *The Five Lessons a Millionaire Taught Me About Life
and Wealth*:

- The median income for American millionaires is $131,000.
- 97 percent own their own homes.
- The average value of their houses is $320,000.
- About half have lived in the same house for twenty years or more.
- Fewer than one in four millionaires owns a new car.
- Fewer than one in five leases a car.
- The average price they paid for a car is slightly less than $25,000.

- For more than a third, their most recent purchase was a used car.
- Only 6.4 percent drove a Mercedes or a Lexus. Less than 3 percent drive a Jaguar.
- 60 percent drive an American-made car.
- 50 percent never paid more than $400 for a suit in their lives, for themselves or anyone else.
- About half never paid more than $140 for a pair of shoes.

Spending Wisely—Becoming a Smart Consumer

Millionaires have instincts and habits that generate and sustain wealth. Those hoping to accumulate wealth understand that carefully considering all expenditures is one of the fastest ways to save money. They understand that freedom and power are superior to momentary pleasure. They do not equate spending with happiness, and given the opportunity to spend or save, they take the greater pleasure in saving. If you want to join their ranks, ask yourself some basic questions before you buy virtually anything:

- **Is this item or service I'm buying really necessary?** Can I achieve the same effect, take care of the same need, or fulfill the same desire for zero money?
- **Can I purchase this item or service at a discount?** Never be afraid to ask merchants or service providers for discounts—if they are offering you the lowest possible price, and if they match the lowest prices available. Often, merchants, car dealers, computer stores, and even real estate agents will drop the price to make the sale.
- **Is this expenditure adding to my wealth or detracting from it?** Buying houses rather than cars that depreciate is an example of this principle.

Make it a habit to never buy anything without giving serious thought about whether you really, really want it. Then, shop around for the best price, and if you cannot make a deal that fits in with your goals, walk away. If you have enough money, and it's something you really want, just make sure you absolutely love whatever you're buying and make sure that you'll continue to love it, or profit from it, for at least as long as it takes to pay for it.

Establishing Concrete Savings and Investment Goals

Once you know your real situation, you want supercede the standard of "just getting by." If you don't create a vision—and a game plan—for your future, your dreams aren't likely to happen. You don't want your goals to be too general, as in simply increasing your income by 10 percent; you want to be specific, as in creating a new income stream based on your ability to create handmade jewelry that you can sell monthly at a local flea market. In other words, you want to set concrete goals that can be achieved.

Push the envelope when you're setting goals. Instead of intending to "save more this month," set your sights on saving $250 (or whatever amount feels out of reach) every month for six months. View it as an invigorating challenge and consciously make choices that support your goals—eat in less expensive restaurants, forego beverages, and go out once a week instead of two; or cut your clothing budget in half and then take pride in finding ways to buy nice clothes at bargain prices. If you reach your goal easily, increase the amount, and look for new areas to trim expenses. Constantly review and change your goals, and get your highs from money being deposited into savings rather than money being spent on clothes, vacations, or cars you cannot really afford.

Creating a Savings Budget

Now that you've done the legwork, select items or activities you can surrender for the sake of building your savings. Even with small amounts added to your investment accounts each month, your savings can grow to be prodigious sums over a few years' time. For instance, at an interest rate of 8 percent, $150 saved per month will become $50,641 in fifteen years. To get you motivated, take a look at what a relatively small sum each month could become in twenty years.

Your Savings over Time*			
Amount saved per month:	$50	$100	$150	$200
5 years	$3,647	$7,294	$10,942	$14,589
10 years	$9,006	$18,012	$27,019	$36,025
15 years	$16,880	$33,761	$50,641	$67,521
20 years	$28,450	$56,900	$85,350	$113,800

Assumes an 8 percent return after taxes and fees

Creating a Game Plan to Achieve Your Savings Goals

Goals without a written game plan to achieve them are just words on paper. Just as it's important to break down dreams into concrete goals, it's also important to break down all the likely steps you will need to take and obstacles you will need to overcome. Here are the tasks involved:

- Identify necessary steps that will lead up to achieving the goals.
- Identify all conceivable obstacles you will have to overcome.
- Write down your game plan for mastering the steps.
- Write down your game plan for overcoming the obstacles.

You may need to supplement your income, at least for one or two years until you get a savings plan established. Put on your thinking cap and come up with as many ideas as you can. Write down everything—don't reject things immediately—and think outside the box. Some examples might include the following:

- Teach cooking or baking classes.
- Take a part-time job at a museum.
- Refurbish furniture and sell it.
- Start a gardening business.
- Sell gift baskets to local businesses around the holidays.

Once you've created the plan, launch it! If it works beautifully, create new goals and the game plans that will achieve them. Get inspired and celebrate your successes. Success builds upon success, and you're the beneficiary!

Monitoring Your Progress

Goals need a timeframe. It's important to stay on top of your fluctuating reality and to assess how you're doing in terms of meeting your goals. Rather than lapse into unconscious—or unexamined—behavior patterns, keep yourself fully conscious and motivated by reviewing your situation at least quarterly. If you are falling short, make any necessary adjustments.

If you are putting away 10 percent of your monthly salary, and can add another 10 percent from additional income streams, you would essentially double your savings, and increase your chances of becoming a millionaire seven years ahead of schedule.

Don't fret much if you didn't reach all your goals; setting goals and achieving them is always a work in progress. If you didn't reach a goal, figure out if the goal is still important. If it is, brainstorm how you will achieve it by the time you next review your progress, and commit to your new plan for achievement.

Creating Money Stashes That Grow

Put your daily change into piggy banks or jars and once a month take it to the bank and deposit it into your savings. You'd be surprised how quickly change can add up to $25 or far more. At least once a week, choose something you can forfeit and place what you would have spent into your savings jar:

- Skip a movie and place the $20 you just saved into your savings jar.
- Skip a cocktail at dinner and place $7 in your savings jar.
- Skip a pedicure and place $30 in your savings jar.

When you have to run to the discount drug store to pick up mascara and nail polish, pay with a $20 bill and then drop what isn't spent into your savings jar. In other words, go from unconsciously spending to consciously squeezing savings wherever and whenever you can, and pat yourself on the back whenever you do. Flip the emotional rush that you used to feel when spending into the emotional rush you will feel when fattening your bank accounts.

Saving Early Can Make You Rich

Chances are that if you're reading this book, you have decades before you retire to grow your assets, which is certainly enough time to create a substantial nest egg. In the world of investing, there's nothing more important than long stretches of time to make your assets grow. For instance, if you put $1,000 into savings today and earn 6 percent per year (after taxes and fees), in ten years you'll have made a 79 percent return; in twenty years you'll have made a 221 percent return; and in forty years your gain will be 928 percent—and your initial investment will have grown to $10,280! If you earn 8 percent every year for forty years, your $1,000 initial investment will grow to be $21,720—which shows you how much difference 3 percent can make. These kinds of potential returns make investing starting as soon as possible the only feasible way for most of us to retire or even be considered rich.

Investing to Make Large Payments

You may have definite savings goals at any age beyond accumulating funds for retirement—like putting your child through college or making a down payment on a home. The earlier you start saving, the better. Once you've accumulated funds, your best bet for securing and increasing your return is to segregate and earmark a portion of your investment portfolio to cover this expense. If you have fifteen years to save, high-risk investments for the first twelve years will create maximum return. Reallocating those funds to low-risk investments—such as bonds, and relatively safe larger-capitalization international and domestic stocks—for the last three years of the saving period will decrease risk and guarantee that you can pay for college or buy your dream home according to plan.

Creating a Diversified Portfolio

Your money will grow faster and you will take on less risk if you maintain a diversified portfolio. Diversification should be done both across asset classes—investing in stocks and bonds and within asset classes—putting money to work in large and small stocks, and low and high-quality bonds.

Stock Category Risk Levels

High Risk	Moderate Risk	Lower Risk
Emerging-market stock	Mid-cap stock	High-quality domestic bonds
Micro-cap domestic stock	High-yield domestic bonds	U.S. Treasury bonds
Small-cap domestic stock	Real estate investment trusts (REITs)	Money market funds
Emerging-market debt	Foreign stock through an index like the EAFE	Large-cap stock

The asset classes below are arranged descending in order of risk—higher-risk investments on the list will tend to have higher returns. Treat the list like a buffet menu. Make your portfolio more diversified, and more palatable, by choosing a range of the assets listed. Based on past returns, the first group of high-risk investments will probably return 8 to 11 percent in the long run before taxes and fees. The second group will probably return between 7 and 10 percent in the long run. The final group, a collection of bonds and money funds, will likely return somewhere between 3 and 7 percent in the long run. If you want to earn 8 percent or more in the long run, keep the amount of your portfolio in lower-risk assets to a minimum.

Investment Goals Based on Age

When you're young, saving and making investments may seem like something you only need to worry about when you're forty. The sad reality, however, is that you reach age forty sooner than you think—particularly when you're busy raising children virtually single-handedly. If you haven't established short-term and long-term goals and actually implemented savings and investment plans, you'll have a lot of expensive catching up to do. Without question, investment plans need to change as one ages, and a savvy investor implements a plan that fits her current needs—while very much keeping an eye on the road far ahead.

Between the Ages of Twenty and Thirty

Time is on your side on all fronts. By establishing healthy savings and investing habits, you can build a very bright future for yourself and your children. Even putting $100 a month into a savings account will build into a sizeable amount. If you set aside $250 a month and you earn no interest on the money, you will accumulate $30,000 in ten years! If you put that same amount into savvy investments, such as money market accounts, certificates of deposit, bonds, stocks, or mutual funds, you should earn higher rates of return, maximizing savings.

ALERT!

If you are twenty-two years old and deposit $4,000 a year ($333.33 a month) into a retirement account growing at an 8-percent annual return, those funds would build to $1 million by age sixty-two. If you wait until you're thirty-two, you'd have to more than double the amount to $8,800 a year ($733.33 a month) to reach $1 million by sixty-two.

If you are between twenty and thirty, you have time to risk weathering the ups and downs of the stock market. Consider the following asset balance:

- Invest 70 percent or more of your retirement funds in stocks or stock mutual funds. Allocate 25 to 35 percent of your stock holdings to riskier classes of stock, such as a mutual fund investing in small-cap domestic stocks.
- Invest 15 to 30 percent of your portfolio in primarily long-term bonds to even out the ups and downs of your portfolio.

Why invest in bonds or other less-risky investments that may provide you with lower returns than stocks? Bonds and other investments that move in response to different factors than stocks help dampen the volatility of your portfolio. A portfolio that returns 8 percent every year without fail will provide you with higher returns over time than a portfolio with more volatility, returning 7 percent one year and 9 percent the next, despite its average return of 8 percent.

Diversification—investing some in stocks and some in bonds—dampens the volatility of your portfolio while potentially increasing returns. It's wise to also diversify within your stock holdings. Investing in a range of stocks— large-cap domestic stock, emerging-market stock, and so on—through a range of mutual funds or exchange-traded funds will often bring higher returns over time, and the balance offers some protection against losses. If you don't have enough money to buy shares in a number of funds and won't be able to save much on a regular basis, choose a broad-based stock index like one that tracks the Standard & Poor's 500 Index or the Wilshire 5000 index. The same advice holds for bonds—diversify your bond holdings by purchasing an index fund or ETF invested in bonds. For more information, review Chapter 12.

One way to be diversified in the right asset classes over time is to invest in a "target maturity" fund. You select the date when you intend to use the money (at age sixty-five, or in twenty years, for example), and an expert money management firm will manage your funds, altering asset allocations and risk levels over time with that "target date" in mind.

Between the Ages of Thirty and Forty

Whether you are twenty-five or thirty-five years away from retirement, time is on your side. Even starting from scratch, there's still time to be a millionaire; however, by waiting longer to get started, you'll need to save $500 per month starting at age thirty, or $1,150 per month at age forty and get an 8 percent return to become a millionaire by age sixty-five.

The good news is that you have decades before you retire, so you can place your savings in higher risk investments that will earn more than 8 percent a year. You'll also have time to recover from a setback if the stock or bond markets stumble. Consider the following asset allocations:

- **Invest 65 to 85 percent of your funds in stock,** including about 25 to 35 percent in risky stock classes.
- **Invest 15 to 35 percent in a range of bonds,** particularly long-term bonds.

Remember to stay diversified within your stock and bond asset classes—not taking too much risk by investing a large part of your portfolio in one kind of stock, especially the stock of one company. On the other hand, as a financially savvy woman, you should always be willing to take calculated risks in the stock and bond markets. There is a place in almost every portfolio for some risky securities. Keep in mind that the sooner the money is needed, and the more important it is to maintaining your standard of living, the lower should be your allocation to very risky securities. In a retirement account at thirty to forty years of age, you have a lot of time and probably don't need the money for decades, so you can technically stomach a lot of risk. On the other hand, investing isn't worthwhile if the swings in your portfolio keep you up at night. You're the best judge about the amount of portfolio volatility you can stand, but remember that the bad months will probably be more than offset by the good ones.

Between the Ages of Forty and Fifty

You're older, wiser, and still have fifteen to thirty years until retirement, key years to grow your assets so that when you reach fifty, sixty, and beyond, you'll have enough socked away to fund your expenses and whatever unknowns you encounter.

Consider the following asset allocation:

- **Invest 60 to 70 percent of your funds in stock.** You still have time to come back from setbacks, and should have some exposure to risk.
- **Invest the remaining 30 to 40 percent in bonds.**

If you're fifty with no savings and want to be a millionaire in fifteen years, you have to save $2,970 per month and invest it so it grows at 8 percent every year.

Between the Ages of Fifty and Sixty

You're aged to perfection, and retirement is just around the corner. If you haven't yet done so, it's imperative that you build a nest egg. Because you will soon begin to sell off parts of your portfolio to fund retirement needs and desires, it's time for you to dial down the risk level of your portfolio. You might consider having 55 to 65 percent of your portfolio in stocks if you are fifteen years from retirement, and a lower percentage each year as you approach the big date. It's still important in most cases to own stock and other risky assets in retirement if you have enough money and emotional security to tolerate the volatility.

ALERT!

S&P 500 index investors lost 25 percent on their stock holdings from April to July of 2002. During market "adjustments," the press jumps on the bandwagon, bombarding the public with bad news, causing many to reflexively dump their entire stock portfolios. If you have diversified your investments within the market and can learn to ignore the skeptics, the market generally rights itself.

If you are less than ten years from retiring, consult with a financial advisor to evaluate your asset allocation plan in detail, focusing on what and how much you will need to have in place before you are able to retire. If you haven't saved enough, you may have to drastically cut back on expenses in order to maintain your lifestyle in retirement. You may have to downsize, trading your present house for a less expensive one or even moving to an area where living expenses are substantially less.

Managing Income Property

Real estate investments can make you wealthy. If you can swing a down payment and convince a lender that you can easily find renters who will maintain the property and cover all, or most, of the monthly mortgage, income property can be a marvelous way to fatten your net worth. Assuming that you don't have higher-cost debt that could be paid off first, you'll want to pay down the loan as fast as possible so that your equity increases.

A commitment to keeping your income property up to code, making sure rent is paid, and that all maintenance and other issues are taken care of is not for everyone. The biggest issues keeping most of us from investing in real estate are the time commitment and the down payment for income property. The responsibilities and risks you have as a landlord include these:

- **Keeping the house in a habitable condition:** Small and large repairs must be handled promptly, which could catch you up short. As you build equity, you could initiate a home equity loan to cover repairs that would only slightly increase monthly mortgage payments. However, you would take on extra risk—if home prices fall, or if maintenance is more extensive and costly than you expect, you could end up "upside down" on your property (owing more on your mortgage than its market value).
- **Screening potential tenants:** You are legally prevented from discriminating based on your tenants' ethnicity, country of origin, skin color, religious affiliation, handicap, gender, or marital status, but you can—and should—choose among potential tenants based on their present income, stability, credit history, personal cleanliness, and references. The risks can be many and varied—from facing extended evictions to dealing with abandoned household goods or destruction of property.

Still, if you can afford it, income property can be a very profitable investment. Once you own one property for a while and have learned the risks and advantages of being a landlord, as well as accumulated equity, you can leverage the purchase of another property through a home equity loan on the first property. If you are managing one property well—and maintaining your own home and paying your debts promptly—lenders will often work with you on future acquisitions. Even Donald Trump started small!

Inheritances Can Make You Wealthy

If you are lucky enough to inherit property, you are essentially being given a cash cow. Here's what you need to know to maximize the windfall:

- **Estate taxes:** According to current tax laws, unless your total inheritance surpasses $2 million, you will not owe estate taxes. The applicable tax law varies by year—for instance, the nontaxable amount of an estate received in 2007 is $2 million, but in 2010 the estate tax will be repealed—so check with the IRS or a tax professional if you are uncertain, or if your gains exceed $2 million.
- **Market value:** When you inherit property, the property's cost basis is adjusted upward to the current market value. You will need a professional appraiser to determine the house's market value when it's inherited. It may make sense to sell inherited property quickly—your gain on the sale will be whatever price you receive, less the stepped-up cost basis of the home, so a quick sale could reduce your taxable gains and the cost of upkeep. The $250,000 tax shelter on real estate gains doesn't apply in this case unless you've lived in the house for two of the five years before it is sold.

If you receive a cash inheritance, and you can afford to indulge yourself in a few luxuries, go ahead and spend 10 to 20 percent of it, but by all means invest the rest in your savings, real estate, or retirement plans. Inheritances can bolster your assets and investments substantially, so it's only smart to maximize the opportunity and use them to build wealth.

Rules for Creating Wealth

If you want to acquire wealth, first and foremost, you have to decide to be wealthy. Choice signals a journey, but it's a commitment to the path that makes all the difference. When people align their intention with their values and establish habits that coincide with their desired outcome—in essence living the decision—the universe (and their own subconscious) lays the groundwork for making it a reality. So decide, already, and get cracking on making your desired outcome a reality. Follow the seven basic rules below, and you'll be well on your way.

1. **Accept responsibility for your financial future.** You are the only person in a position to make sure that you become financially secure. Take control of your finances by getting a clear picture of where you are now and by creating time-based goals and a game plan to achieve them. Commit to your financial plan of action, and review your current situation and short-term financial goals quarterly. Long-term goals and game plans should be reviewed and adjusted annually.

2. **Pay yourself first.** Unfailingly and automatically deposit 10 percent (preferably more) of your paycheck into your savings, and 90 percent of any earnings from windfalls, inheritances, investments, and side ventures. Keep in mind that millionaires tend to save 15 to 20 percent of their monthly income.

3. **Know what your money is doing.** The whole point of amassing money is to use it to generate income. If you manage it well, you may earn more from your investments than you earn from a salary. Reviewing your investment portfolio and filling out your monthly net-worth statement will help you track your investments and maximize wealth-building habits.

4. **Reduce spending.** Instead of blowing $140 on new shoes, or taking on a $20,000 loan to buy a new car, get your kicks from saving, rather than spending, money. Separate essential expenses from expendable expenses, and channel whatever you can save into your investment portfolio.

5. **Earn more at your job.** Commit to being more competent at work by learning new things or getting involved in related functions at your company where you can add value. Make sure that your employer knows

that you've added value with your education or project by showing your superiors that you have the initiative and smarts to make and fully follow through on a plan that helps the firm.

6. **Generate additional income streams.** You need to keep your eyes open for opportunities to generate additional income streams—whether delivering lunch baskets to downtown office complexes, capitalizing on hobbies (decoupage clay pots, handcrafted jewelry, freelance writing), or simply finding a second job. With only a slightly larger time commitment, if you only earn enough to add another 10 percent of your current income to your nest egg, you can potentially double the amount you'll save over time.

7. **Invest wisely.** Make the most of your savings by investing as much as you can in tax-deferred savings accounts like a 401(k) or an IRA. Diversify your holdings so you aren't overly invested in just a few stocks or bonds. Seek to minimize the amount of fees you pay by purchasing the lowest-cost stock and bond index funds available, and limit the number of trades you make to minimize your commissions.

It's not easy to make the sacrifices, but once you become more enthused about how much money you're saving, savvy about the investments you make, and cognizant of where you are on the financial path versus where you want to be, you'll have a far better chance of becoming wealthy and living to enjoy the benefits.

Chapter 11

Deciding Whether to Rent or Own

Homes and cars are the most expensive items you will likely purchase. Owning a home is part of the American dream and can be the fastest road to financial security, but it also comes with some big caveats. The decisions you make—whether you lease, rent, or own and when, where, and how you buy—will have a huge impact on your finances. If you make smart, money-savvy decisions, one day you will be able to afford your dream car or home.

The Pros and Cons of Renting

Although half of American renters say that they rent because of circumstance rather than by choice, renting can, in fact, be a boon to your lifestyle, and in some cases to your finances. If you're a renter, someone else is responsible for the time and money variables necessary to maintain the home. Your landlord, or property manager, is legally required to make sure that your building—including hardware like the toilet and the refrigerator that came with the rental—is in good working order. Maintenance can easily run between 1 and 2 percent of the house's value every year, and the occasional large repair, like a roof replacement, can arrive without warning, throwing your finances into a tailspin . . . if you own the place. Renting can actually save you money and leave you with more time for working, playing, and enjoying your family. Also, if you rent in a town or city with rent control, your landlord is required to keep rent increases to a minimum—sometimes at much less than the rate your paycheck increases—whether or not the value of the home has changed, or whether the landlord made major repairs on the building.

FACT

In Fannie Mae's 2003 Housing Survey, 81 percent of homeowners said that home ownership has been a "very positive" experience, compared to 31 percent of renters who reported a "very positive" experience in rental housing.

Renting makes sense when you plan on staying in the home less than five years. Homes rarely accumulate enough equity in the first five years of ownership to make them the highly profitable investment they become if you live in them for more than that long. If your life is unsettled and likely to remain so, the flexibility of being able to leave with one month's advance notice has distinct advantages—such as being able to buy the right property at the right time, or to transfer to another city for a job opening.

However, renting doesn't make sense for everyone. Without rent control, you may face large and arbitrary annual rent increases. In rare circumstances, a landlord may evict tenants for subjective reasons—such as wanting to move into your home. Finally, as a renter, you don't accrue equity in your home, which for most homeowners translates into the largest asset they own and a major cushion when it comes time to retire.

The Pros and Cons of Home Ownership

Whether you want a country home with a big backyard or a city loft near great restaurants and entertainment, every woman deserves a place over which she reigns as queen. The beauty of home ownership is that you have full control over your home's décor—you can knock down walls and rebuild the kitchen or whatever else you like without asking anyone except perhaps your local building inspector. And, as long as you pay your mortgage promptly, it's yours to enjoy as long as you like.

The reasons for home ownership are substantial. They include these:

- **Equity accrual:** Your home will likely become your largest asset over time. The magic of "forced savings"—the money you put toward paying down the principal on your mortgage—increases your equity, which increases your net worth. Forced savings through home ownership may be your best—and most practical—route to accumulating a retirement nest egg.
- **Tax breaks:** The interest and "points" you pay on your mortgage loan are tax deductible. If you pay slightly more each month on your mortgage than you would for rent, the tax breaks will probably make the larger mortgage payment less expensive.
- **Fixed costs:** Your payments on a fixed mortgage don't increase over time. Costs of maintenance and insurance will rise over time, however.
- **Return-on-investment potential:** Real estate has historically appreciated more slowly and with lower price volatility than stocks and bonds. However, a small down payment will magnify your returns, making even small annual increases in value very profitable.

While a home can be your largest asset, home ownership brings substantial responsibility. In addition to paying a monthly mortgage, you will face insurance, state and local property taxes, landscaping maintenance, routine house and appliance maintenance, and large, unexpected repairs or restorations. Once you own a house, it's crucial that you protect the investment, which can be costly.

Part of every mortgage payment goes to interest, which you don't benefit from, and part goes to principal, which pays down your debt. Over the first ten years of a fixed thirty-year mortgage, you'll pay between 9 and 18 percent to principal, while during the mortgage's final ten years 63 to 72 percent of your payments go to principal.

If you encounter expensive medical problems without insurance, or are unable to work for a long period of time, you could lose your home through bankruptcy, which damages your credit rating for a decade, or more, making it more difficult to borrow—and substantially raising interest rates on credit cards or any other type of loan.

As an owner, your financial tides match those of the market—occasionally ballooning up, occasionally ratcheting down, and occasionally not moving upward significantly for years. However, even in an uncertain market, if you intend to live in the home for at least ten years and have a mortgage with payments you can afford, the timing of your home purchase is much less important.

All about Condos

A condominium, particularly in an urban setting, may be a good place to start. Typically, condos cost 20 to 30 percent less than individual homes, and you may be able to minimize your commute and your maintenance costs—both in terms of dollars and hours. The downside includes adherence to the condominium complex's rules, which may restrict exterior paint or landscaping and may even extend to the number of pets you own. Sound from your neighbor's units may also be a turn-off.

Condominiums usually have additional monthly fees earmarked for building repairs and other communal expenses. Condominium associations may also institute large one-time fees called "special assessments" to pay for major building retrofits or other issues that affect the whole community. Before buying a condominium, ask whether any special assessments are planned or likely—or you could move in just before a large payment is required. Also inquire about the mindset and makeup of the community association that will decide what projects will go forward, which might hinder or help to maintain your investment.

ALERT!

Beware of buying condos in cities where multiple large condominium complexes are being built. Many of them are purchased by investors who will be quick to dump them during a market downturn, and their interiors and views are pretty standard, which means buyers may not care whether they get the condo on the third or fifth floor. When flooded with undifferentiated condominiums, market prices decline.

Buying a Home

Buying a home is both a solid investment strategy and a way to gain stability and enjoyment, but it involves a lot of money and a time commitment. As such, it's wise to make the decision based on meaningful criteria. Begin with a list of what you most want from the home and community in which you will live, as follows:

- **Size:** How many bedrooms and bathrooms do you need?
- **Style:** Are you willing to live in a condominium or mobile home?
- **Essentials:** Storage space and hot tubs can be essential to some.
- **Schools:** Visit and investigate the schools your children will attend.

- **Transportation:** How long will it take you to commute to work? Is there a garage or only street parking? Do you have access to public transportation?
- **Safety:** Is the neighborhood safe for your children?
- **Amenities:** Are there local restaurants, theaters, and other activity centers to entertain your family?
- **Neighbors:** How does the neighborhood look from the street? Your neighbors' slovenliness will diminish the value of your home.

In terms of investment potential, location of the property may be the most important determination. Well-maintained, desirable neighborhoods are worth their weight in gold.

Of course you want to buy a house you love, but a money-savvy woman also wants to protect her long-term investment. Many have made minor fortunes by purchasing the smallest or most run-down house in the best neighborhood. You don't want to buy a house that requires so many repairs it zaps your budget, but you do want to consider the long-term marketability and buy a property that you can afford and that will appreciate in value.

Preapproval

Many people consult with a mortgage lender, who gives them an estimate on what she believes the buyer can afford. This is helpful to you, but if you are ready to buy, going from prequalification to preapproval is advisable. Here's the basic difference:

- *Prequalification* is an estimate a lender calculates based upon simple data you supply about your income, debt, and debt payments about how much you can borrow.
- *Preapproval* is a lender's promise to provide a loan up to a certain amount. Lenders collect and then verify information about your income, debt, and debt payment claims to determine the amount they are willing to loan you for a home purchase.

Preapproval frees you to find a house and negotiate on the strength of the lender's financial backing. It tells the seller's broker and the home seller that you are serious and capable of closing the deal. In competitive markets, the preapproved buyer has a decided advantage. At closing, the lender will probably verify that your income and debt information hasn't changed. The lender will also ask for an appraisal to make sure the property is being purchased for a reasonable amount before the loan is consummated.

Small savings on a large mortgage can add up quickly. Seek out a "lowest-cost bid" for your mortgage through multiple lenders, including your bank and local credit unions that may offer lower-than-average rates. Ask your real estate broker for suggestions, but keep in mind that she may favor lenders for reasons other than reliable low-cost loans.

Online mortgage affordability calculators will give you an idea of the size of a loan you can afford to finance a home purchase. A calculator from a reputable source should include charges for your current payments on other debts, state and local taxes, and home insurance as part of the calculation.

At least three months before you seek preapproval for a mortgage loan, check your credit reports to see if there are any blemishes or mistakes. Using the information in Chapters 6 and 7, make any corrections and clear up anything that will lower your credit score.

Lenders evaluate your monthly income, the stability of your monthly income, your monthly debt payments, your assets, and your credit history to determine the maximum amount they are willing to lend you for a particular home. As noted in Chapter 7, lenders have their own method for computing how much they will loan to you. If you have worked for your current employer for a few years and have a solid credit history, they will probably go as high as 29 percent of your pretax income for mortgage, insurance, and property taxes. However, it's important for you to do your own calculations and decide what you feel you can afford.

Down Payments

For standard home loans, you may be required to invest 10 to 20 percent of the home's value as a down payment to avoid paying private mortgage insurance. However, if you borrow using mortgages backed by the Federal Housing Administration (FHA) or Veterans' Affairs (VA), you may be able to pay 5 percent, or less, of the home's value in a down payment. The FHA or VA may also help lower your mortgage costs.

FACT

If you haven't owned a home within the last three years, if you are divorced and only owned property while married, or if you have only owned a mobile home, you may qualify for an FHA-insured loan. Maximum loans range from $200,000 to $363,000 based on the location of your home. You can calculate your maximum by going online to the U.S. Housing and Urban Development Web site, at *www.hud.gov.*

VA-insured loans are generally offered only to current and past U.S. military personnel who are currently serving, or who served and were not dishonorably discharged from twenty-four months of active duty, including ninety days of service in wartime or 181 days in peacetime. National Guard and Selected Reserves members with at least six years of service are also eligible for VA loans, as are unmarried spouses of veterans who died while in service. The VA will insure loans up to $203,000 and may not require any down payment.

Private Mortgage Insurance

Generally, if you invest less than 20 percent of the home's value in a down payment, you will be required to buy private mortgage insurance (PMI). This can cost as much as $500 per year for every $100,000 of mortgage value to insure the lender against your defaulting on the loan. PMI is automatically cancelled when the amount of your outstanding mortgage falls below 78 percent of the home's purchase value; however, you can contact the mortgage lender when your balance is below 80 percent of the home's purchase value to terminate PMI early.

You may be able to get around PMI requirements by taking out an 80-10-10 loan, in which you pay 10 percent of the home's value, take out a higher-interest loan for 10 percent, and then seek a traditional mortgage without PMI for the remaining 80 percent. This may save you money by eliminating years of PMI payments.

Your Mortgage Options

Lenders typically offer home mortgages that are either fifteen or thirty years with fixed or adjustable interest rates. But the length is negotiable and should be chosen based upon your ability to meet the monthly payments—the shorter the better.

Fixed mortgages lock in an interest rate for the life of the loan, which means your monthly payment will not fluctuate. Adjustable-rate mortgages (ARMs) offer low fixed initial rates that are adjusted upward after a few years. After the first adjustment, increases are limited to an annual "periodic cap" until they reach a specified "lifetime cap." ARMs offer lower mortgage expenses during the first few years, but you need to either make sure you can afford the increased payments or be prepared to seek a long-term fixed rate mortgage when the rate changes. If you only plan on living in your home for five years or less, a 5/1 ARM may be a smart move. This means five years of fixed payments, then a rate that adjusts based on a national or international one-year interest rate standard like the London Interbank Offered Rate (LIBOR) would keep your payments low and save you the need to refinance at a higher interest rate.

ARMs charge adjustable interest rates frequently based on six- or twelve-month LIBOR rates plus a certain percentage, called the margin. Since 1987, six-month LIBOR has usually been between 3 and 7.5 percent, and twelve-month rates have ranged between 3.25 and 7.7 percent. It's best to take out an ARM when rates are historically average or high, as your loan payments will fall if the index interest rate falls. You can look up the current LIBOR and other index rates online, at *www.bankrate.com.*

In June of 2004, the twelve-month LIBOR was 2.1 percent. Homeowners who opted for ARMs then have seen their LIBOR rates raised to 5.7 percent, which means they face monthly interest payments that are 50 percent or more above their original costs. These kinds of payment jumps can be financial suicide, so make sure you are able to afford the "lifetime cap" or highest interest rate allowed under your ARM.

QUESTION?

What is negative amortization?
Negative amortization occurs when unpaid interest is added to your mortgage balance, increasing your future payments. Only consider mortgages with negative amortization features if you are confident that you will be disciplined and able to pay off the loan balance over time.

If your income varies over time—you own your own business or are compensated on commission—an "option ARM" allows you just that, options. You may choose to pay only interest when you don't have the principal payment that month, to pay less than the full amount of interest if you're even more strapped for cash, or to pay full principal payments and interest when you do have the money. Option ARMs and "interest-only" mortgages (with no required principal payments for the first five or ten years) are useful if you have a variable income, but option ARMs can create negative amortization.

Given the volatility of mortgage rates and the leverage you gain by having preapproval, ask your lender if they are willing to guarantee "the best rate possible" when your deal closes. Otherwise, you could fall prey to rising or falling rates between the time when you seek preapproval and the time you close on a house.

What Can You Afford?

The FHA won't approve a loan whose total payments cost more than 29 percent of your gross or pretax income. If you have good credit, you may be able to raise the ration to 40 percent on a fixed mortgage, but if you have substantial debts, be careful not to overburden yourself with payments.

You may be offered mortgages with different interest rates based on the number of up-front fees, or "points," you pay to the lender. Paying one point means that you pay the lender 1 percent of the total loan amount when the loan is made. The more points, the lower your interest rate. If you are certain that you will stay in the house for seven to ten years, paying more in up-front points will probably be your best option.

The details will vary based on the rate break per point, which will vary by lender. For example, if you borrow $200,000 on a thirty-year fixed mortgage and have the option to pay one extra point at the loan's closing in exchange for a 0.25 percent lower interest rate on your loan, you should pay the point if you believe you will stay in the house for more than seven years. Generally, if you plan to stay in your house for ten or more years, paying an extra point or two makes financial sense. You can find out how long you would have to stay in the house to benefit from paying extra points through an online calculator such as the one at *www.rebuz.com.*

Once you acquire a mortgage, one of the smartest moves you can make is to pay 10 percent more than the minimum payment every month. For example, on a thirty-year $200,000 fixed 7 percent mortgage, you could pay off your home in about twenty-three years and save $77,650 in interest.

FACT

The only times it is not a good idea to pay more than the minimum is if you have higher-rate debt, such as credit cards or an automobile loan, that need to be paid down first, or if you are earning a consistently higher rate of return on an alternative investment, such as your personal business.

It is important to understand the amortization schedule for your mortgage. For a thirty-year fixed mortgage with a 7 percent interest rate, 81 percent of the first twelve years of mortgage payments go toward interest, enriching the mortgage lender. Over the next twelve years, 56 percent of your payments go to interest. In the final six years of the mortgage, only 9 percent of your payments are for interest, while the remaining 91 percent is applied to paying down the balance of your mortgage. The same shift between interest and principal credit over time applies to most mortgages (not interest-only mortgages or option ARMs).

Using a Real Estate Agent

Real estate agents are experts at helping individuals find homes that fit their interests, their budgets, and their criteria. They save you time, make your home search more exhaustive and comprehensive, and play on your team. Your agent represents you, and she earns her commission when she finds the home you want at a price you can afford. Your realtor will negotiate with the seller's broker or the seller, if the owner is selling it on her own, to get the best price possible. And the seller pays her commission!

The seller will also have an agent who represents his interests. If you are not using an agent, be wary when revealing financial information to the seller's agent. Give him enough to know that you can afford the property, but don't disclose exactly how much you are willing to pay or you will lose your ability to negotiate. Instead, offer a range that protects your ability to negotiate toward the lower end of the scale. Meanwhile, you can use the seller's broker to show you around the home, learn about the home's history, and reveal the positive and negative aspects of the neighborhood, such as traffic and noise levels, crime rates, school quality, and whatever else you want to know. Always keep in mind that he works for the seller, not for you.

While you'll probably do well with an agent, don't limit your search to her efforts. You can search for homes through the Multiple Listing Service (MLS), which shows details and pictures of available properties online and in print form. You have access to MLS listings online and in print through your real estate agent and online at *www.realtor.com*.

Personal recommendations are the best way to find an agent. However, if you're going to a new community, be aware that when you call or walk into a local real estate office, you will likely be assigned to the next agent on rotation—without regard to her experience, qualifications, or work ethic. You can vastly improve your odds by perusing local newspaper ads—real estate brokers reward their top performers by giving them prominent placement in their ads—and then calling someone with a lot of sales under her belt.

Another option is to buy a newly built home in a community designed and built by a professional homebuilding company. One advantage is that builders like to move the homes quickly and may offer incentives—low down payments or customized upgrades, for example—to boost sales. Newly built homes will also have lower maintenance expenses in their early years. Be sure to research the homebuilder's reputation, using the Better Business Bureau or a local chamber of commerce. If consumers have lodged a lot of complaints against a certain builder, you will know to look elsewhere.

When You're Ready to Buy

Once you've found a dream home you can afford, your agent will contact the seller's agent, who may require "earnest money"—1 to 6 percent of the value of the home in a check or cash—and a contract that indicates the exact amount of your bid and any contingencies. Make sure that the contract gives you a few days to withdraw your bid in case you change your mind. Your "earnest money" will be returned if the deal doesn't go through—usually because you are unable to get the mortgage loan you expected—as long as this is specified in the contract.

Your agent will assist you in offering a realistic bid based on recent sales of homes in the area, one that is adjusted downward from the asking price for extra work required on the home, and upward for special features, like extra bathrooms or a pool. The exact location of the home will be a big determinant of its value, especially in cities where two blocks can mean a price difference of 5 percent or more. In a "buyer's market," when many homes are for sale and buyers are scarce, your agent will adjust your bid downward accordingly. In a "seller's market," you will benefit from being preapproved and bidding high for the house you really want (and can afford).

The seller may accept your first offer, but typically he will counteroffer, asking for a higher price and/or negotiating the terms—for instance, asking that he be allowed to remain in the home for two months. Negotiations usually go back and forth a few times and will likely take a few days. On your end, your agent can and should include some basic contingencies, as follows:

- **Financing:** To safeguard yourself, you want the purchase "contingent upon the buyer's ability to acquire full financing at a reasonable cost." Preapproval can virtually eliminate the need for this contingency and thus helps you snag the house you really want in a competitive market.
- **Inspections:** This contingency is generally reflected with language reading something like "Sale will be contingent upon buyer's inspection of . . . ." Spend the money for competent home inspectors to look for water, termite, and other damage to the home. Also inspect appliances, heating, air-conditioning, and electrical systems. Even if it costs $1,000, your house is a huge investment and you need to be sure you're not buying one that will quickly become a money drain. You can find local home inspectors through the American Society of Home Inspectors online at ✐*www.ashi.com.*
- **Closing inspection:** "Buyer will inspect the property and house just prior to closing." It's within your rights to request a closing-day inspection that allows you to walk around the property and through the home, making sure that the seller is providing the property in "as-promised" condition before the sale finally closes.

One important part of the contract is a written statement that provides full disclosure on the condition of the house—detailing past problems that have been fixed, as well as any issues that have not yet been addressed. In many cases, a seller's failure to offer full disclosure means you have recourse to make them pay for fixing problems after the fact. If you've hired inspectors and studied the full disclosure statement, you will know what you're getting and will be able to judge whether or not it's a good deal.

ALERT!

If the owner is selling the house without an agent, and you choose not to use an agent, it's prudent to hire a real estate lawyer to make sure that all the paperwork and closing issues are well thought through and wrapped up properly. You can find a real estate lawyer by contacting your local bar association.

Keep in mind that the costs associated with buying a home—points on your loan, appraisal fees, title fees, up to six months of local real estate tax your lender may require prepaid, inspection fees, document fees, property title transfer fees, and other charges—usually add 3 to 5 percent to the total cost of the home. Your real estate lawyer or lender will be able to give you an estimate of the closing costs you will be required to pay before you submit your offer.

You will also need homeowner's insurance, which lenders usually require to cover your home, personal property, and landscaping from theft, fires, hurricanes, and other calamities. Homeowner's insurance costs vary based on your home's location, but policies usually cost 0.5 to 1 percent of the value of your home every year—in other words, $500 to $1,000 for every $100,000 of home value insured. If absolutely necessary, you could lower costs by increasing your deductible, which is the amount you are required to pay toward repairs before the insurer pays a claim.

How to Sell a Home

Even though it feels prohibitive, particularly since you will pay the sales commission for your agent and the buyer's agent, when selling an investment as large as your house, it's smart to hire a reputable, aggressive, and professional real estate agent or broker. Whether you love the idea or hate the idea, selling a home is emotional. You need someone with professional savvy who can market your home and negotiate the best deal.

The agent will assume marketing responsibilities, as follows:

- The agent will photograph your home, ask about any and all special features, prepare all marketing materials, and price your home based on current market conditions.
- The agent will advertise your home in a Multiple Listing Service and hold a broker's open house as quickly as possible to increase its visibility.
- The agent will schedule open houses to lure prospective buyers and handle all individual appointments.
- The agent will negotiate with potential buyers, or their agents, make sure all paperwork is handled properly and verify that the buyer's financing is solid.

You may be able to negotiate a lower sales percentage with your broker—most agents ask for 6 percent, but you can frequently bargain them down to 5 or even 4 percent (if they get the buyer's agent to agree to trim their take).

Traditionally, the highest-priced offers and the largest volume of offers will come within the first four weeks of listing. Take advantage by sprucing up your home and readying yourself to field offers.

Making Improvements

Ask your agent what you can realistically do to improve the property. Unless absolutely necessary, avoid expensive upgrades. Instead, rent a storage unit and remove all excess clutter, keeping only what makes the home more attractive. Clean the house thoroughly, plant a few flowers, and touch up interior and exterior paint.

If your house needs a new roof or extensive landscaping, tell your agent you are willing to pay for half of a reasonable bid if necessary to make the sale. Faced with the option of living with the cheapest roof or landscaping you can find, the buyer may be willing to negotiate.

On open house days, bake bread or cookies or use scented candles. Soft lighting and classical music also increase ambiance. Home staging companies—which offer interior decoration—are expensive and best left to those with money to burn.

What About Contingencies?

It's important to be truthful on your "full disclosure" statement, as required by law. If the buyer makes the sale contingent upon your paying for minor repairs, you can usually hire an inexpensive handyman. Failing to disclose latent or unseen problems like seasonal flooding could lead to more expensive repercussions, including expensive lawsuits.

The buyer will usually request that the sale be contingent upon inspections—termite, water, roof, heating and plumbing, and so on. The buyer will arrange and pay for these inspections. However, be aware that inspectors almost always find "problems" that the buyer will then require you to address. Particularly when it comes to termite inspections, ask your agent to recommend inspectors who offer a fair report and counteroffer with a contingency limiting their choices to these known inspectors. Also, to minimize excess charges or surprise upgrades, counteroffer with a contingency that "all reasonable repairs must be approved by seller." The buyer will also have the home appraised. If your agent has accurately calculated its market value, the appraisal is simply a formality—the mortgage lender should approve the buyer's loan.

Buying a Car

After a home, the next-largest purchase you'll make is probably a car. Unlike homes that generally appreciate in value, cars depreciate, or lose value rapidly. For most of us, buying a car is an unavoidable cost of living. One of the most frivolous purchases you can make is a new car, or even more costly, a new luxury car. According to *Consumer Reports*, a car's value drops by one-third to one-half the first two or three years it's on the road. Buying a used car can save you thousands—thousands that could be used to pay down other debt or invested in college or a retirement savings plan.

FACT

When you sell your home, the first $250,000 of gain is not taxed. For instance, if you purchased the home for $150,000, spent $40,000 remodeling it, and sold it for $400,000, your gain—minus the sales' commissions and repairs—will fall well under $200,000, which means you will not owe any taxes on the sale.

As with buying a home, shop for the lowest interest rates, and nail down a preapproved loan for an amount you can realistically afford. That way the seller will know that you are serious and that you can pay for the car, which should help you negotiate the best price. Verify the car's value by checking *Kelly Blue Book* (online at *www.kbb.com*) or by looking up the value through Edmunds.com.

Avoiding Lemons

Most certified car dealers thoroughly check used cars for mechanical issues and offer a guarantee for a certain number of miles and years from the date of your purchase. You may pay more, but the peace of mind can be worth it. *Consumer Reports* publishes an annual *Used Car Buyer's Guide* that provides substantial information on the reliability of different models and model years.

If you buy from a private party, hire a qualified mechanic to inspect the car before you buy it. Also, for about $20, Carfax.com, Autocheck.com, or Cardetective.com will reveal whether an owner has tampered with the odometer or if an insurance company totaled it after a major accident or natural disaster. All you need is the car's seventeen-digit vehicle identification number, or VIN, which can be found on the left side of the dashboard or on the car's frame inside the driver's door.

Buying Versus Leasing

Car leasing has become a huge industry, and you will see tempting ads touting low down payments and manageable monthly rates, but car leasing can be far more expensive than it appears. At the start of a lease, you pay a fixed amount, usually a few thousand dollars, and then monthly payments that are 30 to 40 percent less than what you would pay if you bought the car outright using a loan. At the end of the term of your lease—usually three to five years—you either buy the car or return it. The extra costs of a lease are often clouded by those attractive low monthly payments.

ALERT!

When you purchase a car outright, higher loan payments help you build equity that reduces interest charges; when leasing, you don't build equity and continue to pay interest for the full value of the car. The finance company takes more risk on the value of the vehicle at the end of the lease than it would if it financed your purchase of the vehicle, so you pay more.

You'll also pay an "acquisition fee" of $500 to $600 and high fees if you terminate the lease early. If you don't buy the car at the end of the lease, you may be charged a "disposition fee." Leasers also charge extra for "excessive" wear on the car (using parameters they arbitrarily determine, but will disclose), as well as additional charges for mileage over 12,000 miles driven per year. You'll also pay extra if you modified the car from its original condition—even if the modification added value to the car.

In spite of this cautionary advice, if you decide to lease, don't allow low monthly payments to cloud your thinking. Negotiate the purchase price, the interest rate, and the cost of breaking your lease. Also, you'll want "gap coverage" to cover the difference between what your insurance company will pay for "cash value" of the car and what you will owe on the lease if your car is totaled or stolen, as what you owe could be several thousand more than the "cash value."

JD Power and Associates, a market research firm, found that 64 percent of people who bought luxury cars financed their purchase with a lease, compared to only 21 percent of people who bought nonluxury models. Far too many people lease a car when they covet it but can't afford to buy it outright. First of all, a money-savvy woman will do better by buying a used car that she can afford—and saving her money. If she makes smart investments, one day she will be able to buy her dream car with cash.

Chapter 12

Investing in Stocks and Mutual Funds

12

Whatever your age, investing even small amounts of money on a regular basis can grow your savings many times over. If you save enough and invest wisely, you can not only become wealthy, you will have a healthy financial umbrella for those days life throws you a curve ball—like facing a large, unexpected expense, losing your job, or becoming disabled. In addition, accumulated savings will not only be invaluable when you retire—the cash will be absolutely essential.

How to Establish Realistic Goals

Your current savings, retirement spending needs, and personal goals are unique to your situation. Because different kinds of investments carry different levels of risk and can be expected to provide different rates of return over time, it is important that you consider investing in a set of assets that will best support your goals and that you create a written plan that clarifies your intentions. Your investing plan won't automatically meet or exceed all of your financial goals, but not creating one will almost certainly make you worse off—potentially leaving you unable to meet basic long-term financial needs.

FACT

An asset class is a collection of investments that tend to move up and down together and have similar characteristics. Typical asset classes include domestic stocks, domestic bonds, foreign stocks, real estate, gold, or art.

You can create a state-of-the-art investing plan by adhering to two basic rules: Create and commit to an asset allocation plan, and diversify your stock, bond, or mutual fund holdings.

Your Asset Allocation Plan

Creating a plan to diversify your assets is one of the most important decisions you can make. Give serious thought to various asset classes (gold, commercial real estate, stocks, bonds, and so on) in terms of their level of risk and how long you are willing to wait for returns, and then allocate your assets to balance risk and the rate of return. It's important to write down your plan—you'll need this to stick to your plan when markets fall and doubt creeps in. Asset classes like domestic stocks or bonds typically have wider variants of fluctuating risk and return than real estate or precious metals.

Diversify Your Holdings

Don't put all your eggs in one company basket or mutual fund. Creating a diverse stock or mutual fund portfolio (mixing large-cap, small-cap, international growth, and bonds) decreases volatility, or risk. A class of investments that all go up at the same time and then down at the same time limits your return and increases your risk. If you diversify stock or mutual fund investments, some will be up while others are down, increasing your portfolio's return while decreasing its risk level.

Choosing Asset Classes

When it comes time to select asset classes, and to figure out the allocation of your available investment funds within each class, you first need to determine how long it will be before you need to spend your invested money. The longer you have, the more risk you can take. If the time is short, you may want to keep your investments liquid—easily retrieved without incurring harsh penalties—and limit your investments in risky asset classes.

Investors define "risk" as the level of investment volatility. If one stock goes up or down 2 percent while another goes up or down 1 percent, the first stock is considered riskier even though it may increase your proceeds (returns) over time. Greater fluctuations in value increase the risk that a downturn may limit your ability to meet timely short-term payments.

If you are deciding between two investments with the same return, your choice is obvious: Choose the less risky investment. The same logic has historically resulted in riskier (more volatile) asset classes, like small-cap stocks, returning more than less-risky securities, like bonds. You should expect a higher return over many years' time on more volatile asset classes; however, you always risk losing a substantial amount of money in the short run by buying into the riskier asset classes.

The Virtues of Long-Term Investments

Obviously, the longer your money is invested, the more money you can make. Although long-term investments like real estate, business, or art do well as asset classes and are an important part of your diversified portfolio, individual stocks and mutual funds that hold dozens—or even hundreds—of individual stocks can also be very rewarding long-term investments. Stocks are riskier than bonds, but stocks should also return more in the long run.

Stocks and Mutual Funds

The concept and use of stock indexes is very important when considering investments. Each index is a single number that increases or declines based on the movement of stocks in the index. Essentially, an index is the value of a portfolio of the stocks that are held in that index. The Standard & Poor's 500 ("S&P 500"), the most widely followed stock index, consists of 500 of America's largest companies. The Dow Jones Industrials Average, sometimes referred to as "the Dow," is made up of thirty very large companies, all of which are also tracked by the S&P 500. The NASDAQ market index tracks more than 3,100 stocks that trade on the NASDAQ stock market and is more volatile than either the Dow or the S&P 500.

Common Stock

A share of common stock is an ownership interest in a company. If you start a vintage clothing store with two friends as equal partners, you have in effect created three "shares" of stock in the store. The same ownership structure applies to publicly traded companies like IBM, Wal-Mart, or McDonald's. In the case of McDonald's, for example, if you own 100 shares of the company (at a current cost of about $4,000), you would own a 0.000008 percent ownership interest in the company and have 950,000 partners.

Ownership of common stock entitles you to possible gains from two different sources: dividends and appreciation in stock value. Dividends are paid quarterly or annually. Dividends are not guaranteed, and company management can decrease or increase them at any time. Companies typically pay dividends out of earnings. If the company's earnings increase substantially, the company will probably increase its dividend payment.

Dividends are subject to federal and state taxes. The federal tax rate on most dividends is currently 15 percent, but this rate is likely to increase in the future—the Jobs and Growth Tax Relief Reconciliation Act of 2003, which provided tax relief on dividends, is set to expire on January 1, 2009. Also, long-term stock gains are generally taxable at 15 percent at the federal level, while short-term gains (under one year) may be taxed at your ordinary income tax rate, potentially as high as 35 percent, but these rates may also change after 2010.

You might consider reinvesting your dividends back into the stock that paid them by using a company's dividend reinvestment program ("DRIP"), a low-cost way to accumulate more of the company's shares. More information about DRIP plans is presented on page 166.

Common stocks are risky. They are not insured by any government agency, and they can rapidly decline in value. In an extreme case, you could lose your entire investment. However, from 1926 to 2002, a diversified portfolio of large-cap common stocks returned 12 percent per year, or 6 percent more per year than long-term treasury bonds, and they and other categories of stock will likely continue to outperform less-risky bonds and cash over the long run.

ALERT!

High-turnover mutual funds often increase your tax bill faster than your returns. Save them for tax-free retirement accounts, like IRAs, where rapid turnover won't result in taxes on realized stock gains.

Mutual Funds

Mutual funds are stock portfolios managed by a firm that commingles your funds with other investor funds and then invests them en masse. Instead of owning individual stocks, you purchase shares in the mutual fund. You can place an order for a mutual fund with your broker at any time, but your investment will only occur at the end of that day's trading—after the mutual fund company has accounted for that day's gains and losses. You buy into a mutual fund at its net asset value (NAV), which is the market value of the securities held by the mutual fund.

Many mutual funds attempt to earn the same return as major market indexes. If you invest in stock funds, you are investing either directly or indirectly in stock market indexes, which spreads your portfolio across hundreds of stock investments. It's far less risky than investing all of your funds in one or two risky stocks.

ALERT!

Most mutual funds are open-ended and can be purchased and sold at net asset value (NAV). Closed-ended funds do not accept new investments and may trade above or below NAV. It's generally a bad idea to purchase a closed-ended fund above its NAV—it has the same effect as paying a "load" fee on an open-ended fund.

Mutual funds generally fall into two categories:

- **Actively managed mutual funds:** Funds that are staffed by money managers and analysts who attempt to buy and sell the right stocks at the right time to beat the return on a particular stock market index.
- **Passively managed funds, or index funds:** Funds or index funds that track a market index as closely as possible, making them similar to index exchange-traded funded (ETFs, detailed on page 167).

Actively managed funds allow you to bet on the expertise of a team of professionals. However, few mutual fund management teams beat the return on the S&P 500 in the long run, and actively managed mutual funds tend to charge high fees. Many actively managed funds also trade stock frequently, which will leave you on the line for taxes on realized gains.

If you are considering investing in a mutual fund, ask your broker to order the mutual fund's prospectus. (You can also find one online.) The prospectus will give you important information about the manager and how long the manager has run that fund—investment philosophy and portfolio composition may have changed with a new manager in charge. The prospectus will also give you details about the fees the fund charges. Look under the heading "Shareholder Fees" for the fund's fee structure, which may or may not include the following:

- **Load fee:** The charge to buy into the fund
- **Redemption fee:** The charge to sell shares
- **Management fee:** The charge to pay analysts and portfolio managers
- **12b-1 distribution fee:** The charge to cover marketing costs and other expenses

All these expenses can add up quickly. If you hold an actively managed high-fee fund for ten years, the fees could easily cost you 15 percent. When it comes to mutual funds, fees matter!

The National Association of Securities Dealers (NASD) has an online mutual fund fee calculator that you can use to compare the total fees you would pay over time on up to three different mutual funds. You can access this information at ✑*www.apps.nasd.com.*

If you are considering buying shares in a mutual fund for a taxable account, make sure you investigate the fund's "turnover rate" (the percentage of stock owned in a given year that was sold during the year). It's typically "hidden" in a table deep in the prospectus. The higher the turnover rate, the more likely it is that you will have to pay taxes on the fund's distributions, which may include short-term gains taxable at high ordinary income rates. If a mutual fund holds its average investment for three years, its turnover rate will be 33 percent. In a taxable account, it's best to hold funds that have lower turnover rates to avoid paying your returns out as tax payments.

Target Maturity Funds

If your head is spinning about creating an asset allocation plan for yourself, and you're hesitant to hire a financial advisor, particularly if your retirement lies far down the road, you might want to opt for a target maturity mutual fund. Managers of these funds change the allocation between stocks and bonds over time. If your retirement date is decades away, for instance, they invest larger portions of assets in higher-risk securities like small-capitalization and foreign stock as well as a range of fixed income securities.

ALERT!

Target maturity funds often invest in mutual funds managed by the same company, which means you might pay a reduced fee for target maturity fund management but also unwittingly pay full mutual fund management fees. Essentially you end up paying two fund management teams while only reaping the rewards for investing in one—a good deal for mutual fund management, but not for you.

As your target date approaches, the asset allocation gradually shifts to lower-returning and less-risky securities like large-cap domestic stocks and higher quality, shorter-term bonds. When you choose a reputable target fund manager, you don't have to worry about rebalancing your portfolio. Barclays' Lifepath Portfolios, which currently charge a total fee of about 1.2 percent per year, appears to be a lower-cost option in the industry.

Blended Funds

Blended funds typically invest in a mix of stock and bonds in fairly fixed proportions over time, offering another way to gain immediate broad portfolio diversification. Fees for blended funds vary, but they can be high. You can always make your own blended fund by purchasing low-cost exchange-traded funds (ETFs, discussed on page 167) and rebalancing the asset allocation of your fund annually.

If you want simple investing, Vanguard's Wellington Fund (VWELX) is a blended fund that allocates 60 to 70 percent of its assets to stocks and 30 to 40 percent to bonds. The vast majority of mutual funds charge more than 0.50 percent per year in fees; the Wellington Fund charges 0.29 percent per year in fees. Vanguard requires relatively high initial investments when its funds are purchased directly through the company; however, you can frequently buy into Vanguard's funds with lower minimum investment amounts through Charles Schwab and other brokers.

ALERT!

When a broker seems to strongly favor a certain mutual fund, make sure you know whether the fund charges a "load" fee or sales charge. Mutual funds with a load fee frequently charge investors 1 to 3 percent of the investment upon purchase—most of which goes to the broker making the recommendation.

Index Funds

An index is in essence a portfolio of stocks. The S&P 500 tracks 500 stocks, while the Dow Jones Industrials tracks thirty stocks. Index funds are mutual funds that attempt to earn the return of a certain index for investors. Because indexes include a wide assortment of stocks or bonds, purchasing index funds immediately provides you with a diversified stock or bond portfolio.

Exchange-Traded Funds

Exchange-traded funds (ETFs) are portfolios of investors' commingled funds run by a professional investment management company in the same way as an index mutual fund; however, you buy and sell ETFs like stock. ETFs and most mutual funds track broad stock market indexes—lists (baskets) of thirty or more stocks held as if in a single portfolio. The advantages of ETFs over mutual funds include the following:

- ETFs frequently have lower management expenses than mutual funds tracking the same index. ETFs are purchased and sold as a stock, which means you pay commissions when the shares are bought and sold; a mutual fund may or may not charge a commission. Still, mutual funds usually have higher fees.

- When mutual funds sell a stock at a profit, they generate taxable gains that you must pay taxes on in the year the gain is recognized. ETF holders recognize capital gains only when they sell their investment, which usually decreases tax liability.
- Mutual funds are priced daily, at the end of the day. ETFs are actively priced during the day, which means you can purchase or sell them any time during stock market hours, allowing you to jump (or dump) on the best price.
- While thousands of mutual funds compete for your dollars, ETFs are fewer in number, and thus easier to research and select.
- Because ETFs track indexes, they are standardized except for fees, simplifying your homework to finding the one with the lowest fees.

If you are buying into a mutual fund or ETF that tracks a broad U.S. market index, make sure that the ETF or mutual fund company charges no more than 0.50 percent per year in fees. ETFs and mutual funds exist that track the S&P 500 and charge under 0.20 percent per year in fees. In a world where mutual fund managers find it very difficult to out-perform the S&P 500 index (and the average mutual fund charges about 1.4 percent in fees), buying an ETF or mutual fund that tracks the S&P 500 and that has an ultra-low expense ratio is a smart way to invest in stocks.

FACT

Standard & Poor's Depositary Receipts ("SPDRs," pronounced "spiders"), an ETF tracking the S&P 500, trades like a stock under the symbol SPY. Annual fees on SPY are only about 0.1 percent, making the commission you pay your broker on the purchase and sale of shares likely lower than the fees you would pay a mutual fund tracking the same index.

You can research ETFs through your brokerage firm, or online at the ETFConnect or the American Stock Exchange Web site (*www.etfconnect .com* or *www.amex.com*). Before you buy an ETF, compare it with other ETFs that invest in largely the same stocks to find the one that charges the lowest fees. You can find all the information you ever wanted and more about the ETF you are considering by going to the Web site of the ETF sponsor (such as *www.ishares.com*, *www.vanguard.com*, or *www.barclays.com*) and downloading a prospectus.

Because all of this information can become mind-boggling, it's a good idea to review the differences between ETFs and mutual funds:

ETFs Versus Mutual Funds*

ETFs	Mutual Funds
Low management expenses	May have high management fees
No loads or sales fees	May have high load and sales fees
Bought or sold like a stock	Bought or sold only at the end of the day
Investor pays a commission to purchase	Brokers may waive commissions (for a limited number of mutual funds)
Taxed on gains only when you sell	Annual distributions require annual tax payments
Tracks indexes	May track indexes or practice active portfolio management

* Information applies to open-ended mutual funds.

Core Funds

Some mutual fund companies sell core funds. Typically, core funds track a single asset class like large-cap domestic stocks or corporate bonds. These may or may not attempt to track a leading market index like the S&P 500. Don't let yourself be influenced by the word "core" in the name; it is put there in an attempt to sell more shares of the fund. You are in control of your own portfolio, and you get to decide which funds or ETFs make up the core of your portfolio.

Large-Capitalization Value Funds

Large-cap value funds usually invest almost entirely in domestic stocks with market capitalizations greater than $5 billion that also are considered "value stocks." There are as many opinions about what constitutes a "value" in the stock market as there are investors, but generally value stocks are those that trade at low price-to-book and price-to-earnings multiples relative to the average stock.

Large-Capitalization Growth Funds

Large-cap growth funds are mutual funds that typically invest in domestic companies with market capitalizations greater than $5 billion. These businesses are also expected to grow faster than the average publicly traded company.

FACT

Market capitalization is the total value of common stock owned by investors. Large-capitalization ("large-cap") companies generally have a market capitalization greater than $5 billion; "small-cap" companies have a capitalization under $2 billion; "mid-cap companies" fall somewhere in the middle; and "micro-cap" companies have a market capitalization under $200 million.

Mid-Capitalization Funds

Mid-cap funds generally invest in companies with market caps between $2 billion and $5 billion dollars. You can also find mid-cap value and mid-cap growth funds. Why would you choose mid-cap or small-cap funds over large-cap? Investors generally require a higher return on riskier investments, which means that you are likely to earn higher returns in the long run on mid-cap stocks than you are on less-risky large-cap stocks, and also more on small-cap stocks than mid-cap stocks.

Small-Capitalization Funds

Small-cap funds invest in companies with market capitalizations less than $2 billion. At times you may be holding mid-cap stocks in a small-cap fund because the stock has risen substantially. Small-cap value and growth funds are also available.

International or Global Funds

International or global mutual funds invest primarily in markets outside of the United States. International mutual funds that are actively managed may charge high fees, so it is worthwhile to make sure you know how high the fees are for a particular international or global fund. You can also invest overseas through exchange-traded funds (ETFs).

The most widely followed international index is the Morgan Stanley Capital International Europe, Australasia, and Far East (EAFE), which tracks about 1,100 stocks in twenty-one developed markets outside of the United States and Canada. The EAFE doesn't include stocks in riskier emerging markets like Egypt, China, and Slovenia, among others.

Market capitalization is determined by the price required to buy 100 percent of a company's shares. So if Company A has 100 shares trading for $10 each, its market capitalization is $1,000 ($10 × 100). If Company B is trading at $100 per share, but it only has five shares, its market capitalization is $500 ($100 × 5).

Load and No-Load Mutual Funds

Load mutual funds can be purchased through your broker or directly through the mutual fund company, who then charges a commission and an additional "load" fee. This is a flat fee charged either when you first buy into the fund ("front-end sales load") or when you sell your shares in the fund ("deferred sales load"). The load is paid to the broker selling the fund; it's a hidden commission, and it can be large. The U.S. Securities and Exchange Commission allows mutual funds to charge a maximum of 8.5 percent, but most load funds charge 1 to 3 percent.

No-load mutual funds can be purchased through your broker or directly through the mutual fund company, although they may charge a commission. If you are considering a mutual fund with a load and find an equivalent no-load fund, buy the no-load fund.

Variable Annuities

A variable annuity is a contract between you and an insurance company. You buy into the variable annuity either in a lump sum or over time, and in return you receive payments over time from the insurance company. The amount of the payments depends on the investment results you achieve by investing in mutual funds offered and managed by the annuity. Variable annuities are usually sold to retirees who want a fairly regular stream of income. They can be complex arrangements that provide insurance and mutual fund companies with large profits at your expense. Unless you're approaching retirement age, you're likely to fare better with other investment choices. You'll read about the advantages—and major disadvantages—of variable annuities in Chapter 16.

Individual Investing

Individual investing simply means that you buy individual stocks. Investing in individual stocks exposes you to all the best and worst parts of the stock market. On the positive side, you will learn about investing in public companies. The knowledge you gain would be a valuable heirloom to pass on to your children.

The negative side of investing in individual stocks is the time commitment, which will be more substantial as you go along. There is also a fairly substantial learning curve when you start. You're also competing against professionals, who are paid very well to spend all day trying to buy and sell stock better than you do. As a result, it is difficult to make more than you would if you only purchased shares of exchange-traded funds (ETFs) or mutual funds that track broad market indexes.

DRIP Investing

Dividend reinvestment programs (DRIPs) occur when large companies allow stockholders to reinvest their dividends by using them to purchase additional shares. In most cases, if your dividend is less than the value of one share of the stock, you are able to purchase less than one full share. If you have a small amount of money to invest in a particular stock, DRIPs can let you grow your stake over time without having to pay brokerage commissions on the purchase of additional shares.

The downside to DRIPs is that while you won't receive dividends as cash, you will be taxed on the dividends received in the program. The company operating the DRIP program will also frequently charge administrative fees—though these are usually less than brokerage commissions if you have a small stake in the company.

Do Your Research

Now you know something about investing, have some idea of the sorts of assets you'd like to invest in, and you are ready to take the plunge. It's time to get busy and do some basic research on various companies. You can find this information online and in newspapers like *Barron's* and the *Wall Street Journal.*

ALERT!

Beware of hot tips and inside scoops. It isn't enough to like a product or the celebrity endorsing it. Before making a major stock purchase, you need to know more about the company's overall financial stability: whether its competitors are underpricing it or grabbing more market share; whether it's facing rising operating costs or other challenges its management cannot control.

Researching Mutual Funds and ETFs

You can find information about mutual funds through your brokerage firm, which should have a searchable database online of the mutual funds available, as well as information about those funds' stocks, bonds, and other holdings, along with data on the fund manager's investment style, the fund's turnover, and fees. This information is also available in a prospectus provided by the mutual fund management company, which you can order through your broker or view online.

You can find mutual fund listings in Morningstar's annual *"Morning-star 500,"* a list of mutual funds that includes information about each fund's investing "style" (for instance, small-cap value), expenses charged, results achieved in the last few years, along with a profile of the investment manager and Morningstar's estimate of tax-adjusted returns on the fund. Morningstar also grades each fund with a frequently cited star rating: Five stars indicate that a fund has posted excellent returns in the past on a risk-adjusted basis. *Barron's* and the *Wall Street Journal* also periodically publish lists of mutual funds that provide a wealth of useful information.

Your broker or financial advisor is probably your best resource for unearthing the goods on particular mutual funds. Charles Schwab and E-Trade both offer a wide range of noncommission mutual funds (where the fund either pays the broker for the referral, or the broker makes money managing the fund), which also frequently have very low initial investment requirements. Both brokers have online tools to help you sort through the thousands of mutual funds offered.

A company's price-to-earnings (P/E) ratio is the price of the company's stock divided by its earnings per share, or "EPS" (usually for the latest twelve months). Faster-growing companies tend to have higher price-to-earnings ratios, and they may be called more expensive because of their higher-than-average P/E ratio. However, it often makes sense to pay more for a company that is growing more quickly.

Is This Company Investment-Worthy?

Standard & Poor's, a respected provider of credit ratings, provides free access to a searchable database of its credit ratings for many public companies online at *www.sandp.com.* You can also check the company's finances on the Yahoo!Finance Web site (*www.finance.yahoo.com*). Enter the one- to four-letter "ticker symbol" of your stock, then click on the "Key Statistics" link. This will show how much money the company makes per share, as well as its price-to-earnings and other key valuation ratios. You can find more in-depth information by browsing the investor-relations section of a company's official Web site. Investor presentations will give you insight into the company's strategic direction, and recent earnings announcements are the way the company's management team communicates its business progress to investors.

The U.S. Securities and Exchange Commission (SEC)

The U.S. Securities and Exchange Commission (SEC) maintains a financial filings database called "EDGAR" (online at *www.sec.gov*). EDGAR is an excellent source of in-depth, reliable information. Look for a detailed discussion about the company's operations in its annual financial filings, known as "10-K" forms, as well as in its quarterly filings, or "10-Q" forms. These financial filings include a section titled "Management's Discussion and Analysis," where management discusses the company's operating strengths and weaknesses over the preceding quarter or year. This information can greatly deepen your understanding of where the company actually makes its money, as well as the challenges and opportunities it faces. Check out competitors so you know what and how their peers are doing and how that might affect your favored company over time.

Chapter 13

Protecting Your Assets

Insurance can be costly, and when you're writing a fat check, it can feel like a luxury. However, now that you are making wise investments, paying down your debt, increasing your income, and building a retirement fund, it's time to reassess what you are doing to safeguard those assets. While allowing adept sales pitches to sway your decision is not a good idea, insurance is not a place to slash costs. The educated consumer wants to secure her assets and protect her loved ones without overpaying.

Why You Need Insurance

It's one thing to generate income and accumulate assets, but it's another to take care of them. You have responsibility to your children—and yourself—to protect your assets. You must read through all the fine print, learn the basics, and then talk to experts who can put the proper insurance protections in place.

If you have a valuable possession, or earn a high income, insurance salesmen will go overboard to sell you multiple policies. While some insurance isn't needed, or simply isn't affordable, you do need some basic types of insurance. The primary ones include these:

- **Health and dental insurance:** This allows you and your children to receive the preventative care and necessary treatment you deserve.
- **Life insurance:** This provides funds to pay for your funeral expenses, pay off the mortgage, fund college, and pay your children's living expenses until they are capable of taking care of themselves.
- **Homeowner's or renter's insurance:** This protects the structure of your house and its contents from unforeseen events such as fire, theft, or adverse weather.
- **Car insurance:** This protects you and your children in case you are involved in an accident or in case of theft or damage to your vehicle. It also protects you from being sued for your assets if you are the cause of an accident.
- **Disability insurance:** This provides a percentage of your current level of income in case of illness or accident.

In an ideal world, you would have maximum insurance coverage. In reality, you may have to make crucial decisions between what you really need and cannot afford to be without and what you can realistically afford.

Health and Dental Insurance

Health and dental insurance is an absolute must. Hopefully you, or your children's father, will have coverage through an employer. Working fathers are often required by law to carry their children on their employer's health plan until the children are eighteen, or older if the children attend college full time. If he has this option available, make sure you take advantage of it, and don't be afraid to go to court to do so. It could save you thousands of dollars over the years and guarantee your children the coverage they deserve.

If neither you nor the children's father can acquire health insurance through an employer, you will need to find a plan you can afford that will cover and protect you and your children. In general, your health insurance options are as follows:

- **HMOs:** Health maintenance organizations require a primary care doctor and usually one hospital within their plan. Co-pays range from $10 to $15 for doctor's visits and prescriptions. They can be sufficient for families that are generally healthy, and they are cheaper than plans with more options.
- **PPOs:** Preferred provider organizations give you a greater range of doctor selection and choices about whether or not you see a specialist or have certain medical tests. You will have a larger selection of doctors and hospitals, but you pay a higher premium, and typically higher co-pays if you see a doctor outside the plan or opt for branded prescriptions.
- **Catastrophic coverage:** Premiums are much cheaper, but you will have a high deductible—$2,000, $5,000, or $10,000—which means you pay everything until the deductible is met. If you are really strapped for money and this is all you can afford, it will protect you from bankruptcy if a tragedy occurs or anyone becomes gravely ill.
- **Government assistant plans:** If you have a low income and cannot afford health insurance, you may qualify for state children's health insurance programs (SCHIP) or federal Medicaid assistance. Amazingly, six out of ten families who are eligible never apply. In most states, if you earn less than $36,000, your children are eligible for low-cost—and sometimes free—medical coverage. Under Medicaid, a mother earning less than $17,600 per year who also has one child less than six years old qualifies for free health coverage for her child. Check out *www.cms.hhs.gov/schip* and *www.insurekid snow.gov* to see if you qualify.

When it comes to health insurance, it pays to stay current with coverage vernacular and to search for any means of saving money—without sacrificing coverage.

Flexible Spending Plans

Flexible spending plans are optional plans that employers may be able to offer employees. Basically, you determine a set amount for your employer to withhold from your pretax wages that you can then spend to cover medical and dental costs that your insurance doesn't cover. This saves you 15 to 35 percent a year on co-pays, deductibles, braces, caps, laser eye surgery, over-the-counter medications, and other health care expenses.

Much like credit reporting agencies, a medical information bureau collects personal medical data and then sells it to life, health, and disability insurance companies. The information they gather may or may not be accurate, and it may not even belong to you. Log onto ✎*www.mib.com* or write to MIB, P.O. Box 105, Essex Station, Boston MA 02112, to request a copy of your report. If you find errors, ask them to make corrections.

The only catch is that you have to determine an amount for the entire year. In many cases, funds not spent within 14.5 months are forfeited to the government. Still, it's wiser to start small and adjust upward than not to participate at all. This can be a real boon, particularly if you know in advance that you or one of your children will need braces or glasses in the next year. Even if the deadline was approaching and you still had $400 in the account, you could buy over-the-counter drugs, such as aspirin, or prescription sunglasses to use up the funds. Just be sure to save all your receipts so you can document your spending.

COBRA and HIPAA

Consolidated Omnibus Budget Reconciliation Act (COBRA) is a plan employers are legally required to offer employees who are fired or who leave for any reason, even if it's to transition into part-time work. Employers who employ more than twenty people must offer you (and your children, if they have been covered under the plan) health coverage at their cost, plus 2 percent, for a period of eighteen months. Legally separated, divorced, or widowed spouses are eligible for thirty-six months. However, you must accept the offer within sixty days (thirty days if your spouse died), and don't wait! You won't be able to find independent coverage cheaper, and COBRA protects you, and your children, during transitions.

The Health Insurance Portability and Accountability Act (HIPAA) was created to protect your access to health insurance. Under HIPAA, anyone leaving a group insurance plan is guaranteed coverage as long as you were covered for at least twelve months and switch health care providers within sixty-three days.

Take advantage of COBRA and HIPAA to ensure that you and your children will not be turned down or made to wait for coverage. Allowing a break in insurance gives insurance companies the opportunity to deny coverage, or withhold specific coverage, on the basis of pre-existing conditions.

Health Savings Plans

If you are self-employed, you can open a health savings account (HSA) that combines high deductible, catastrophic health insurance with a tax-favored savings plan. You make a tax-deductible contribution each year to the HSA to cover medical bills. If you don't use the funds, they will accumulate. The maximum amount you can contribute changes annually—currently it's around $5,500 for a family. This option is best for healthy families who have enough money to cover basic medical expenses. Talk to your financial advisor and an insurance broker about whether this plan is a smart move for you.

How to Save Money on Health Insurance

If you and your children are in good health, you can opt for a large deductible. It's a gamble, but may be worth the risk. You can find the best prices by comparison shopping on the Internet. Many health insurance sites offer side-by-side comparisons that will give you an idea of what to expect.

THE EVERYTHING GUIDE TO PERSONAL FINANCE FOR SINGLE MOTHERS

When you've done your homework and are ready to purchase, find a reputable broker.

Life Insurance

Most savvy money investors recommend term life insurance for parents. Term means that you pay a set fee per month for a policy that provides a set amount of coverage over ten, twenty, or thirty years. Term insurance is cheaper than whole life, universal life, or variable universal. As long as you choose a term that covers your children's expenses until they become adults, it's sufficient protection.

ALERT!

Even if it's tempting, never lie on insurance applications. Most policies have clauses that will nullify the contract if you have failed to provide accurate information. If you have a crisis and they discover that you've lied, you could lose the policy, any anticipated coverage, and all the premiums you paid.

Some insurance agencies will suggest cash-value policies that combine life insurance with an investment as a way to save for college, but it also means you will be paying for insurance and an investment. In fact, you will most likely save money and maximize college fund savings by buying term life insurance and managing your college and retirement funds separately.

How Much Life Insurance Do You Need?

The Consumer Federation of America recommends that you buy eight times your annual income to cover living expenses for twenty years, or nine times for thirty years. If you want to cover college expenses, add $100,000 per child. Then deduct the value of any life insurance provided by your employer.

Computing Term Life Insurance Needed

	20 Years	30 Years.
Your Income	$40,000	$40,000
Multiplier	× 8	× 9
Subtotal	$320,000	$360,000
College	$200,000 (2 children)	$200,000
Less Employer	$25,000	$25,000
Total Life Needed	$495,000	$535,000

If your children's father is carrying life insurance that will adequately safeguard them, you may feel comfortable reducing your life insurance, but make sure you review this with him annually and ask for verification that your children are the beneficiaries of his policy.

ALERT!

When you name your children as your life insurance beneficiaries, the proceeds do not have to go through probate and are not taxable as part of your estate. However, minor children cannot legally receive the proceeds. Make sure you assign a "property guardian" or "custodian" to receive and manage the funds until they reach age eighteen or an age you or your state laws specify, such as twenty-one or twenty-five.

How Long Should You Carry It?

The longer the "term" (five, ten, fifteen, twenty, or thirty years), the higher the monthly premium, but it's wise to weigh whether a slight premium increase is well worth the extra coverage. If you're in your twenties or thirties and your children are toddlers, definitely opt for a thirty-year term. If you're in your forties and your children are in elementary school, the twenty-year term may be sufficient. Ideally, you want coverage either until you reach retirement or until your children are earning a decent income. If you've invested well, your retirement fund should replace the need for life insurance upon retirement.

Another form of term life insurance available to young parents is annually renewable term life insurance (ART). These term policies are renewable up to age eighty. Although they cost less in the first few years, they cost more in the long run than the other term policies, particularly when prices rise annually. If you're in your early twenties, you may want to buy an ART for ten years and then switch to a thirty-year term policy.

If you have a special-needs child, you have special life insurance needs. You can still buy term insurance, but you'll want one that can be converted to a cash-value policy. This way you can keep a policy in place that protects your special-needs child for the rest of your life at a fixed cost.

How Much Does It Cost?

Insurance companies typically offer volume discounts—lower prices per $1,000 once you exceed a certain level of coverage. Price breaks usually occur in $250,000 increments. If you fall between a break, and if you can afford the higher cost, opt for the higher amount.

Prices can vary widely. The young and healthy win the lowest rates, but no matter your age, it's wise to comparison shop on the Internet. Be wary of sites that require your telephone number or agents that hard sell cash-value or other life insurance options. Sites such as *www.term4sale.com* will compare 150 insurers to give you a concrete idea of the range of prices. Once you've chosen a policy, you can go on that company's Web site to find a local agent, or go to *www.insure.com* to see a list of agents in your area. (See "How to Research Insurance Options" later in this chapter.)

If your employer offers free "portable" (so you can take it if you leave) or "convertible to cash" life insurance, take it and then supplement it with another policy. If the employer's life insurance isn't free, and you're relatively young, you may score lower rates on your own.

Home and Mortgage Insurance

For home insurance, you want a "replacement-cost" policy that will cover the costs of rebuilding your house if it burns to the ground. Don't buy "resale price" coverage—it includes the value of your land, which will not be damaged in a fire. Make sure the face value of the policy increases every year to cover inflationary costs, and consider "extended" or "guaranteed" coverage to cover 25 percent more than the policy's face value. Cash-value insurance may cost less, but it can leave you underinsured. Ask your agent what you can do to bring the costs for "replacement-cost" policies down—installing smoke detectors, for example. In lieu of home insurance, renter's insurance will cover the costs of replacing your possessions in case of fire, damage, or theft.

ALERT!

Insurance companies are increasingly using credit scores to judge customer reliability and responsibility. They will compare your credit payment habits with their best customers and make judgments that can raise or lower rates. If your credit rating is low, it's wise to clean it up before shopping for insurance. (See Chapters 6 and 7.) If it's stellar, bargain for lower prices.

Car Insurance

Yes, you need car insurance! But you do have options that can keep the price affordable. Here's a brief rundown of what you do and don't need:

- **Liability and property damage coverage:** This covers injuries or damage you cause to other drivers, passengers, pedestrians, and property. Liability coverage usually specifies three numbers, such as 100/300/75. The first number is the amount your insurance company will pay if one person is injured ($100,000), the second the total amount they will pay if more than one person is injured ($300,000), and the third number is the maximum they'll pay for property damage to property, such as a fence, a house, a sign, or a mailbox ($75,000). It's expensive coverage, but don't skimp, particularly if you have a lot of assets that someone could come after.

- **Medical:** If you have sufficient health insurance, you don't need this. Opt for zero or minimal coverage.
- **Collision and comprehensive:** Collision covers the cost of damage to your car if you cause an accident, and comprehensive covers random damage or theft. If your car is old, you can adjust the amount downward, but keep in mind that the cost of repairs can be high. If your car is new, your loan agreement may require a certain level of coverage, but you can still opt for a high deductible.
- **Uninsured or underinsured motorist:** This covers your expenses if someone without any or sufficient insurance hits you. Check to see if your state covers any of these costs; opting out is a gamble. The Insurance Information Institute estimated that 13 percent of accidents are the fault of an uninsured driver.

It makes far more sense to raise your deductibles to keep premiums low than it does to minimize the levels of coverage. Your chances of not needing the coverage are greater than what it will cost you if you do.

How to Keep Your Car Insurance Rates Low

If you have an excellent driving record, you may qualify for the lowest rates available. Amica (800-992-6422) offers low car insurance premiums to safe drivers, but you have to meet their rigid standards to qualify. Also, anyone with military experience, or who has a family member (parent or spouse) who served in the military, is eligible for reduced rates through USAA (*www.usaa.com*). Another option is to minimize coverage, but there are smarter (and safer) ways to lower your car insurance premiums:

- **Drive safely.** Two moving violations in a year will raise your rates substantially for the next three years. Obtain a safe driving pamphlet from your state's driver's license bureau, read through it, and abide by its laws.

- **Contest traffic tickets.** Even if the issue is debatable, many jurisdictions are not prepared to send a representative to court, which means you avoid those pricey points that boost insurance rates.
- **Pay all fines promptly.** The DMV can suspend your license, which will hike premium prices substantially for three years. Plus, they could report your delinquency to credit reporting agencies.
- **Take a defensive driving course.** You can save as much as 10 percent for three years.
- **Check your policy annually.** Benchmark birthdays can lower your rates. Women's rates go down at age twenty-five, unless they marry earlier. In some states, an early marriage qualifies a woman for adult rates.
- **Lower your mileage.** Mileage less than 5,000 to 7,000 miles per year earns lower rates.
- **Avoid SUVs.** Companies will charge 5 to 20 percent more for SUV coverage. Ditto for sports cars.
- **Drive cheap cars.** If you buy a car that is cheaper to repair and that is not particularly attractive to thieves, you will be eligible for lower insurance rates.

Finally, always remember to ask about discounts. Not smoking, having a clean driving record, using antitheft devices, installing anti-lock brakes, automatic seatbelts, airbags, and having good grades or not using a cell phone in the car can all lower your rates—but you have to ask!

Disability, Long-Term Care, and Children's Life Insurance

If you can afford extra coverage, having disability insurance is highly desirable. Long-term care insurance becomes more important as you approach fifty. Carrying life insurance on your children may be proposed to you as a viable savings plan, but it is, in fact, usually a luxury.

Disability Insurance

While you may be entitled to short-term state and long-term federal disability protection, if your employer offers additional disability insurance, it's wise to take advantage of it. State disability generally covers up to one year. Federal disability extends coverage beyond a year, but it is extremely restrictive and difficult to obtain. Typically, disability insurance pays approximately 60 percent of your pretax income. If you pay for the policy, you won't owe any taxes, but if your employer pays for the policy, you will owe taxes on the income. If you are solely responsible for your children, or if you earn a high salary, disability insurance is a worthy expense. Although it's essential for anyone in a high-risk profession, anyone can quite suddenly become disabled—approximately one in eight people will suffer a serious disability. If you can afford it, buy it.

Most auto and homeowners' policies have an upper limit on how much liability coverage they provide. If you have a lot of assets, a personal liability or umbrella liability policy offers extra protection. Fortunately, you can generally find one that costs $200 to $300 for $1 million of coverage.

Long-Term Care

Long-term care insurance is purchased to cover the expense of full-time nursing or nursing home care. If you're young and in good health, long-term care insurance can wait, but if you have the money, the younger you are when you purchase one, the better chance you have of keeping premiums lower. In general, you need to address this when you are approaching fifty.

Children's Life Insurance

Some people purchase life insurance for their children as a savings plan. Unless the policy pays a substantial interest rate, it's better to consider placing the same amount into a savings or money market account instead.

How to Research Insurance Options

The Internet is a great way to compare rates, but it's wise to also call local brokers and to check with friends, coworkers, and relatives. Rather than jumping at the lowest price, you'll want to make sure you're dealing with a reputable firm that will be there when you need them. However, be aware that vast differences in price for equal coverage are common, and the best way to get the optimum price is to shop around.

FACT

Even the cost of basic insurance can vary widely. Consumer surveys have found insurers who will inflate their insurance policy rates at a price 400 percent higher than their competitors. You can save a lot of dough just by shopping around and knowing what's within reason.

Explore policy and cost options on the Internet (*www.insure.com* or *www.accuquote.com*); or call Termquote (800-444-8376) or Quotesmith (800-556-9393) for multiple comparisons; or find a local independent broker who isn't locked into one company. After you've researched your options, make sure you are buying from a reputable company by assessing the following:

- Are they financially sound?
- Are their prices competitive?
- Do they have a good customer service record?
- Do they pay benefits promptly?

Weiss Ratings, Inc., provides reliable insurance company ratings (*www.weissratings.com*) for around $15 for an individual company and a comprehensive analysis for around $50. You can also log onto *www.insure.com* to see if Standard & Poor's has given a particular insurer an AA or above. You can also go to *www.ambest.com* to see if the insurer has earned an A- or higher. To check for consumer complaints, the National Association of Insurance Commissioners at *www.naic.org* will link you to your state's insurance department. Once you have selected the company, read the policy thoroughly before purchasing.

How to Find a Reputable Broker

The best way to find a reputable broker is to ask people in your community—coworkers, church members, friends, family. You can also call your local chamber of commerce and the Better Business Bureau to see if anyone has filed complaints. Having a one-on-one relationship with a good broker can be profitable and rewarding for you both. A reputable, smart broker will help you make decisions that benefit you and your children. Take the time necessary to make sure you're working with someone you trust, and when you find her, consider placing all of your policies under one umbrella.

Naming Guardians and Beneficiaries

When you are responsible for children under the age of eighteen, two of the most important decisions you make are these:

- Who is the beneficiary of my insurance policies and retirement plans?
- Whom do I want to take care of my children in the event of my death?

Anyone you name as a beneficiary on insurance policies or retirement plans will remain the beneficiary, no matter what you express verbally or even what you record in a formal will. It's vital to review your choices every five years, or whenever your circumstances change, to make sure you have the names and the proportions the way you want them.

If you have minor children, when it comes to naming a guardian or guardians, there are two primary questions you need to answer:

- Who will take day-to-day physical custody of my children?
- Who will manage their money and property (including insurance proceeds)?

Oftentimes one person will fulfill both of these roles, but if not, you need to specify the delineation in your will. Also, you may not want your children to assume control of the money and property at age eighteen, in which case you may want to create a trust that oversees the financial aspects until they finish college or reach milestones, such as age twenty-one or twenty-five.

Upon your death, your children inherit your net worth—any assets you own minus liabilities against them, including credit card debt. The first step in safeguarding your children is to know your net worth, and then to protect them through proper planning and strategic choices. Begin at the beginning—compute your net worth, and then work toward raising your net worth.

In most cases, the remaining parent assumes custody of the minor children, but you can establish a guardian for their financial and property inheritance. You may also want to name a guardian in case your ex-husband dies before the children reach eighteen. If you do not want the children's father to gain full custody, you can name a guardian and then write a letter explicitly stating your reasons for doing so. In the event of your death, the court would review the documents and make a decision about whether your children would be better off under the care of your named guardian. If you are adamant that your children's legal father should not have custody, consult with a lawyer.

Wills and Trusts

A will is a legal document that determines how your money and property will be distributed upon your death. When you create your will, you designate an executor who will be responsible for guiding your will through probate and distributing the proceeds. You also designate beneficiaries, those who will benefit from the proceeds of your estate. An astonishing two out of three Americans die without having a will or a trust in place that determines how their assets will be distributed upon their death! If you die without a will, the state you live in will decide how your money and property will be distributed. Usually, the state divides your property equally among all of your family members and hires an expensive probate lawyer at your estate's expense to make decisions you could easily have made.

ALERT!

Know your state laws. In some states, anyone who signs your will as a witness cannot inherit anything, despite what your will says. Also, hand-written wills are legal in some states but not in others. Unless they are properly witnessed (the rules for which differ by state), typewritten wills are usually tossed out, and videotaped wills are invalid in most states.

If you have dependent children, creating a legal will is essential. Not only do you need to provide for their financial welfare, you need to designate guardians. Avoid any ideas of hastily writing down instructions and presuming it becomes a legal will. State laws vary, and what you think will suffice very often absolutely will not. Wills have to go through probate court. The simpler you keep the will, the less it will cost to distribute your assets to your heirs, but having a legal will drawn up by a lawyer will keep the cost of probate lower and better serve your intentions.

Unless your financial holdings are complicated, most of the time a simple will is sufficient. You can use forms found on the Internet or in books that help you gather all pertinent information, create a list of all your assets, cover all your bases, and clarify your wishes. Once you've created a first (or second, or third) draft, do yourself and your children a huge favor and consult with a lawyer. You don't have to select an expensive lawyer, or draw out the process. If you've done your homework well, a lawyer can draw up a legal will and process it for a reasonable fee ($500 to $1,000). A lawyer will also make sure you've covered everything a will needs to cover. It's safeguarding your children, and, therefore, a worthwhile expense.

If your children are under the age of eighteen, it's very important to specify whom you want to take care of them and their inheritance. A durable power of attorney gives the authority to someone you trust to make legal decisions regarding your estate; an executor processes your will through probate; a guardian is someone you designate to take care of your children.

Basic requirements for a will are as follows:

- You have to be at least eighteen years old and of sound mind.
- Your will must be typed or computer printed.
- It must state clearly that it is your will.
- You must leave property to at least one beneficiary and appoint at least one guardian for minor children.
- You must sign and date your will in the presence of at least two witnesses, who do not have to read your will but must sign it as a witness to your signing.

As stated earlier, laws vary state by state. If you're going to draw up a will yourself, make sure you know the laws in your state and abide by them. In general, wills have to be neither notarized, nor submitted to the court, nor stamped with any legal imprint prior to your death.

Living Trusts

A living trust is a document that assigns a trustee to handle your estate in the event of your death. It's essentially a will that doesn't have to go through probate. You create a list of your beneficiaries, the name of a guardian or guardians, and how you wish matters to be handled. You then draw up a living trust that allows your designated trustee to distribute your estate according to your wishes.

QUESTION?

Do I have to worry about estate taxes?

In general, estate taxes will be minimal. Currently, estates valued at less than $2 million are not subject to federal estate taxes, but this limit fluctuates annually and may revert back to $1 million in 2011. If you are worried about paying extensive state taxes, or you have an estate over $2 million, an attorney can help you distribute your assets in ways that minimize taxes.

A living trust makes more sense if you own a business or have complicated real estate holdings. It is possible to name yourself "trustee" and to name a "substitute" who will take over when you die or become incapacitated, but doing so means you have to transfer your house title and all other assets to yourself as "trustee" and sign all your checks in a way that clearly indicates this position. Trusts are revocable—meaning you can change your mind at any time, but they can be expensive and unnecessary. Beware of seminar leaders who warn of probate nightmares. Ask your financial consultant or your lawyer if you need a living trust. If so, do the legwork ahead of time and save money without sacrificing your children's welfare.

Neither a will nor a living trust has to be complicated. In both cases, the most important information you need to gather is the following:

- **A list of all your assets:** Write down everything you want to pass on to your children or family, including real estate, bank accounts, safe deposit boxes, money market accounts, corporations or businesses, vehicles, insurance policies, retirement plans, commodities, stocks, bonds, artwork, precious metals, antiques, collectibles, and computer equipment, right down to jewelry, books, china, silverware, and even clothing.
- **A list of all your liabilities:** These will be deducted from your assets to establish the net worth of your estate. You may want to designate how the liabilities are to be paid, but at the very least, you need to know the real net worth of your estate.
- **A list of beneficiaries:** Gather all insurance policies, bank account applications, and retirement fund documents, and review the beneficiaries named and the proportion of distribution.
- **Guardian(s):** Indicate one or more people that you want to have physical custody of your children, and the name(s) of the person(s) you want to manage your children's inheritance until they reach an age you designate. Backup guardians are a good idea.
- **Trustee(s):** Name the person you want to designate as trustee of your living trust and the person(s) you want to have durable power of attorney or to serve as your health care proxy. You will also name

one or two "successor trustees" in case your chosen trustee dies before fulfilling her duties.

- **Executor(s):** An executor is the person you designate to handle the probate and distribution of your will. You assign this person the legal responsibility for the carrying out the terms of your will, including establishing an estate bank account, processing probate, filing taxes, and distributing proceeds. Executors are frequently paid for their services; you affix a price and specify it in your will.

It's your job as a single mother to make crucial decisions that directly affect your children's welfare. In the event no will has been created, a legal system that may, or may not, make the best decisions will be in charge of your estate. Spare your children. Do all the research required, and then create a will or a living trust that will safeguard their future.

Living Will

A living will, also called a health care directive, is a legal document that directs doctors and your family what to do if you are permanently unconscious, irreversibly brain damaged, suffering from dementia, or dying and unable to speak or make decisions. While it feels gruesome, imagine how your children would feel if they were ever asked to make a decision about whether you lived or died. Spare them the anguish and make these decisions for yourself.

Also, it's wise to name a health care proxy or assign "durable power of attorney" to someone you trust to give and receive medical information and enforce your living will. Choose someone you trust implicitly, someone with exceptional judgment who would stay calm under dire circumstances and who has your best interests at heart. It's ideal to select someone who lives close to you, but if your most trusted person lives 1,000 miles away, choose her and make sure she's listed on your emergency information. This prevents strangers from overriding your living will.

Your living will normally comes into play when you have one of the following situations:

- You are close to death from a terminal illness or are permanently comatose.
- You cannot communicate your own wishes orally, in writing, or through gestures.
- The doctor in charge has been notified that you have a living will.

Thus, it is wise to give copies of your health care directives to your attorney, your primary-care physician, your close relatives, and your local hospital.

You can find forms on the Internet or in books that will help you sort out all the issues and make firm decisions. Do this when you are formulating a will and save money by having your lawyer draw up the documents at the same time.

Put Your Financial Papers in Order

Wills do not have to be officially recorded or filed in a court, which means it's up to you to keep yours in a safe place. If you keep all your important papers such as insurance policies, birth certificates, mortgage papers, house deed, and your will in a safe deposit box, make sure your executor has access to it. It's perhaps wiser to keep them in a waterproof and fireproof box at your home, as long as the executor knows where to find it. It's also wise to include any and all papers that would assist in handling your estate—a list of all credit card numbers, bank accounts, retirement funds, insurance policies, and creditors. Make it a habit to review these documents annually and update any information so that you'll have everything in order in case of an emergency.

Chapter 14

Affording Child Care

As a single mother, it is a real challenge finding and paying for child care that meets your and your children's needs. Although a whopping 72 percent of parents plan to use some form of child care within their child's first year, options are limited and costly. In a Babycenter.com poll, more than half of 9,500 parents reported researching child care options before the baby was born. In another Babycenter.com survey, 30 percent of 2,070 parents needed a month to find day care, while 36 percent needed three months.

The Family and Medical Leave Act

Under the Family and Medical Leave Act of 1993 (FMLA), you may be entitled to a total of up to twelve weeks of unpaid leave during any twelve-month period for the following purposes:

- The birth and care of a child
- The adoption of a child or caring for a foster child
- The care of a spouse, child, or parent who has a serious health condition
- A serious health condition that leaves you unable to perform the essential functions of your job

In general, you are eligible for FMLA leave if the following apply:

- You work for an employer engaged in commerce, or in any industry or activity affecting commerce, that employs fifty or more employees.
- You have worked for the employer for at least twelve months.
- You have worked at least 1,250 hours during the twelve-month period immediately preceding the start of the leave.
- You work at a site where fifty or more employees employed by the employer live within seventy-five miles of that work site.

FACT

According to the U. S. Department of Education, 19 percent of kindergarteners through eighth grade spend unsupervised time before or after school at least once a month; other studies report that 5 million school-age children are essentially latchkey children. The American Academy of Pediatricians recommends constant adult supervision until a child is eleven or twelve.

Under certain conditions, an employee may use the twelve weeks of FMLA leave intermittently. Unless it's an emergency, the employee is required to report her (or his) intention to take the FMLA leave at least thirty days before it begins. The law then requires your employer to return you to the same job, or an "equivalent position with equivalent benefits, pay, status, and other terms and conditions of employment." An employee who takes FMLA leave is also entitled to maintain health benefits coverage by paying the employee share of the premiums on a current basis or paying upon return to work.

FACT

In a 2005 survey of 7,700 parents who used child care options, 26 percent used private in-home care; 20 percent used home-based day care; 30 percent used a day care center or preschool; and 24 percent relied on relatives.

Check with your human resources department or your supervisor to see if you are eligible for FMLA leave. Also, ask if your company provides "dependent care reimbursement accounts." Some companies offer this as a benefit to their employees to help defray child care expenses.

Day Care Options and Their Costs

Depending upon your child's age or needs, you will have a variety of options for long-term child care. Unfortunately, child care costs can be expensive. Costs for full-time care can range between $125 and $650 a week, depending upon the type of care, your location, your children's ages or needs, and other factors. Each choice has its pros and cons, both financially and personally. Since you'll want to weigh the choices before selecting one that will work best for your children and you, presuming you have the luxury of time, it's wise to explore all the options three to six months ahead of when you'll need it.

Considering Your Options

Before you narrow down your choices, it's important to take stock of your situation, including your children's ages, personalities, needs, and your location, flexibility, and all the factors that can enter into the decision about child care. Here are the primary factors you'll need to consider when selecting day care:

- **Your children's ages:** Many day care centers will not take children under the age of three months; others require children to be potty trained. Once your children are in school, you may find after-school programs that will reduce your costs substantially.
- **How many of your children need day care:** Day care centers may offer reductions for families with two or three children in their care. Or you may select family day care for a toddler and an after-school program for your school-age child.
- **If they have special needs:** If you have a child with special needs, child care will likely cost a premium. Nannies, au pairs, or full-time babysitters may be your best option.
- **Your work schedule:** If you work locally and have a traditional eight-hour schedule, day care centers may meet your needs. If you commute long distances or frequently work overtime, home-based care may be your only choice.
- **Your budget:** If you're like most people, you will need to create a realistic budget and find the best option available within your price range.
- **The location and size of your home:** If you have a large home in the country, home-based care makes sense for small children. If you live in a large city, you may have many excellent options, but you'll probably pay a premium for them.
- **Your and your child's comfort level:** Parents and children may have strong feelings about group care situations versus having the children in their own environment. It's important to honor those feelings and to trust your instincts when it comes to knowing what's right for your child.

Child Care Costs

Child care costs can vary widely depending on where you live and how much care is available, but some monthly cost estimates are as follows:

Estimated Monthly Costs for Child Care

Option	Approximate Cost (2006)*
Nanny	$1,600 to $2,600, plus agency finder's fee
Live-in nanny	$1,200 to $1,500, plus room and board
Au pair	$1,160, plus room and board, plus initial expenses
Day care	$500 to $1,250
Family day care	$700 to $1,000
Share-care	$1,300 to 1,600

Source: Parent Savvy

Home-Based Care

You can hire someone to care for your children in your home—nannies, au pairs, housekeepers, babysitters, or relatives. Home-based care is ideal for infants and small toddlers. Unless you have a grandmother, sister, or friend who works for little to nothing, however, it is generally an expensive option. Nannies and au pairs make more sense when you have more than one child or if your home is big enough that you can exchange room and board for a large portion of the cost.

Family Day Care Centers

Often you can find mothers in your community who take care of other people's children so that they can stay home with their own. While they often have a lower child-to-adult ratio, they may not be required to meet the same strict licensing requirements of larger, commercial day care centers. You are also dependent upon someone who could become sick or move.

Day Care Centers

Day care centers typically offer a structured environment run by licensed teachers, who may or may not have specialized in early childhood development or education. The centers are subject to governmental licensing, which means they are inspected and monitored by your state government. Studies have shown that children under the age of five who attend day care centers and preschools often develop advanced social skills, as well as language and academic skills. On the con side, these centers can be rigid and often close early, limiting their viability for commuters.

Preschools

Preschools are very similar to day care centers, but they focus on your child's academic, social, and physical development. Generally, preschool centers accept children between the ages of three and five. "Graduates" transition into elementary school systems when they are ready for kindergarten. Preschools may have very limited hours and may adhere to a highly structured routine that might not fit your child's needs.

Share-Care or Babysitting Co-ops

Mothers in family neighborhoods often form babysitting or share-care co-ops. The obvious advantages are that you know the caretaker and that costs are low, but you may have to rotate care.

Workplace Care

If you're extremely lucky, you may work for a firm that has on-site day care for employees' children. To find out which companies offer this, call your local chamber of commerce, or find a copy of *Working Mother* magazine's annual "Top 100 Companies." If your company doesn't have one, and there are a number of working mothers or fathers who would appreciate the service, pitch the idea to your boss.

Extended Day Care

There are usually reliable programs available that take care of children after school. Many schools offer programs, as do churches and local youth organizations. You may even be able to find programs geared toward music, dance, art, sports, computers, or anything else that holds particular appeal to your child.

Backup Options

No matter your choice of day care, you will have days when backup care will be necessary—when a child or caregiver becomes ill, during summer vacations, nontraditional holidays, and so on. As you search for the best situation, keep your eyes open for backup alternatives. During the summer, churches, community centers, youth organizations (such as YMCA, YWCA, or Boy's Club of America), and parks and recreation departments often sponsor daylong summer camps that not only take excellent care of your children, but also offer a wide range of healthy activities.

The Pros and Cons of Nannies Versus Au Pairs

If you want to keep your young children at home, hiring a nanny or an au pair may be the route to go. In general, a nanny is someone you hire through an agency or a personal reference. She may or may not live with you. Also, she may or may not assume other household duties, such as laundry or light cleaning. An au pair usually exchanges live-in child care at a lower hourly wage for the opportunity to live and work in the United States for a set period of time. Some au pair agencies are regulated by the U.S. State Department.

The Pros and Cons of Nannies

Although they are undeniably expensive, hiring a personal nanny has many advantages, and a few pertinent disadvantages.

The Pros and Cons of Nannies

Pros	Cons
One-on-one care in your home	You rely on one person
Your child may form a close attachment	A nanny may abruptly quit
Scheduling flexibility	A nanny's lingering illness may disrupt your schedule
Avoiding a morning rush	Unsupervised care, unless you hide a nanny-cam

Pros	Cons
May help with housework	May not have transportation
Available to include activities	Children may be more isolated
Available to care for sick children	Expensive and complicated payment requirements

The most restrictive aspects to hiring a nanny include the exorbitant cost and the fact that nannies are neither licensed nor regulated by any governmental agencies. This means parents are responsible for the process of ferreting out reliable, trustworthy nannies. Although it certainly behooves all parents to hire nannies from reputable agencies that research their employees' backgrounds, as well as obtain and check extensive references, this also increases the expense.

ALERT!

When hiring a nanny, take time to research the range of prices paid in your area (typically $11 to $15 an hour, dependent on educational or experience level, or $1,200 to $1,500 a month for a live-in nanny). Also make sure you know the federal and state laws that will apply to taxes and overtime. Even if you use an agency, you'll need the comparisons in order to know if it's the right price for you.

Nevertheless, for many single mothers, a nanny can be the answer to their prayers. If you have a large house, ideally with a private room and bathroom, and more than one child, you can lower nanny expenses by offering room and board. You need to realize, however, that doing so rarely means you are hiring a full-time housekeeper and babysitter. Nannies expect a schedule and would likely consider additional time spent with the children as cause for increased pay.

Decisions that could affect the cost include these:

- **Level of educational or formal training:** All nannies should have CPR and first aid training, but insisting on a degree in child care or early childhood education can boost the price significantly.

- **Level of experience:** Obviously nannies with vast experience warrant a higher salary, but keep in mind that having a young nanny can have its advantages—she'll have a higher energy level and not be so set in her ways, for instance.
- **Live in or live out:** You can pay less for a live-in nanny, but you have to weigh the convenience or inconvenience and what works best in your situation. Federal law does not require you to pay overtime to a live-in nanny, but state laws can differ.
- **What services you request:** If you want your nanny to do the laundry, run errands, pick up the children or shuttle them to and from activities, work longer hours, or cook, the price will rise appropriately.
- **Hours needed:** Some states require that you pay overtime after eight working hours per day; other states require overtime for any hours worked over forty in one week.

Agency fees can vary, but they are generally a flat fee or a percentage of the nanny's annual salary for the first year (usually ranging from $1,500 to $3,000). Nannies are usually paid well above minimum wage (approximately $11 to $15), and keep in mind that you will be required to comply with federal and state employment laws. You will pay Social Security, Medicare, and state unemployment taxes. You will also be required to file an I-9 and a W-2 at the end of each year. Depending upon which state you live in, you may have to pay for worker's compensation insurance, and, if the nanny will be driving your car, additional insurance costs. You can hire a payroll service to handle the paperwork for a reasonable monthly fee (less than $30 a month) that would calculate and deduct taxes, help you make quarterly payments, and assist you in filing all necessary paperwork.

ALERT!

If you hire an illegal immigrant or a nanny "off the books," you risk an IRS audit that could cost you hundreds, or thousands, in back taxes and penalties. When you pay a nanny "on the books," you not only comply with the laws, you make it possible for her to receive Social Security benefits, as well as worker's compensation and unemployment benefits.

If you're finding and hiring a nanny without going through a placement agency, it's money well spent to perform a comprehensive background check. By shopping around, you should be able to find out everything you need to know for a reasonable fee—around $100. But be sure you have permission from the prospective nanny, as required by the Fair Credit Reporting Act (FCRA).

The Pros and Cons of Au Pairs

Au pairs are nannies who come to the United States for a one- or two-year cultural exchange. A number of governmental agencies match parents and au pairs, who are legally allowed to work forty-five hours a week for less than you would pay a professional nanny—around $6 an hour for a live-in au pair, compared to $11 and up for a nanny. Au pairs are generally between the ages of eighteen and twenty-six and are required to have a high school education and to be proficient in English. If you have an infant under the age of two, au pairs are required to have 200 hours of infant-care experience. Au pairs are also required to have eight hours of safety training and twenty-four hours of child development education.

The Pros and Cons of Au Pairs

Pros	Cons
Half the cost of nannies	You pay airfare and agency placement fees
One-on-one attention	Two-year maximum stay (most leave in one year)
No limit on number of children	Cannot work more than forty-five hours per week
No federal or state taxes due	Cannot perform household duties
Screened by government agencies	Cannot interview in person
Scheduling flexibility	Cannot work more than ten hours in one day, or overnight
Cultural exchange works both ways	You pay $500 for educational allowance

An average au pair can cost a whopping $14,000 a year, which equates to about $270 per week, including agency placement fees and educational allowance. You will also need to provide a private room and live within one hour's drive of an agency. You can find a list of reputable agencies through the U.S. State Department Web site, at *www.exchanges.state.gov.*

The Pros and Cons of Day Care Centers

Day care centers can cost between $500 and $1,250 per child, per month, depending upon your location, competition for available spaces, the number of children you have, and how many hours per day they will be in day care.

The Pros and Cons of Day Care Centers

Pros	Cons
State licensed	Limited flexibility
Cheaper than home-based	Limited one-on-one interaction
Stimulating atmosphere	Susceptible to spreading of viruses
Multiple caretakers	You'll have to keep child home when sick
Supervised care	Usually won't take infants under three months
Educated caretakers	May be too structured for your child

Even though day care centers have to obtain a state license and undergo state inspections, licensure only means that a center has met the minimum requirements. You will want to talk with other parents, your pediatrician, or anyone else who might know a center's reputation and reliability. Once you've narrowed your search, take time to meet personally with the director and its staff. Some questions to ask include the following:

- What are the age requirements?
- Are you licensed by the state?
- Are the caretakers licensed teachers? Are they degreed in early childhood education?

- Do you have flexible hours?
- What is the child-to-caretaker ratio?
- Do you have a curriculum?
- Do you include social and physical activities?
- Will my child receive individual attention?
- What do you do to minimize the spreading of germs?
- Do you have provisions for emergency situations? A doctor on call?
- Do you have restrictions on illness? Fever? Rash?
- What happens if I'm late?

When you narrow down your choices again, it's time to ask questions about costs. Make sure you ask the following:

- How much do you charge per child?
- Will I have to pay during vacations?
- Are there extra costs (for art supplies, food, day trips)?
- Do you require parent participation?
- Do you charge penalties for being late to pick up my children?
- What is your payment schedule? Do you have a grace period for late payments?
- Do you offer any scholarships or grants for low-income parents?
- If you require a deposit, is it due in a lump sum, or can I pay it in monthly installments?
- What is your cancellation policy?

Once you've found the ideal day care center, it's wise to play by their rules and to make sure you arrive on time, pay on time, and show appreciation for a job well done. They are nurturing your children, and a good caregiver is worth her weight in gold.

The Pros and Cons of Family Day Care Centers

Family day care centers are often far cheaper than commercial or larger day care centers. They may also have more flexibility, but they do have drawbacks.

The Pros and Cons of Family Day Care Centers

Pros	Cons
Inexpensive	Unsupervised caretaker
Home environment	Very lax state licensing requirements
Caregiver is also a parent	May not have any early childhood education or training
Smaller child-to-caregiver ratio	Usually dependent on one caregiver
Scheduling flexibility	Caregiver, or her child, might be sick
Not subject to employee taxes	Will need backup for vacations

The National Resource Center for Health and Safety in Childcare and state law usually require a low caregiver-to-child ratio for home-based day care centers. Solo providers are usually limited to no more than two children under the age of two. If you know the provider and feel comfortable with her parenting style, this could be the best solution, particularly if your budget is tight. Just make sure you ask a lot of questions and observe the circumstances going on around you when you visit.

How to Lower Child Care Costs

One option for saving money is to enter into share-care arrangements with other families. If you work part-time or if your schedules mesh perfectly, you might be able to share a nanny or babysitter with another family. You would ideally seek someone like-minded with children close to yours in age, temperament, and activity level. The convenience of sharing costs and having a backup could make this work financially and on every other level. Although some nannies might balk at watching an extra child, or two, you can sweeten the pie by offering broader benefits, such as health insurance, and still keep expenses lower than they would be if you hired your own nanny.

Having relatives or friends available to care for your children can save you substantial sums of money, but you may end up with steep emotional costs. If you go this route, you may avoid problems if you treat the arrangement professionally. Make sure you have a formal agreement that states the hours needed, rate of pay, vacation time, and overtime. Even if they offer to watch your children for free, you can avoid misunderstandings by creating a list of expectations and offering a quantifiable reward program.

If you're really strapped for money, you could call your local AARP office to see if they have a list of elderly citizens in your neighborhood that might like to "adopt" a grandchild. You can also post listings on bulletin boards or in your local paper. If you're new to a neighborhood, it's worth a neighborhood sweep to see if anyone is interested in a watching your school-age children for several hours after school. You'd want to research backgrounds and obtain references, but finding someone this way could save you a tidy sum.

The National Association for the Education of Young Children (NAEYC), a nonprofit center that offers educational programs for day care centers, has developed a stringent optional accreditation process. If a day care center boasts an NAEYC accreditation (only 10,000 out of 100,000 centers have gone through the laborious process), you can rest assured they have exceeded national standards.

The only other concrete options involve reducing your work hours, moving closer to where you work, telecommuting, or convincing your boss to contribute to child care costs. Keep in mind that paying for child care "on the books" may actually save you money. You can take advantage of child care tax breaks and dependent care spending accounts. Read about these tax advantages in Chapter 17.

Chapter 15
Funding College

According to 2004 U.S. Census figures, Americans over the age of twenty-five with only a high school education earned an average of $26,104. Those with a two-year degree earned $32,383; and those with a four-year degree earned $42,087. In today's world, your children need to go to college, yet college can be prohibitively expensive. Although you may think it unimaginable that you would be able to afford a college education for your children, starting early and taking advantage of college-fund savings accounts can secure your children's opportunity.

Weighing Your Options

According to the College Board's Annual Survey of Colleges, four-year private university tuition, fees, room and board charges averaged $29,026 in 2005. Public four-year college costs were $12,127, and two-year college costs were $8,100. Even though many four-year college students get scholarships, loans, or grants that cover 15 to 30 percent of their annual costs, the overall costs remain daunting.

If you have five years before your child starts college and can earn an 8 percent return on investments, investing $140 per month will provide $10,000 for her college fund; with ten years, contributing $60 each month to the college fund accumulates $10,000; and fifteen years only requires $30 dollars per month to provide $10,000.

In the last ten years, public and private four-year college costs increased about 2.5 and 2 percent, respectively, above the rate of inflation. If this trend continues, in ten years you can expect that college costs will increase 5 to 7 percent per year—totaling about $50,000 per year for the average private four-year college; $22,000 per year for the average public four-year college; and $14,500 per year for the average two-year college. So, if you want to pay a large part of your children's college expenses, the earlier you start planning, saving, and investing, the better.

The two best ways to save for your child's education are to open a Coverdell education savings account and/or a section 529 college savings plan. Their basic allowances and qualifications are as follows:

- You can contribute $2,000 each year to a Coverdell account. Funds in the account grow tax-free, and the funds can be spent on almost any education-related expense for your child as soon as she starts first grade.
- You can deposit significantly larger annual amounts in 529 plans earmarked for college expenses. The plans allow new contribu-

tions until the account value reaches a certain level that varies by state—most of the the lowest limits max out at $235,000; the higher limits max out around $300,000. To retain tax-free status on gains, you must spend withdrawn funds on tuition, room and board, fees, books, supplies, and equipment used for college and graduate school—not for any earlier education expenses.

- You can deposit funds into a section 529 plan that allows you to pre-purchase four years of tuition at today's prices at one of your state's public universities or one of a number of private schools. Deposits are limited to the cost of tuition and required fees for five years.

Educational savings bonds are a safe, tax-advantaged option, but they typically don't accrue enough interest to bolster savings. Custodial accounts are an option; however, they don't offer tax advantages and can be problematic if your children obtain ownership at age eighteen or twenty-one and squander the funds. Using your Roth IRA to fund your child's education is also possible, and it may be reasonable if you are at least age 59.5 when your child attends college. Still, this approach isn't generally recommended because withdrawals from the account are counted by financial aid formulas as parental income and could limit access to additional financial aid. Also, using your Roth IRA may create a situation in which you have to choose between your retirement savings and your child's education.

Coverdell Education Savings Accounts

If your 2006 modified adjusted gross income is less than $110,000, you can contribute a maximum of $2,000 per year, per child, to a Coverdell account in a given child's name. Total annual contributions per child can be as much as $2,000 from all parties gifting. The minor can also fund his/her own account, but the total from all sources per year cannot exceed $2,000. Gains and interest on investments in the account grow tax-free for the life of the account. You won't be taxed on withdrawals at the federal level (or, in most cases, by the state) as long as the money is spent on qualifying educational expenses for things required for your child's education from the day your child starts first grade. These include the following:

- A computer
- College, graduate school, and private school tuition, fees, and books
- School uniforms and supplies
- Room and board
- Private school tuition
- Academic tutoring

The range of expenses covered make a Coverdell account an attractive way to save to cover expenses at almost all points during your child's education.

If you withdraw funds from a Coverdell account that you don't spend on qualified education expenses, you will have to pay ordinary income tax at a relatively high rate on a pro-rata share of earnings on the withdrawal, as well as a 10 percent penalty on the same withdrawn earnings. For instance, if you withdraw $1,000 from an account with a total value of $10,000 and account gains of $5,000, you would owe taxes and penalties on $500 of gains. Coverdell account advantages and constraints are as follows:

- If your MAGI exceeds $95,000, the maximum amount you can contribute will be less than $2,000 per year. In this case, consult a tax advisor, or look up your maximum contribution through the IRS (*www.irs.gov*).
- Coverdell contributions are considered gifts to your child. If you are gifting more than $12,000 (or the current limit on tax-free cash gifts), the funds will be subject to high gift-tax rates. Direct tuition payments are not subject to gift taxes.
- Since the federal financial aid formula views Coverdell accounts as a parent's asset, investments don't impact financial aid as much as assets held in the child's name, such as a custodial account.
- You retain control of account investments, but your child legally owns the account assets, which means that you cannot spend account funds to cover a financial emergency.

- You can fund your child's Coverdell account until she turns eighteen, and she has until the age of thirty to deplete the funds. Otherwise, gains will be taxed at ordinary income rates, and a 10 percent penalty will be levied on gains before the account assets are disbursed to your child.
- You have leeway to invest in almost anything, including individual stocks, bonds, and mutual funds.
- If you decide that you'd rather have a 529 plan than your Coverdell account, you can transfer account assets to a 529 account at will. (You can't, however, transfer assets to a Coverdell account from a 529 account.)
- Your child has to be enrolled in school for at least half the number of units that would qualify her for full-time status to withdraw funds without incurring taxes and penalties.
- If your child has a developmental disability, the child's Coverdell account assets can be used to hire a physical therapist without incurring taxes or penalties on account withdrawals.
- Provided her school's students are qualified to receive federal financial aid, your child's Coverdell account can fund her overseas and trade school expenses. Go online to *www.fafsa.ed.gov* for a complete list of eligible schools.

The only drawback to a Coverdell account is that you can only contribute $2,000 a year. Thankfully, you have other options that you can choose instead of—or in addition to—a Coverdell account.

Section 529 College Savings Plans

Since 1996, parents have had a choice between two kinds of 529 college savings plans to pay for their children's education. You can establish a 529 plan that will function as an investment account in which gains and interest aren't taxed, or you can establish a 529 prepaid tuition plan, which allows you to purchase blocks of college tuition (by semester) for your child at today's prices.

Both types of 529 plan offer excellent savings opportunities and share common features. For example, 529 plans have no income limitations or age limitations on the contributor or the beneficiary. As far as taxation, contributions are considered gifts, meaning that if you gift over $12,000 in one year (or the current limit on tax-free gifts) to a single beneficiary, the donor, rather than the recipient, is technically required to pay gift taxes for annual gifts over $12,000. New legislation allows withdrawals from 529 plans that are spent on qualified educational expenses to be tax-free and penalty-free indefinitely.

Maximum contribution amounts are dictated by each individual plan. With the exception of state-sponsored prepaid tuition plans, limits usually exceed $235,000, making 529 plans an especially good way to save a substantial amount for your children's college expenses. Before you deposit large sums of money into these accounts, it's good to know that you cannot borrow against a 529 plan.

ALERT!

Financial advisors may try to sell you a 529 plan with a "load" or sales charge, which may be hidden in the fine print and not mentioned. The load is usually 1 to 6 percent of the amount you invest in the plan. To avoid these "hidden" costs, tell the financial advisor that you'd like to research options on your own and hold off until you find a "no-load" 529 college savings plan.

Both plans generate from either an individual state or educational institution. States and educational institutions are the only groups allowed to create 529 plans. Plan management is often delegated to a major financial firm like T Rowe Price, Fidelity, and Vanguard; however, many states run their own programs. Each plan is unique in terms of the investments it allows as well as its various restrictions and fees. To make the right decision for your situation, obtain the "offering circular" from the plan sponsor and thoroughly review plan details before you open the account.

Because all 529 plans are created with unique terms by either a state government or educational institution, it's prudent to weigh all the costs, limits, and benefits of investing in each plan. Consider whether you will receive state tax credits or deductions for your contribution to the plan. Research things like the list of schools that are covered directly by the plan, what happens if your child attends a school not covered by the plan—including what fees you may owe, what happens if your child receives a scholarship, and what happens if your child doesn't go to school at all. You can invest in 529 plans offered by a state other than the one you live in, so you may want to compare a range of plans in other states. You can find out more about the details of specific plans through *www.collegesavings.org* and *www.saving forcollege.com.*

QUESTION?

What happens if I withdraw funds from both a 529 plan and a Coverdell account in the same year?
You have to split your qualified higher education expenses (QHEE) between the accounts to determine whether any taxes are due. If you spend $5,000 on tuition and other QHEE during a year, the total amount of QHEE you can cover between the two accounts is $5,000; no double counting is allowed.

Though your contributions to a child's 529 prepaid tuition plans are treated as gifts for tax purposes, you are able to change the beneficiary on the account at will and to control investments in the account. If your first child hasn't used all the credits in a prepaid tuition plan, a second child can benefit from the unused credits; or, if you plan to take classes at a qualified university for classes, you can name yourself as the beneficiary. Changing the beneficiary on a 529 plan is not a taxable event, though you may be required to pay a fee.

Managing a 529 Plan

A 529 plan functions similar to a Roth IRA. Your deposits are not deducted from your gross income on your tax return; however, you may receive modest state tax credits or deductions in a given year. The monies you deposit into your 529 plan are limited to one or a few investment options offered by the plan—usually stock and bond mutual funds—and your savings grow tax-free until you're ready to withdraw them to cover qualified educational expenses. If you choose an investment-type 529 plan, you have the potential to earn a higher return than you would with a prepaid tuition plan; however, you also take on stock and bond market risk in the process.

You can avoid paying taxes and penalties on earnings in your 529 savings by spending the account's assets on "qualified higher education expenses," (QHEE), including college and graduate school tuition, room and board, mandatory fees, books, supplies, and even computers or other equipment required by the school. The school receiving the funds must also be eligible to disburse federal financial aid. (See *www.fafsa.ed.gov* for a list of qualified schools.) The list includes overseas, technical, and trade schools, as well as traditional universities and junior colleges.

For federal financial aid purposes, 529 plans are treated as assets of the parent rather than the child. This means your child has increased ability to receive financial aid when she has a certain amount of money in a 529 plan than she does with the same amount in a custodial account in her own name. Also, even after the child reaches age eighteen or twenty-one, you maintain control of the account. You can withdraw funds not spent on education by paying a 10 percent penalty and taxes on the profits accrued.

529 Prepaid Tuition Plans

The 529 prepaid tuition plan allows you to purchase tuition credits at any school that has signed up to take part in your state's plan. Because tuition has risen much faster than inflation for decades, this can be an attractive way to finance your child's education, but there are caveats.

Generally, your child cashes in the credits by attending a school in the plan (in most cases, a state university), and tuition (and in some cases also room and board) is paid by the plan. If your child wants to attend a college not covered by the plan, the plan usually pays the value of your child's tuition credits directly to the other institution. If that institution has lower tuition and fees than state schools, the plan will usually pay the lower amount. Since you may sacrifice funds in this situation, you should evaluate whether the best option is simply to cancel the contract and obtain a refund.

Seemingly, prepaid tuition guarantees that your child will be able to afford tuition and fees at the preferred state school and limits investment risk; however, when their prepayment investments didn't grow at the same rate as college-cost inflation (5 to 7 percent annually), or their plan didn't attract a critical asset mass to make it self-sufficient, a few states cancelled their contracts, which left investors to find an alternative plan in another state. Other limitation and benefits of a 529 prepaid tuition plan include the following:

- Plan terms vary by state.
- Most require that either the child or a parent be a resident of the state offering the plan.
- Refunds from the plan for any reason can engender significant fees.
- Most plans only provide for undergraduate-level tuition and mandatory fee payments.
- You are likely to pay numerous fees, including enrollment fees and annual maintenance fees.

To avoid investing in 529 prepaid tuition plans that are in danger of folding, look for a plan that has many other investors and a large amount of assets. Check out the College Savings Plans Network's "Statistics Warehouse" Web site (online at ✍*www.collegesavings.org*), as well as the Web site ✍*www.savingforcollege.com*. Both include side-by-side state-sponsored 529 plan comparisons, which are excellent starting points for further research.

Another option is to investigate the Tuition Plan Consortium (online at *www.independent529plan.org*), a plan sponsored by hundreds of private colleges that joined forces to create a 529 prepaid tuition plan that covers future tuition payments at member colleges. Participating colleges include Amherst, Case Western Reserve, University of Chicago, Hampshire, MIT, Mount Holyoke, Princeton, Stanford, Tulane, Wellesley, and many others. The plan does not charge annual fees or exit fees and allows you to buy tuition credits at a 1 percent discount to their current price, a valuable benefit if you're interested in a prepaid tuition plan. If you sign up for automatic bank or payroll transfers, accounts can be funded with as little as $25 per month.

Custodial Accounts

Established in some states under the Uniform Gifts to Minors Act (UGMA), and in others at the Uniform Transfers to Minors Act (UTMA), parents or guardians are allowed to establish custodial accounts. These are simple trust accounts opened for someone under twenty-one years of age and controlled by the custodian, usually one of the account holder's parents, until the child reaches adulthood. A deposit into a child's custodial account is considered a gift to your child; however, you, as the custodian, are responsible for managing the account assets until your child reaches age eighteen or twenty-one, depending on the state you live in. Currently, you are allowed to gift $12,000 tax-free per year. When your child reaches the relevant age, she owns the account, and you will no longer have legal control over how she chooses to spend the money you intended for college. Once gifted, the money cannot be reclaimed, even if you find yourself in dire financial straits.

It's best to use tax-advantaged account options like a 529 savings plan to fund your child's college expenses rather than a custodial account for three reasons:

1. If your child has a custodial account, the account will reduce her available federal financial aid by 3.5 times (in 2007) more than the amount that it would be reduced if she had the same amount of funds in a 529 plan. One way to avoid this penalty under current law is to transfer custodial account assets required for college to a 529 savings account before your child applies for financial aid.
2. Custodial accounts owe taxes on all realized gains; 529 account earnings are not taxed.

3. No matter your child's age, you maintain control of 529 plan assets; at age eighteen or twenty-one, your child owns the custodial account and could conceivably spend the funds on clothing, a car, a tropical vacation, or entertaining her friends, rather than on college expenses as you envisioned.

Even at age eighteen or twenty-one, children are not likely to understand the financial sacrifices you made to accumulate college funds or to spend them wisely. To avoid disappointment, it's advisable to choose plans that remain under your control.

FACT

A child under age fourteen will earn tax-free gains on the first $850 in investment income (interest, dividends, and capital gains), and pay taxes at her marginal tax rate for the next $850 of investment income. Any investment income in her custodial account over $1,700 will be taxed at your marginal tax rate. After age fifteen, all gains in the account will be taxable at her tax rate.

Education Savings Bonds

You can also purchase government-backed bonds—Series EE and Series I bonds—that earn tax-free interest income as long as the bonds are eventually used to pay for qualifying college and graduate school expenses. The U.S. government guarantees both bond types, so you have almost no risk of losing money; however, interest rates will be lower than most investment alternatives. Qualified college and graduate school expenses include tuition and mandatory fees for a degree-granting college or graduate school or any school eligible to disburse federal financial aid (See *www.fafsa.ed.gov* for a list of qualified schools.)

Series I bonds increase in value based on the level of inflation measured by the Consumer Price Index (CPI), plus a return over inflation, while Series EE bonds are guaranteed to at least double in value within twenty years—which equates to a 3.5 percent minimum annual return.

To purchase these bonds and take full advantage of the federal tax breaks, you must be at least twenty-four years old and have a modified adjusted gross income (MAGI) below $63,100 (for 2006). If your MAGI falls between $63,100 and $78,100 when you cash in the bonds, you will receive a partial federal tax deduction. You can purchase up to $30,000 of each kind of education savings bond each year. They can be purchased through most brokerage firms or direct from the U.S. Treasury Department (online at *www.treasurydirect.gov*) in denominations as low as $25.

Local and state governments do not impose tax on education savings bond gains. You are required to hold Series I and EE bonds for at least twelve months. If for any reason you sell the bonds within five years of original purchase, you will lose the most recent three months' interest paid on the bonds. Finally, education savings bonds can be transferred tax-free into a 529 savings plan, but you still forfeit the most recent three months' interest if you redeem the bonds within five years of their purchase.

Education Reward Programs

Some credit cards offer education reward programs that work in the same way as money-back, store-credit, or airline-miles programs. When you purchase goods or services from businesses partnered with the rewards program, they typically deposit 1 to 5 percent of the purchase into your child's 529 account. You can also sign up friends, family, godparents, and others naming your child the rewards beneficiary, which can potentially increase your child's college savings by thousands of dollars over the years.

Two established education reward programs are BabyMint (*www.baby mint.com*) and Upromise (*www.upromise.com*). Both programs include a list of disclaimers and qualifications for when and how you can claim your rewards, so be sure to read and understand the steps you need to take to actually earn—and cash in—rewards. Even though you cannot save money by spending money, it makes sense to reroute 1 to 5 percent of a purchase price—on something you needed and would buy anyway—into your child's college funds.

The Hope Credit

The Hope credit is a nonrefundable credit that can be used to offset taxes you owe for qualified expenses up to $1,000, plus half of expenses over $1,000, with a maximum credit amount of $1,500. Qualified expenses include tuition and required fees for you or your dependent to attend the first two years of a qualified postsecondary school (eligible to disburse federal financial aid) and required books or supplies purchased directly from the college or school.

To avoid limiting your child's access to financial aid, buy the bonds in your name, and hold them until the year you begin paying pay for her college or graduate school expenses. If you spend less than the full amount of the Series I and EE bonds you sell in a given year on qualified expenses, you'll have to pay taxes on the remainder of your gains.

You or your dependent must also be enrolled in at least half of what's considered a full-time workload at the school for at least one academic period (quarter, semester, or trimester) during a the calendar year, and must be enrolled in a program that leads to a degree, certificate, or credential for at least one full academic period during the year. Anyone convicted of a felony drug possession or distribution charge is not eligible for the credit.

The Hope credit is reduced if your modified adjusted gross income is between $88,000 and $108,000 (for 2006; these figures are adjusted annually for inflation), and it isn't available if your income exceeds $108,000. To calculate how much your credit will be reduced or to find more information about the Hope credit, consult IRS Publication 970, or visit the related Web site online, at *www.irs.gov*.

Lifetime Learning Credit

Education expenses that qualify for the Hope credit also qualify for the lifetime learning credit; however, the lifetime learning credit is not restricted to the first two years of the student's higher education. The two credits have the same key qualifying income levels as well. The credit is for 20 percent of up to $10,000 of qualifying expenses per family tax return, up to a maximum of $2,000 that may be attributable to qualifying expenses from more than one child in the family.

You cannot claim the Hope credit and the lifetime learning credit in the same year. But if you have more than one student in the family (including yourself), you could use the Hope credit for one and the lifetime learning credit for the other. If your child or you are in the first two years of college, if the relevant qualifying expenses are under $7,500 for the calendar year. If you have to decide between the lifetime learning credit and the Hope credit, given current tax law, the Hope credit offers greater financial rewards. If qualified expenses paid are over $7,500, the higher-limit lifetime learning credit ($2,000 maximum) is the better choice.

The lifetime learning credit has fewer qualifying restrictions than the Hope credit. For instance, the student is not required to pursue a degree or certificate, and the student remains qualified regardless of whether she has a felony drug offense on her record.

Federal Student Aid Programs

About 60 percent of undergraduates enrolled full-time in college receive federal, state, or school grant aid. If you pay interest on a nonfederal loan that you are liable for, you are able to deduct the interest on your taxes. Scholarship money used for tuition and course-related expenses are tax-free; however, funds used to pay room and board are taxable.

For all federal aid programs, your student must file the Free Application for Federal Student Aid (FAFSA), each year. The FAFSA filing establishes the expected family contribution (EFC) for your child, a figure used commonly in federal financial aid calculations. You can file the FAFSA either online (*www.fafsa.ed.gov*) or by submitting a paper form obtained from your local high school or college.

When the college to which your student applies receives her FAFSA filing, she will be mailed a "financial aid package" listing the available aid programs for which she is eligible, including federal loan programs, school scholarships, and state grant programs. The financial aid package will include instructions for how to apply to each available loan or grant available. If you have any questions about your eligibility or how to go about securing the loans and grants offered, contact the financial aid office at the college.

A variety of federal student aid programs exist, as described in the following sections.

ALERT!

Your student's college may offer Supplemental Education Opportunity Grants and Perkins Loans on a first-come, first-served basis. To make sure you don't miss out on these programs, find out the earliest possible day to submit your student's FAFSA documents to the college(s) of her choice, and submit all requested information via the Internet (using the *www.fafsa.ed.gov* Web site) as close as possible to that date.

Pell Grants

Since they are outright subsidies that do not have to be repaid, Pell Grants are the most popular form of student aid—traditionally claimed by approximately 5 million students each year. Pell Grant awards are based on the cost of attending the specific school and the student's EFC. For the 2006–2007 school year, the EFC cutoff is $3,851. (When the EFC is greater than this figure, the student is ineligible.) Grants can go as high as $4,050 each year to qualifying students. The U.S. Department of Education posts an annual grant eligibility form on the department's Web site, at *http://stu dentaid.ed.gov*.

Supplemental Education Opportunity Grants

Families with low EFCs are eligible to claim a Supplemental Education Opportunity Grant ("SEOG") as additional support for college expenses. SEOG awards can also reach $4,000 per year and do not have to be repaid. Schools typically grant these awards on a first-come, first-served basis, so submitting applications as soon as possible is crucial to obtaining support. According to guidance from the U.S. Department of Education, Pell Grant–eligible students with the lowest EFC are the first to receive these grants. The next group to receive funds is non-Pell students who have the lowest EFCs.

Stafford Loans

If a student has demonstrable financial need (as documented on her FAFSA) and is enrolled at least half-time, she may qualify for a low-interest Stafford Loan. Undergraduate students who are someone's dependent for financial aid purposes are able to borrow progressively larger amounts—in 2006, loan amounts were $2,625 in the student's first year, $3,500 in the second year, and $5,500 for each of the third and fourth years. Undergraduate students who aren't someone's dependent can borrow up to $6,625 in their first year, $7,500 in their second, and $10,500 in their third and fourth years; however, the federally subsidized portions of these loans are offered only up to the maximums for dependent students. Post-graduate and professional students (such as those at medical or law school) can receive $18,500 in loans for each year of study, but no more than $8,500 can be subsidized.

There are two varieties of Stafford Loans. Banks, credit unions, or other traditional lenders provide Federal Family Education Loans ("FFEL"), and the U.S. Department of Education offers Direct Stafford Loans. FFEL loans must be repaid by between ten and twenty-five years after graduation; Direct Stafford Loan recipients must repay between ten to thirty years after graduation.

PLUS Loans

Parent Loans for Undergraduate Students ("PLUS") are available to families (including the parent of the dependent child) that pass a credit check. Your school may offer two kinds of PLUS package: Direct PLUS loans are offered by the U.S. Department of Education, and FFEL PLUS loans are offered by nongovernment lenders. FFEL PLUS loans are offered to parents of dependent undergraduate students enrolled at least half time, up to a maximum of the total cost of attendance, less other financial aid received. Interest rates are low and change every year. You'll have between ten and twenty-five years to repay loans outstanding on a FFEL PLUS loan.

Direct PLUS loans are offered with the same requirements as FFEL PLUS loans; however, FFEL PLUS loans allow repayment based on the amount of income you earn. Families can select an "income-sensitive" repayment plan with higher payments when family income is higher and lower payments when income is less.

Perkins Loans

Undergraduate and graduate-level students with "exceptional" financial need, as defined by the college, can obtain federal Perkins Loans, whose interest rates hold steady at 5 percent. Eligible undergraduate students can borrow up to $4,000 per year through the program, or up to $20,000 total. Graduate students can borrow up to $6,000 per year, up to a maximum of $40,000, including undergraduate loans outstanding under the program. Graduates have a nine-month grace period and then ten years to pay off the loan. Your school will likely disburse Perkins Loans on a first-come, first-served basis, so it's imperative that students apply as soon as possible.

Federal Work-Study

The federal work-study program offers part-time employment to students with financial need to offset their college expenses. Usually students work directly for their college, fulfilling a variety of roles, but they may also work for an unrelated public agency or private nonprofit. In limited cases, they are able to work with private, for-profit employers when the job is relevant to the student's course of study.

Other Ways to Maximize College Savings

The most important, and, incidentally, least expensive, way for you to help prepare your child for college is to stress the importance of your child's excelling academically, athletically, or in other activities she enjoys (all of which will help her win scholarships and grants). Encourage your child's development, teach her that college will help her achieve whatever she desires, and cultivate the idea of college as a necessary rite of passage to adulthood. If you do this, she may become motivated to work harder in high school, to work harder to help raise funds for her college education, and to make sacrifices that will allow you to channel additional money into her funds.

You can also encourage your children to become proactive in funding college by encouraging contributions such as the following:

- They could take summer jobs and deposit 50 to 75 percent of their earnings into their college fund.
- They could go to a state college. If they want to attend a state college in another state, they could move to that state and attend junior college there for two years before transferring to the preferred state college.
- They could attend a community college for two years before transferring to the college of their choice.
- They could adjust their expectations and attend a college that allows them to live at home or with relatives.
- They could work part-time while attending college.
- They could participate in work-study programs while attending college.

If you cannot adequately fund college savings plans, make sure your child's father contributes at least as much as you do. Devote at least a small percentage of child support to fund the account, and ask your family to donate 20 to 25 percent or more of what they would spend on gifts for the children to their college funds. It's also completely reasonable to reward your children with deposits into their account every time they bring home a good report card, or to offer to match whatever savings they are willing to contribute. These days it takes commitment and discipline to save enough to send your children to college. Consider it a noble sacrifice, research your options, and be inventive.

Chapter 16

Funding Your Retirement

Even if retirement seems like a distant star, planning for retirement has become an issue that few can afford to ignore. Government programs—Social Security, Medicare, and Medicaid—that have traditionally supplemented retirement are rapidly diminishing. Few will receive enough government support to live a comfortable lifestyle, much less take care of their basic needs, including health care. As a single mother, the responsibility to plan for your retirement falls squarely upon your shoulders. The sooner you face reality and begin, the better you will fare in your twilight years.

Take Control of Your Retirement Savings

According to Laurence Kotlikoff and Scott Burns, authors of *The Coming Generational Storm*, a seminal work on the state of America's Medicare, Medicaid, and Social Security systems, America's triad of social systems has the potential to bankrupt the country in the coming century—it's that bad. The country, according to Kotlikoff and Burns, can right the budget gap by increasing federal income taxes by 69 percent, or cutting Social Security and Medicare benefits by 45 percent. The end result will likely be a combination of tax increases and Medicare, Medicaid, and Social Security cuts. Because of the government's large projected budget strains over the next few decades, there is a good chance that if you retire in 2020 or later, you will receive fewer benefits in aggregate from Medicare, Medicaid, and Social Security than your parents did.

FACT

Today, most retired Americans are dependent upon the government, churches, or their families to support them. Most work until retirement age and have little to no money in the bank. Almost a third of all retirement-age people have no substantial accumulated assets, and more than two-thirds of all current retirees rely on Social Security for at least half of their retirement funds.

These are dour statistics and absolute proof that you cannot rely on "traditional" government programs—Social Security, Medicare, and Medicaid—to pay your bills in retirement. Now, more than ever, everyone has to invest for retirement.

The only way to secure your future is to implement a savings plan designated for retirement funds. If your employer offers a retirement plan, jump in with both feet. If not, by all means, open individual retirement accounts (IRAs) and make a commitment to fund them to the maximum amount allowed per year, or at least the maximum you can reasonably afford. You cannot afford to limp along—saving some months, and depleting your savings in others. If you are not contributing regularly to your retirement savings, you need to take control of your spending habits now.

Tax-Advantaged Retirement Savings Accounts

Luckily, you have opportunities—through an employer or individually—to contribute to tax-advantaged savings accounts that allow you to grow your retirement savings tax-free until the time of retirement, or upon early withdrawal. The only drawback is that early withdrawals from the accounts (before you are age 59.5), will be taxed on some or all of the withdrawal, depending upon the type of account. Plus, you will pay a 10 percent early withdrawal penalty.

It's in your best interest to put as much of your retirement savings as you can into tax-advantaged accounts. As shown in the table below, you will have far more money over time in a tax-advantaged account. If your employer matches your contributions, your savings will be that much higher when retirement rolls around.

The following is a table of approximate extra savings accumulated in tax-advantaged savings accounts relative to taxable accounts based on your annual rate of return.

Years until withdrawal	10	20	30	40	50
Rate of return	6%	11%	23%	36%	51%
Rate of return	8%	13%	29%	46%	65%
Rate of return	10%	16%	34%	56%	81%

Keep in mind that a little incremental annual return becomes into a lot of extra account value over time. For instance, given an extra 0.5 percent every year for thirty years (8 percent returns versus 8.5 percent returns), the ending value of a $1,000 investment is $10,063 versus $11,597—a 15 percent difference.

Employer-Sponsored Defined-Contribution Retirement Plans

The majority of American companies still offer "defined-contribution retirement plans" for their employees. But in this era of cutbacks and downsizing, some companies have begun diminishing, or even completely eradicating, retirement benefit plans. So, if you are lucky enough to work for an employer that offers retirement benefits, especially if they offer to match whatever funds you contribute, celebrate your good fortune and pony up as much cash as you can. Let's review the types of employer-sponsored plans, and their benefits or drawbacks (which will be few).

401(k) and 403(b) Plans

401(k) and 403(b) plans are employer-sponsored savings plans that allow you to save current income without paying current taxes on the savings. 401(k) plans are offered by private companies; and 403(b) plans are offered by public, educational, and nonprofit organizations. Employers typically offer 401(k) and 403(b) retirement plans as an employee benefit. Basically, the employer deposits additional income into a 401(k) or 403(b) retirement plan and uses a "plan provider" to invest the funds on your behalf. The income and the return on investment are not taxed until you withdraw the funds. Also, and even more importantly, particularly in the case of 401(k) plans, many employers offer "matching contributions" up to a certain level. For instance, an employer may pay fifty cents for every dollar you put into the plan, until your contributions reach 10 percent of your annual salary. Your employer's matching contributions are also not taxed until you withdraw the retirement funds. Your employer will typically require that you stay with the company for a certain time before your funds are "fully vested," or become 100 percent yours. (Vesting is discussed in detail later in this chapter.)

When you change employers, you can transfer the retirement funds tax-free to a new employer's 401(k), 403(b), a state or local government deferred compensation plan (457 plan), or to a new IRA. Maximum contribution levels can be as high as 100 percent of your income in a given year, up to $40,000—unless your income lands you in the top 20 percent salary-wise at your firm. If so, there are special rules for "highly compensated employees" that become applicable.

FACT

The 403(b) plans are tax-sheltered retirement plans with distinct differences from 401(k) plans. These specialized plans are offered to teachers, hospital workers, and employees of nonprofit organizations. Also, to keep plan costs low, 403(b) plans may offer investment options limited to fixed and variable annuities.

Each plan may offer investing choices—usually stock, bond, and money market mutual funds. However, you can frequently trade individual stocks, bonds, and other mutual funds by using the plan's "brokerage window" option. However, you may be assessed fees for this option.

Plans are regulated by the Employee Retirement Income Security Act (ERISA), which means that employers and financial institutions providing investment options and administration (the "plan provider") have a fiduciary responsibility to act in your best interest. In reality, this means that you will receive at least a summary of the retirement plan and annual account updates. Most plans now go beyond the minimum, allowing Internet access to current plan values and information about investment returns.

These company-sponsored retirement plans have additional very attractive features:

- Employers can direct deposit all contributions—what you don't see, you don't miss, and can't spend.
- Unless you owe money to the IRS, or to an ex-spouse as part of a court-brokered divorce settlement, your creditors generally cannot touch your 401(k) funds if you declare personal bankruptcy.
- You may be able to borrow funds from the plan, allowing you to access the plan's value before retirement (borrowing from retirement plans will be discussed in depth later in this chapter).

Although they are largely good, 401(k) and 403(b) plans do have some limitations. For example, your 401(k) plan may charge administration fees on top of the fees levied by the mutual funds offered within the plan (usually less than 1 percent of your assets), which will reduce your financial returns. Plans with fewer than 100 participants may be assessed "wrap fees," which at the high end can reach 1.5 percent of assets per year—compromising your ability to grow your retirement assets.

Also, your employer may not make its matching contributions until the end of the relevant year's tax-filing deadline, which means you may wait for matching contributions until the second half of the year following the year you made the related contribution. The sooner the funds are deposited, the sooner you begin earning additional money.

Some of the other "negatives" include these:

- If you withdraw funds prior to age 59.5, you will pay a 10 percent early withdrawal penalty, plus taxes on the amount as "ordinary income." The taxes and penalty can easily absorb 40 percent of your funds. At age 59.5, you can withdraw funds without incurring penalties, but you will still owe taxes.
- If you are one of the highest paid employees at your firm, falling within the top 20 percent, you are considered a "highly compensated employee" and are limited to contributing up to 2 percent of your gross income over what the lowest 80 percent of wage earners in your firm contribute on average as a percent of their gross income. For instance, if the lowest-paid 80 percent of employees at your firm contribute an average of 5 percent of income to their 401(k) plans, you would be able, as a highly compensated employee, to contribute 7 percent or less of your gross income.
- If you belong to a union that hasn't specifically negotiated for members' access to the plan, you can't join your employer's 401(k) plan. Some plans also exclude hourly workers, temporary employees, nonresident aliens, and those under twenty-one years of age.

Finally, 401(k) plans are limited by the documents your employer created to govern the plan. Limitations may include your inability to borrow against your account and trade individual stocks and bonds. You can lobby your employer to change the plan's features, but your employer controls the outcome of requests for change.

Vesting Periods

Your 401(k) or 403(b) plan will come with a vesting period, which is the time period over which you earn ownership to the matching contributions your employer has made to the account. Any funds you contribute are automatically yours. There are two types of vesting periods. "Cliff vesting" means you receive full ownership of matching contributions at one time; "graduated vesting" gives you ownership of a certain percent of matching contributions each year.

Typically, graduated vesting means that you acquire ownership in incremental percentages according to the length of employment. Laws regulate the minimum amount of vesting of matching contributions: Cliff vesting must happen within three years of the matching contribution, and graduated vesting must start within two years and be complete within six years.

If your employer offers matching contributions to your 401(k) plan—paying a certain amount into the plan when you contribute—by all means make maximum use of the offer, and continue to deposit beyond the matching number if at all possible. There are few, if any, other safe, easy, and legal ways to earn 10 to 100 percent (depending on the generosity of your employer) on your money.

For instance, your employer may offer a 401(k) plan with graduated vesting that happens evenly over five years. This means that if you leave the employer three years after your employer makes a matching contribution to your 401(k), you are able to transfer 60 percent of the employer's matching contribution to the new 401(k), 403(b), 457, or IRA. Even though you don't have full ownership of matching contributions until they vest, you can invest the contributions as soon as they are deposited in your account.

If your employer terminates its 401(k) plan, if you reach the "normal retirement age" defined in the plan (usually sixty-five years old), if you die or become disabled as defined in the plan, or if your employer lays off 20 percent or more of its employees (including you), your 401(k) funds automatically become fully vested.

Nonmatching Contributions

Some employers offer "nonmatching contributions," which means that they establish a set amount of money, usually as a percentage of your salary, that the employer will deposit into your 401(k) or 403(b) retirement plan each year. Your employer would pay nonmatching contributions whether or not you contributed to your own 401(k) plan. Nonmatching contributions usually take longer to vest—a maximum of five years for cliff vesting plans, and a maximum of seven years for graduated vesting plans.

FACT

According to a 2004 Employee Benefit Research Institute (EBRI) survey, only 40 percent of workers had taken time to estimate their retirement needs; yet 68 percent believed they would have enough money. Workers aged twenty-five to thirty-four save far less than other age groups, and 75 percent of workers under age forty-four reported giving little to no thought to how they will manage their money in retirement.

The maximum amount you can contribute to your 401(k) plan is 15 percent of your annual salary until it reaches a certain number. In 2006, the maximum allowable for employees age forty-nine years and younger was $15,000, and $20,000 for employees fifty or older. Maximums are adjusted for inflation so they should be reviewed annually. If your employer makes a contribution to your 401(k), that amount is not added to your contribution when calculating your maximum annual limit, so by all means, contribute as much as you can afford until you reach the limit. Retirement plans are one place where maxing out your options is one of the smartest financial decisions you can make.

Borrowing from a 401(k) Retirement Plan

Many 401(k) plans allow loans, limited by law to a maximum of 50 percent of the employee's vested balance or $50,000—whichever is lower. Loans must be repaid within five years, usually in equal monthly payments, unless they are for the purchase of your primary residence. If you borrow to buy your primary residence, you may benefit from relatively low loan rates. However, you won't benefit from the tax deductibility of interest on a traditional home loan, and you usually have to repay the loan within twenty-five years.

As long as you can afford payments, these funds could be used to pay off expensive short-term debts, but you will pay a one-time fee when the loan is made (usually about $50), and may pay annual service fees (also around $50). Interest rates are usually "prime rate" plus 1 percent, with payments deducted from your paycheck. If you leave, or are fired by your employer, you will have to pay off the loan. If you aren't able to fully pay off the loan, remaining balances will be treated as an early withdrawal from your 401(k), meaning you will pay "ordinary income" taxes and a 10 percent early withdrawal penalty unless you are over age 59.5. Interest on the loan is payable to your account, but you may earn less on your own payments than you would if the funds remained invested in stock and bonds.

Alternate Employer-Sponsored Plans

Some employers offer different options to bolster your retirement funds. These plans also offer opportunities to substantially increase your retirement savings, so it pays to review the benefits available and to take full advantage of them. Self-employment options are discussed later in the chapter; keep in mind that some small employers may offer the types of plans outlined in that section.

Defined-Benefit Plans

A defined-benefit plan guarantees employees a certain payment schedule when they retire. In the old days, defined benefit plans were considered the Cadillac of retirement plans because the guaranteed payments were likely to be higher than any returns employees might have earned on stock, bond, or other investments. Plus, the employee didn't have to fund the plan, only reap the rewards. If your employer has this type of plan, you may feel lucky—particularly if you will likely work for the same employer until you retire and if the company is rock solid.

Defined benefit payouts usually increase steadily based on the time you've served with the firm and your average, or highest, salary over your last few of years of employment. Most plans offer incentives for employees to work until age sixty-five, and those who don't have reduced payments for the life of the support.

ALERT!

Some companies make matching contributions by offering employees company stock, but you should always be wary about becoming overly invested in one stock, no matter how hot your company is at the moment. If something goes wrong and a lot of your wealth is tied up in company stock, you could lose most, if not all, of your retirement savings.

If you are eligible for a defined benefit plan, it's important to know its vesting schedule. Similar to some tax-advantaged accounts, defined benefit plans have either cliff vesting schedules, which allow you ownership of a certain level of benefits at one time, or graduated vesting, which awards you ownership of the plan's benefits gradually over time. If you change jobs or are fired before some or all of your benefits are fully vested, you will lose any claim to the nonvested benefits.

If your firm offers a defined benefit plan, seek out a human resources person at your firm and ask for clarification on what the specific benefits are and how quickly you become vested. Make sure you know the consequences of changing jobs or losing employment. If you receive an attractive job offer at another firm, make sure you weigh the new retirement plan against the benefits of your current defined benefits plan. Sometimes the defined benefits plan offer "assets" that far outweigh an increased salary being offered elsewhere.

Profit-Sharing Plans

Profit-sharing plans are usually offered along with a 401(k) and allow contributions only from employers. Your employer may contribute between 0 and 25 percent of your income each year to the plan, to a maximum of $44,000 in 2006 (adjusted annually for inflation), with benefits beginning to accrue no later than two years into your employment. Vesting restrictions apply, with the most common vesting schedule being 20 percent per year starting in the second year of employment. Investment earnings grow with taxes deferred until you withdraw funds. You'll be charged a 10 percent penalty for withdrawals from a profit-sharing plan before you reach age 59.5. There are two main differences between this type of plan and a 401(k). The maximum you're allowed to put into profit-sharing, tax-advantaged retirement accounts in total is higher, and profit-sharing plans can have longer vesting periods, up to seven years. They both grow tax-free and are taxed as ordinary income when you withdraw funds from the plan.

Employee Stock Ownership Plans (ESOPs)

With an Employee Stock Ownership Plan, your employer puts shares of company stock into the account. You can become rich through an ESOP if your company's stock does well over time, but you'll also usually end up with an extra-large position in your own company's stock. You have no control over the shares in an ESOP until you've been with the company for a while, usually ten years, and are over age fifty-five. If you've been part of the plan for at least ten years, at fifty-five, you have the option to sell 25 percent of your holdings, and at sixty, you can sell a total of 50 percent for diversification purposes. Contributions aren't counted as income in the year made, and plan assets grow tax-free until you withdraw funds. Tax treatment of withdrawals is complex, so seek help from a tax professional.

Vesting options of ESOPs can be cliff vesting after three years, or graduated vesting for a maximum of six years, starting in year two. Dividends paid on company stock in your account may be paid out to you, in which case they are treated as part of your income. The downside of ESOP plans is that your path to riches—an oversized position in your own company's stock—can lead to a large retirement shortfall if the value of your company's stock doesn't increase at a reasonable rate over a long period of time. Be ready to diversify into stocks and bonds not related to your company's performance when you reach fifty-five and sixty. Remaining invested largely in any one company's stock is very risky.

Contributions aren't included in the employee's income in the year they are made, and value grows tax-free until the employee takes distributions from the plan. At that point distributions are taxed, but the rate varies. Vesting can be "cliff" or "graduated," with a three-year cliff option or six-year graduated option (starting in year two, with five years of 20 percent vesting).

Individual Retirement Plans

Individual retirement plans allow any income-earning citizen to start a tax-advantaged retirement account with many of the same benefits and drawbacks as company-sponsored retirement plans. Whether or not you're covered by a defined benefit plan or by another plan that relies on the trustworthiness of many different managers at your company, individual retirement accounts are a great way to build a separate investment account that puts you in the driver's seat.

Individual Retirement Accounts (IRAs)

Unlike employer-sponsored plans, you are responsible for opening a traditional individual retirement account (IRA) and making annual contributions. Contributions reduce your gross taxable income, and IRA investments grow tax-free until withdrawn, at which point they are taxed as ordinary income. As with 401(k) and related plans, in the event you file for bankruptcy, your IRA assets should be protected from seizure.

Contributions to your IRA can be as high as 100 percent of your gross income, not including investment gains and dividends, up to $4,000 per year if you're under fifty years old, and $5,000 per year if older. These limits increase in 2008 to $5,000 and $6,000, respectively. If you have more than one traditional IRA, these limits apply to the total contributions you make in a given year to the accounts. Contributions can be made to your IRA at any time during the related year through the date for filing your tax return for the year, excluding extensions. The date changes, so always check when your contribution is due early in the year.

If you're single or "head of household" for tax purposes, are covered by an employer's retirement plan, and earn a "modified adjusted gross income" (MAGI) of more than $60,000, you cannot deduct your IRA contributions. Contribution maximums are reduced below the $4,000 to $5,000 threshold when your MAGI is between $50,000 and $60,000 and you're covered by an employer's plan

When computing your IRA maximum, MAGI includes wages, salaries, commissions, self-employment income, alimony, and separate maintenance payments received under a decree of divorce or separate maintenance. Earnings not considered taxable income include earnings from property, interest and dividend income, pension or annuity income, and deferred compensation.

FACT

According to the Federal Reserve, 53 percent of workers aged fifty-five to sixty-four have no retirement savings account. That's zero retirement savings! Of the 47 percent who do have a retirement fund, the median amount saved is $25,000, about a tenth of what you need to be able to retire and live somewhat comfortably, but certainly not luxuriously.

If you change jobs and your new employer doesn't offer a 401(k) retirement plan, you can "roll over" your funds from the previous employee-sponsored retirement plan into a new "Rollover IRA." Rollovers should directly transfer the account funds from the original plan into the new IRA within sixty days. If you don't roll all the assets into the new account within the allotted time, the shortfall will be taxed as ordinary income and you'll face the 10 percent early withdrawal penalty.

Unlike 401(k) plans, you cannot borrow from an IRA, nor can you sell property to an IRA, use the IRA to secure a loan, or use the IRA to purchase property for personal use.

As long as you have earned taxable income in a given year, you can continue to contribute to an IRA until you are age 70.5. You can withdraw funds from your IRA when you reach age 59.5 without incurring a penalty. If you have not begun tapping the account, you are required to start taking distributions from your non-Roth IRA by April 1 of the year following the year you reach age 70.5.

Other IRA qualifications or restrictions include the following:

- If you make more than $110,000, you can't contribute any funds.
- If your modified adjusted gross income is between $95,000 and $110,000 and you file taxes as single, head-of-household, or married filing separately, and you didn't live with your spouse at any time during the year, your maximum contribution is restricted.
- You cannot borrow money from your IRA.
- If you receive an IRA as part of a divorce or separate maintenance decree, the IRA becomes yours, and the transfer is tax-free.
- If you were divorced or legally separated within a year, and didn't remarry before the end of the calendar year (December 31), and you contributed funds to your ex-spouse's IRA that year, you cannot deduct any contributions you made to your ex-spouse's IRA.
- If you inherit an IRA from someone who wasn't your spouse, you can't roll the funds over into your own account. You'll be required to withdraw funds over time, and withdrawn amounts will be taxed as ordinary income.

If you are making your contribution around tax time, it's very important to specify which year the contribution covers. Be sure to tell the brokerage firm that holds your IRA whether it's for the year just passed or the current year. Although many people fall into the habit of only making contributions when submitting taxes days before the IRS deadline, keep in mind that the earlier in the year contributions are invested, the greater financial returns you can potentially earn.

Roth IRA

A Roth IRA has the same basic requirements and restrictions as a traditional IRA but with some crucial differences. With a traditional IRA, you fund the account with pretax dollars (by deducting the contribution) meaning you pay less in taxes up front. With a Roth IRA, you fund the account with post-tax dollars (by not deducting the contribution), which means you'll pay more in immediate taxes. However, unlike a traditional IRA, you will not pay any taxes on Roth IRA interest earnings or capital gains—as long as you do not withdraw funds within five years of depositing them and are over age 59.5 at the time of withdrawal. If you do withdraw funds before those requirements have been met, you will be required to pay a 10 percent early withdrawal penalty and taxes on withdrawn gains and any interest income. The benefits increase substantially if you are young and have many years to acquire gains.

The Difference Between Traditional and Roth IRAs

The amount you can contribute, the early withdrawal penalty, and most other aspects of the Roth IRA are identical to the traditional IRA, with a few exceptions:

- With a traditional IRA, you cannot contribute to IRA accounts past age 70.5; with a Roth IRA, you can continue to contribute to the account at any age.
- With a traditional IRA, you have to begin liquidating the funds by taking at least minimum annual withdrawals at age 70.5; with a Roth IRA, you do not have to begin withdrawing funds at age 70.5.
- With a traditional IRA, early withdrawals (before age 59.5) are taxed as ordinary income and incur a 10 percent penalty on the amount withdrawn; with a Roth IRA early withdrawals (before age 59.5, or less than five years after the account was established) incur a 10 percent penalty and only the gains are taxed.
- With a traditional IRA, upon deposit, you do not pay taxes on contributions; with a Roth IRA, upon deposit, you pay taxes on contributions.
- With a traditional IRA, upon withdrawal after age 59.5, you pay ordinary income taxes on contributions, plus taxes on interest

earnings and capital gains; with a Roth IRA, upon withdrawal at age 59.5, you do not pay taxes on the contributions, interest earnings, or capital gains.

You can convert a traditional IRA into a Roth IRA if your MAGI for Roth IRA purposes is less than $100,000 and you aren't married, filing a separate return. You would pay full ordinary income taxes on your funds in the year of conversion, but you wouldn't have to pay again when you withdraw after you reach age 59.5. It may be worthwhile to convert to a Roth IRA if you have a year with low earnings or large tax deductions and a relatively small traditional IRA, so you can take advantage of your personal exemptions and deductions. However, the taxes you'll incur are high enough that if your account is substantial, you should consult with a tax professional to see whether conversion of your IRA to a Roth IRA is best for you.

Using Your Roth IRA to Pay for College

If you are at least age 59.5 and have had your Roth IRA for at least five years, you can withdraw contribution funds and interest earnings or capital gains tax-free and penalty-free to fund your child's education.

"Qualified higher education expenses" or QHEEs consist of the following: tuition, fees, books, supplies, and equipment required for the enrollment or attendance of a student at an eligible educational institution, as well as for special needs costs incurred by, or for, special needs students in connection with their enrollment or attendance. The qualifying student needs to be enrolled at least half time. Room and board constitute QHEEs.

However, if you are not age 59.5, or have not had your Roth IRA for at least five years, you can use your Roth IRA funds for "qualified higher education expenses" (QHEEs) without incurring the early 10 percent withdrawal penalty as long as enough QHEEs are paid out of pocket. QHEEs can be paid tax and penalty-free using a Roth IRA to the extent that they are not covered by payments from Coverdell ESAs, tax-free parts of scholarships and fellowships, pell grants, employer-provided educational assistance plans, veterans' educational assistance plans, and any other tax-free payment (other than a gift or inheritance) at any age. Taxes are owed under any circumstance when money is withdrawn before age 59.5 from your Roth IRA.

If you will be age 59.5 or older when your child attends college or graduate school, saving for your children's education in your Roth IRA might make sense. If you withdraw funds at age 59.5 or later and the funds are used for qualified college or graduate school expenses—tuition, mandatory fees and equipment, books, and supplies—the withdrawal won't be taxed. You can also withdraw funds from your Roth IRA tax-free if you are at least age 59.5 and paying for your own college or graduate school expenses. To qualify for favorable tax treatment, withdrawn funds must be used to pay for expenses at a school authorized to disburse financial aid. (See *www .fafsa.ed.gov* for a list of eligible schools.)

Since mothers tend to be overly generous in regard to their children, funding a 529 plan or a Coverdell account is a more direct and conflict-free way to make sure that your children will be able to afford higher education without draining your retirement resources.

As always, if you withdraw funds from your Roth IRA before you reach age 59.5, you'll owe ordinary income taxes on the share of earnings that you withdraw from the account. Basically, Roth IRA contributions are funds that are contributed post-taxes so you never owe taxes on the contributions, but if you withdraw any funds prior to age 59.5, or prior to having the Roth IRA five years, you do owe taxes on the investment gains. However, if the withdrawn amount is spent on qualified educational expenses, the standard 10 percent early withdrawal fee does not apply. The amount of earnings attributable to early Roth IRA withdrawals is taxed at high ordinary income rates, making early Roth IRA withdrawals a bad choice in most cases, even when paying for college expenses.

Since funds withdrawn from a Roth IRA count as income on financial aid applications and are weighed more heavily in financial aid formulas than your assets, your child may not receive as much financial aid as she would if you weren't adding Roth IRA funds to the mix. Also keep in mind that using Roth IRA funds to pay for your child's college expenses means you may eventually have to choose between keeping your retirement funds sufficient to cover your needs or funding your child's education.

Self-Employed/Small-Business-Owner Retirement Plans

If you have a highly profitable business, recent laws have created fantastic retirement fund options that are a real boon for accumulating wealth in your retirement accounts. On the flip side, as a business owner, the total responsibility for securing your retirement falls on your shoulders. Luckily, you have several options that will allow you to deposit more money into your retirement accounts than most.

HR 10 Plans

HR 10 Plans are a form of defined-contribution plans, a class of "qualified plan" available as an option for the self-employed. You can create a "money purchase" HR 10 plan that requires an inflexible, defined percent of your business income saved per year, or a "profit-sharing" plan that allows changes in the amount of business income you pay into your—and your employees'—plan accounts. You must be self-employed to be eligible for an HR 10 retirement savings plan—meaning you are a sole proprietor, a partner in a business, or own an LLP or LLC. You are not eligible if you own an "S" or "C" corporation.

You must declare the percentage of your income you'll put into a "money purchase" HR 10 plan the year the plan is created; as long as the plan exists, you must stick to your investment target. You are able to change the percentage of your business income that you save if you have a "profit-sharing" HR 10.

If you have employees and you contribute to your own HR 10 plan in a year, you generally must contribute to the HR 10 plan accounts of all your employees. If you retain control of HR 10 plan investing and don't do a good job, you can be held responsible for breach of fiduciary duty over your employees' retirement funds, something you want to avoid at all costs.

FACT

If you are eligible, you can contribute more money to an HR 10 plan than to other tax-advantaged plans. For 2006, you can contribute up to $44,000, or 25 percent of self-employment income, for a "money purchase plan" or up to $44,000, or 20 percent of your business income, for a "profit-sharing plan."

If you qualify, you can maximize contributions to tax-advantaged retirement accounts by contributing a moderate level of business income to your HR 10 each year, and adding more to tax-advantaged IRAs when you have extra funds.

Retirement Plan Contribution Maximums, 2006 to 2008				
	Traditional and Roth IRA*	**401(k)**, 403(b), 457 Plans**	**SIMPLE IRA**	**Keogh****
Less than 50 years old	$4,000	$15,000	$10,000	$44,000
Over 50 years old	$5,000	$20,000	$12,500	$44,000

* In 2008, traditional and Roth IRA maximums will change to $5,000 and $6,000 for individuals less than and greater than fifty years old, respectively.

** HR 10 and 401(k) plan maximums change with inflation every year

Savings Incentive Match Plan for Employees (SIMPLE)

The Savings Incentive Match Plan for Employees (SIMPLE) can be set up either as an IRA or 401(k) in the name of each employee covered by the plan. SIMPLE plans have lower contribution limits than 401(k) plans (usually 1 to 3 percent of an employee's income), but administration tends to be less costly to plan members. SIMPLE plans are only for employers with 100 or fewer workers who earn at least $5,000 in a given year and who aren't covered by another retirement plan.

SIMPLE plans have' other benefits and limitations, including these:

- Maximum contributions in 2006 were $10,000 for those under age fifty, and $12,500 for those over age fifty.
- Employee and employer matching contributions are put into the account on a pretax basis—no taxes are paid until you withdraw funds.
- If other employees receive funds for the year, all employees who earned more than $5,000 in a given year must generally receive an employer's matching contribution.
- Matching contributions are required to be either dollar-for-dollar up to a maximum of 3 percent of the employee's total pay, or 2 percent of the employee's pay, whether she contributes to the plan or not.
- All contributions vest immediately in a SIMPLE IRA and a SIMPLE 401(k).
- Early withdrawals are treated as ordinary income and incur a 10 percent penalty. In the first two years of deposits, you would incur a penalty of 25 percent, plus pay ordinary income tax.

Simplified Employee Pension (SEP) IRA

A simplified employee pension (SEP) IRA is a tax-advantaged retirement plan option for the self-employed, typically used by those with fewer than ten employees. This option is perhaps most advantageous for sole proprietors or small partnerships who want maximum benefits and limited paperwork.

As a business owner, the contributions you make to your profit-sharing SEP IRA can go as high as 20 percent of your self-employment net income (defined as income less expenses, one half your self-employment tax, and the deduction for the contribution to your own SEP IRA), up to $44,000.

However, calculating your SEP IRA personal maximum contribution limit is tricky. The IRS provides two separate forms on its Web site (online at *www .irs.gov*) to facilitate the process. Some SEP IRA limitations and benefits include the following:

- Contributions are always deductible, no matter what your income or whether you participate in other retirement plans.
- Employer contributions to employees' SEP IRA accounts are typically discretionary until they have been employed for three out of the last five years.
- Distributions from SEP IRAs are generally subject to the same tax rules as those for traditional IRAs. (See IRS publication 560 for more details, available online at *www.irs.gov*.)

Be aware that if you establish a SEP IRA for your small business and have employees over the age of twenty-one who have worked for you for at least three of the last five years, you will have to contribute an equal percentage to their accounts. For example, if your eligible income was $50,000 and you opt for a 10 percent contribution, you will have to deposit $3,000 into the SEP IRA of an employee earning $30,000. Also, whatever funds you deposit into an employee's SEP IRA are immediately 100 percent vested, which means they can quit and take their funds one month after you open their account.

Chapter 17

Maximizing Your Tax Advantages

Being a single parent has its challenges, and most of them leave holes in your pocketbook, but it also has a few well-deserved tax advantages. Without going into IRS speak, this chapter explains the tax advantages unique to single parents. However, to make sure you are maximizing your dollars, you'll also want to consult with a tax advisor or review generic tax laws annually. What you don't want to do is to miss out on tax breaks that can bolster your savings, your retirement plan, or your child's college funds.

Special Tax Breaks for Single Parents

The tax code is complex, but it's not impossible to decipher, especially when you use a tax preparation software package like TurboTax (used by many financial professionals), or rely on a tax preparation professional. You should know that any alimony you receive is taxable. Child support payments you receive are not taxed, nor are they deductible for the person who pays them.

Alimony you receive won't have taxes withheld from the gross amount, so you usually need to have your employer increase your tax withholding or else pay quarterly or annual estimated tax payments to avoid a fine from the IRS at the end of the year. You are required to pay estimated tax payments if the amount of taxes withheld for you during the year is less than either of these two amounts: 90 percent of the tax shown on your current year's tax return, or 100 percent of the tax shown on your prior year's tax return. You can calculate your estimated taxes for the year with IRS Form 1040-ES.

Although you cannot deduct the legal fees and court costs for actually obtaining a divorce, you may be able to deduct the cost of legal advice related to taxes or legal fees paid to negotiate alimony. You may also be able to deduct the cost of home appraisal, actuaries, and accountants whom you used to obtain income, such as through alimony, or tax advantages. IRS Publication 504, "Divorced or Separated Individuals," provides guidelines.

You may be wondering whether you should itemize your expenses or take your standard deduction. In general, itemization will save you money if you have large medical and dental expenses, home mortgage interest, casualty and theft losses, job expenses, a small home-based business, or have made large charitable contributions during the year. The IRS publishes Form 1040, "Schedule A & B Instructions," every year to clarify what payments can be included in your itemized deductions.

The tax code has two options for single parents that can lower the taxes you owe. You can file as "head of household" or as "qualifying widow with a dependent child." Both options substantially raise the income bars that put you in higher income tax brackets. In 2006, single filers earning more than $30,651 typically fell in the 25 percent tax bracket. (You'll need to check this annually.) When filing as "head of household," a single mother has to earn $41,051, and a "qualifying widow with dependent child" has to earn $61,301, before getting higher "standard deductions." In 2006, for example, single filers could claim a $5,150 standard deduction; "head of household" filers could claim $7,550; and "qualifying widow with dependent child" filers could claim $10,300.

To file as "head of household," you must be "supporting" your child on your own, which means you are either unmarried or living apart from your spouse and filing separate tax returns. Child support payments are not considered taxable income; however, a single mother would have to pay more than half of the child's expenses during the year, including child support payments received, which most are. To file as "head of household," you and your children must meet the following requirements:

- The child must be your biological, step, foster, or adopted child.
- The child must live with you at least 50 percent of the year. (If she attends school away from home or travels for long periods, but you are still supporting her, she qualifies.)
- The child cannot provide more than half of support (from trust funds, earned income, or inheritances). Check with the IRS if you are unsure about this provision.
- The child must be under the age of nineteen, though there are exceptions: If she is a full-time student under the age of twenty-four; if she is permanently and totally disabled; if she is not claiming herself on a separate tax return.
- You must pay more than half of the cost of maintaining a home for yourself and your child for the year.

If your child doesn't meet all of the above requirements, but she does meet the requirements for the dependent exemption (see "The Dependent Exemption" later in this chapter), you may still be able to file as "head of household." Consult with a tax advisor or review IRS Publication 501, "Exemptions, Standard Deduction and Filing Information."

To file as a "qualifying widow with dependent child," your spouse must have died within the past two years or within the past three years ended December 31 of the tax year for which you're filing. Your children must also meet the following requirements:

- You can claim the dependent exemption for your child.
- You were entitled to file a joint return with your spouse in the tax year that your spouse died (even if you didn't actually file a joint return that year).
- You did not remarry before the end of that tax year.
- You paid more than half of the cost for maintaining a home for yourself and your child for the entire tax year.

You can file a joint tax return in the year your spouse dies and then file as "qualifying widow" for the next two years.

QUESTION?

What is the Earned Income Tax Credit and how do I qualify?
The Earned Income Tax Credit (EITC) offers tax credit to financially challenged parents. If your earned income is less than $31,030 with one dependent child, and $35,263 with two children or more, you may qualify. A worksheet for figuring this credit is included in the book of instructions that accompanies the standard 1040 tax forms. The IRS will also calculate it for you, or you can consult with a tax advisor.

Tax Deductions Versus Tax Credits

Here are some basic tax phrases that will assist you in understanding how each of the following tax breaks will most benefit you. A tax deduction is a reduction in your taxable earned income. If your taxable income is $30,000, you can deduct the $3,300 dependent exemption from that income to reduce your taxable income to $26,700.

A tax credit is a post-tax deduction in the amount of taxes you owe. If you owed $3,500 in taxes, you could use the child tax credit and deduct $1,000 per child from the amount of taxes to be paid, reducing your taxes to $2,500 if you had one child, to $1,500 if you had two, and so on.

A refundable tax credit occurs when you overpaid your taxes throughout the year. You can add the refundable tax credit to the amount you're owed for overpaying taxes for the year. You can even get a refund for your tax credits if you owed no taxes for the year. Hypothetically, if a single mother with one qualifying dependent child files and owes $0 before the credit, she could possibly be refunded $1,000, but the IRS requires a few conditions be met before a refund is granted. Form 8812, "Additional Child Tax Credit," will help you calculate the actual refund and whether you qualify.

The Dependent Exemption

Regardless of whether you itemize your deductions, the dependent exemption offered qualified parents the opportunity to claim $3,300 per child in 2006. When you add a new child to your family, you can claim the exemption for that year, even if the child was born or adopted on New Year's Eve. Typically, the parent with whom the child lives for more than 50 percent of the time claims the dependent exemption. If you share joint physical custody, some parents agree to alternate the deduction from year to year.

FACT

As of 2006, the federal government began phasing out higher income restrictions on dependent exemptions. By 2010, regardless of your income, all parents will be able to claim full personal and dependent exemptions. Until then, if your adjusted gross income exceeds $150,500 (single) or $188,150 (head of household), you can check with the IRS to see if you are now eligible for a partial exemption.

However, it behooves you to make sure you are not surrendering this tax asset too quickly. After a divorce or separation, fathers generally have higher incomes than mothers. If you didn't negotiate who would take advantage of the dependent exemption at the time of your divorce or separation, it generally makes sense for you to receive the deduction.

If the father balks, use it as a bargaining (but not a punishing) chip. No matter what he thinks, the reality may well be that you earn far less, have fewer deductions, and provide more than 75 percent of your children's care. The mere fact that he has a higher income means that you need the deduction more than he does. It might also make sense to review the situation annually. If you really don't need the deduction, offer it to him in return for depositing half of his savings into your child's college funds.

ALERT!

If you are rightfully entitled to the dependent exemption, your former partner cannot use it unless you file IRS Form 8332, "Release of Claim to Exemption." This form allows you to designate whether you are transferring the exemption for one year or for another length of time.

The dependent exemption is a valuable tax asset and something you should do your best to use. If you must surrender it to the children's father, use it as bargaining chip, as mentioned above, asking that he deposit half of his savings into your child's college funds.

To compute the value of the dependent exemption to your former spouse, make sure you multiply the exemption by his tax bracket. For example, if the father's income will be taxed in the 25 percent bracket, he would save $825 (based on $3,300) per child. If your income falls in the 10 percent bracket, you would save $330 (based on $3,300). Base your negotiation on what he would save, in the first example, pegging $413 into your children's college funds.

To qualify for the dependent exemptions, all of the following requirements for eligibility must be met:

- The child must be your biological, step, foster, or adopted child. There are exceptions. If you are providing more than half of her support, if she lives with you the entire year, if she meets the other requirements, and if no one else is claiming her as an exemption, you may still be eligible for the exemption. Also, a child placed for adoption but whose adoption has not been finalized is eligible. (Consult with a tax advisor or call the IRS to confirm.)

- The child must live with you at least 50 percent of the year. (If a child is born at any time during the year, she is eligible for the exemption. If she attends boarding school, but you are still supporting her, she qualifies. Other exceptions may exist; call the IRS to confirm eligibility.)

- The child is under the age of nineteen. There are exceptions: if she is a full-time student under the age of twenty-four; if she is permanently and totally disabled; if she is not claiming herself on a separate tax return.

- The child must be a U.S. citizen or a resident of the United States, Canada, or Mexico.

- Your adjusted gross income must be within the limits established by that year's tax code (less than $150,500 in 2006).

The IRS provides free booklets annually that provide eligibility guidelines. You can find them online at *www.irs.gov* or by calling your local IRS office.

FACT

Even if you are receiving a refund, you may be able to add a portion of the child tax credit to the refund amount, increasing the amount you'll receive from the IRS. To determine your eligibility and compute your amount, obtain Form 8812, "Additional Child Tax Credit," and the complementary IRS booklet. To increase the benefit, add the amount gained to your child's college fund account.

Child Tax Credits

Regardless of whether you itemize your deductions, and regardless of whether you take the dependent exemption, the child tax credit allows qualified parents to subtract a set amount ($1,000 per child from 2006 to 2010, slated to fall to $500 thereafter) from their total tax bill.

To qualify for the child tax, you must meet all the requirements for the dependent exemption, with two changes: the child must be under the age of seventeen, and your income must be within the limits established by that year's tax code. As your income increases, the exemption decreases proportionately. If your modified adjusted gross income exceeds $75,000 (as of 2006), you are not eligible. To maximize this advantage, make sure to review the annual IRS *Child Tax Credit* booklet, or ask your tax advisor.

Child Care and Dependent Care Tax Breaks

If you qualify, you have additional tax credits available. Basically, a child care tax credit allows you to deduct 20 to 35 percent (depending upon your adjusted gross income) of the first $3,000 you spend per dependent child, per year for qualified child care. A dependent care account allows your employer to set aside a certain amount in pretax dollars to be spent on dependent care per year; this amount cannot be greater than your earned income for the year. You can use both credits to reduce your tax bill, but sometimes the greater benefit comes from selecting one over the other. (See Dependent Care Accounts later in this chapter for more information on how these tax breaks compare.) The IRS outlines its requirements in Publication 503, "Child and Dependent Care Expenses." Basically, the qualifications that must be met for both are as follows:

- The child must be considered your dependent.
- The child must be under the age of thirteen or physically or mentally not able to care for herself.
- The parent must work part-time or full-time outside of the home or be a full-time student.
- The childcare provider must be a licensed day care provider, preschool provider, or legal nanny, and must not be someone you can claim as a dependent. The caretaker can be over eighteen years old and a child of the taxpayer if not a dependent, however. Other rules

apply if the father of the child is paid—IRS Publication 503 has more information.

- The time spent must be used working, looking for work, or attending school full-time.
- The payment must be for child care only—not for household chores.

Child Care Tax Breaks

The total amount of your child care credit cannot exceed your earned income for the year unless you have significant physical or mental limitations that impair your ability to work or study. If you have no income but are a full-time student, you may still be eligible for a child care tax break of $250 for one child or $500 if you have more than one child.

Before hiring a caretaker or placing your child in a day care center, make sure that you acquire the necessary information. Without proper documentation, your payments aren't likely to qualify for this tax break. If the child care provider is a tax-exempt church or school, you can still claim the tax break by writing "tax exempt" in the proper space on the tax form.

Preschool expenses qualify for the child care tax breaks, but once a child enters first grade, you cannot include educational expenses, such as a private school. Unless they are full-time students, stay-at-home mothers are not eligible for child care tax breaks.

Note that you will be required to provide the name, address, and Social Security number or employer or taxpayer ID of the child care provider, as well as the exact amount paid on the IRS Form W-10, "Dependent Care Provider's Identification and Certification."

Dependent Care Accounts

If your income puts you in the 28 percent tax bracket and your employer offers the option, you may want to opt for a dependent care account in addition to, or in lieu of, the child care tax break. Note that these accounts must be established by an employer and are limited to your earned income. They also involve planning and paperwork, but if you earn enough money, they can be well worth the effort. For instance, if you set aside $2,500 and are in the 25 percent tax bracket, you immediately save $625 in federal taxes. You also pay less in Medicare and Social Security taxes and may pay fewer state and local taxes.

If your employer offers a dependent care account, jump on board, but make sure you understand the following basics before establishing the account:

- Your child care provider must meet the qualifications described in the preceding section.
- You should fund the account based on the maximum you are allowed to deduct. The IRS determines the maximum amount that an employer can set aside. Though this amount changes from year to year, it can never exceed your earnings in any given year.
- Budget carefully. Any funds not spent will revert to your employer at the end of the year.
- Save your receipts and submit them to your employer promptly for reimbursement.
- Review, make any adjustments, and, if it's working for you, make sure you re-enroll annually.

Dependent care account contributions are deducted from the permitted child care base of $3,000 per child. In some cases, it might make more sense to use only the child care tax break. For example, if you contributed $1,500 to a dependent care account, you would deduct that from your $3,000 base. That would leave you with $1,500, of which 20 percent, or $300, is deductible. If you eliminated the dependent care account, on the other hand, 20 percent of $3,000 leaves $600 deductible.

Health Care Tax Breaks

As a single mother, you have basically two options. You can open a flexible health spending account funded by pretax dollars through your employer, or, if your employer doesn't offer comprehensive health coverage, you can open a health savings account using pretax dollars to cover a high deductible or to pay health care expenses. If you make a lot of money, or if you or your children have extreme medical expenses, you may be among those rare people who benefit from medical and dental deductions. Even though health care premiums are probably your highest medical expense, you cannot use health savings accounts or flexible health spending accounts to cover their costs. Here's what you *can* do.

Flexible Health Spending Accounts

If your employer offers health spending accounts, you can set aside pretax income to cover your out-of-pocket expenses, including deductibles, co-pays, prescriptions, over-the-counter medications, humidifiers, eyeglasses, and so on. Your benefits administrator can provide you with a list of covered expenses.

Typically, you make payments to the account throughout the year, but you are not restricted as to when you can submit expenses for reimbursement. If you have a dental procedure in February that will be covered by the $4,000 (maximum for 2005) you allocated for the year, you can submit the bill in March and be reimbursed promptly. However, you will need to keep meticulous records so that you don't exceed your budget, and you'll want to calculate the annual contribution carefully—any funds not used at the end of the year are returned to your employer.

Health Savings Accounts

If you do not have employer-sponsored comprehensive health insurance, or if the only health insurance you have has a high deductible ($2,000 minimum for a family), you can open a health savings account that will offer tax breaks. These accounts have distinct advantages:

- You are allowed to contribute the amount of your deductible, or $5,250 for a family, whichever is smaller, into a savings account every year.
- The amount you invest can be entered as a deduction on your tax return.
- Any payments for medical or dental care are claimed as an exemption on your tax returns. (If you spend the money for nonhealth related expenses, you'll owe income taxes on the amount withdrawn and may pay a penalty of around 10 percent.)
- Monies in the account earn tax-free interest.
- You can carry balances into the next year.

For more information and to find a bank near you to open an account, go online to *www.hsainsider.com*. You can use checks or withdraw funds to pay any expenses, but you will need to keep all receipts.

Medical and Dental Deductions

You can only benefit from these deductions when your out-of-pocket medical or dental expenses are greater than 7.5 percent of your adjusted gross income and you itemize your deductions. You can read more about all of your options in IRS Publication 969, "Health Savings Accounts and Other Tax-Favored Plans."

Ways to Maximize Your Tax Advantages

In general, you also need to maximize your tax advantages by adopting some—and preferably all—of the following practices:

- Familiarize yourself with tax laws and stay current on annual updates.
- In late December, take time to plan your upcoming financial year to gain maximum benefit. Planning for major expenses by opening health savings accounts, for example, or adjusting exemptions, as needed.
- Double-check all itemized deductions to make sure you aren't missing a legal deduction. If you haven't checked past reports in the last three years, take them to a tax consultant for review. You may be

able to obtain a refund if any legal deductions have been missed, such as an earned income credit.

- Hire a professional accountant or tax consultant (such as seasonal firms that specialize in tax preparation) every year, or at least every two to three years, to make sure you are not overpaying taxes. If your income tax returns aren't complicated, costs will range from $100 to $150 and are well worth the price.

- Don't overpay. If you ended up with a large return, you overpaid your taxes in the past year and allowed Uncle Sam to earn the interest that could have been fattening up your savings account. Consider claiming more exemptions on your W-4.

- Avoid last-minute surprises. If you underpaid and owed taxes upon filing, consider claiming fewer exemptions or open a savings account allocated to paying taxes upon filing so that you'll earn interest and avoid a last-minute crunch to fund a tax payment.

- Keep meticulous records throughout the year. Set up a filing system to accumulate and organize all pertinent documents and receipts. Take time to make notations on receipts and match up receipts with credit card or bank statements.

- Acquire a home equity loan for major purchases, such as a car or home remodeling. Home equity loan interest is tax deductible, but it only makes sense when used for a "good debt" (as described in Chapter 6), and not when used for disposable goods like clothing, televisions, or vacations.

- Pay yourself first! Make contributions to your retirement plan early in the year so that you accumulate interest throughout the year and avoid that mad April 15th dash to the finish line. Waiting until April 15th means you lose fifteen months of interest and appreciation.

- Don't report income that is tax exempt, such as gifts (in 2006, up to $12,000 from one person), inheritances (under $2,000,000 until 2008), group life insurance payments deducted/withheld by an employer, and child support payments.

These are just a few of the tips you can use to lower your tax nut, but it is highly advisable to research your particular circumstances and to consult with a tax advisor if you have complicated or confusing questions.

Chapter 18

Teaching Your Children about Money

Along with everything else, the responsibility for teaching your children about money falls to you. Your children need to know how to earn money, how to make responsible decisions about money, and how to manage, save, and invest money. Unless you make concerted efforts, their thoughts, ideals, and goals will arise from what you show them through your actions, rather than what would help them avoid your mistakes. They will unconsciously adapt—unless you work to raise their consciousness and to impart wisdom and clarity on the subject.

The Benefits of Starting Early

Now that you have probed your own attitudes and are becoming fiscally conscious, it's time to ponder a desirable, intentioned financial education for your children. If you wait until they are older to teach them about money, not only do you risk their resistance, you will have missed many opportunities to help them form healthy attitudes and habits. Obviously, you'll want to tailor the lessons to their age, but by all means start early!

For instance, as soon as a child can count, you could introduce her to money concepts by playing games with pennies, nickels, dimes, and quarters. Preschool children aren't ready to add or subtract, but you can teach them the names of the coins and play counting games by spreading five pennies, three dimes, and two quarters across the table and asking them to pick up combinations of particular coins. Board games such as Chutes and Ladders and Candyland also reinforce counting.

Around age three or four, you can teach your child to "play store" by letting her exchange paper money for goods or having her find coupons in the Sunday sale flyers for foods she likes. At the grocery store, give her the responsibility for finding the matching food and handing the coupons to the cashier. For children under the age of five or six, you are basically teaching counting skills and planting a seed that will help them understand basic economic and financial concepts down the road.

Around the age of six, children are ready to learn mathematical concepts. According to scientists, they have formed a "mental number line" that allows them to distinguish between sizes and numbers, which means the more complicated construct of increasing numbers and quantities are now interlinked. This "conceptual construct" helps them compare numbers.

By the time they are eight, children are beginning to understand the dynamics of subtraction and addition required to make change. It's a good time to provide a weekly allowance that they earn by performing simple chores and that they use to buy treats or toys. Start small and adjust the amount of work and the amount of money upward as they mature. It's also a good time to take them to a bank and explain how adults work to accumulate the money that goes into their checking or savings accounts, how banks work, and how ATMs work. Many children presume ATMs magically dispense money and that you can just withdraw whatever you need; it's a good idea to give them a very basic introduction to reality-based economics. As you increase their allowance, open a savings account for them and tell them that 10 percent of their allowance will now go into this account so that it will grow. Show them the statements and explain how their money is growing.

How to Develop a Wealth Consciousness

Although you want your children to become financially and psychologically independent—and to do well in life—it's also important to teach them that success is not measured by the amount of money you make, or by consumption. If you want your children to develop positive values, teach them to measure their success by these standards:

- How they feel about themselves.
- Whether they are achieving the goals that are most important to them.
- How they operate in the world.
- The values they hold.
- How they support and encourage those around them.
- Their passion for the work they do and the life they live.

If you teach your children to measure their worth in terms of the security and happiness they generate for themselves and those around them, and teach them savvy money-management skills, they will live a wealthy life—rich with promise, dreams, and fulfillment of their dreams. If you want them to be wealthy, teach them to constantly ask themselves some deep questions. Are they are growing, learning, exploring, and enjoying life? Are they more focused on feeding their souls than feeding their piggy banks?

Are they responsible citizens who manage their lives well and contribute to society? If they can answer with a resounding "yes," they will be on the right track because these practices will create true wealth.

It is also very important to teach children how to earn, manage, save, intelligently spend, and invest money. Rather than teaching them to become top-notch consumers, why not teach them to become investment-savvy owners? Even a young child can understand that owning a piece of FAO Schwartz will make her richer than buying toys. You can order a stock certificate and have it framed for her so that she can show their friends that she owns a piece of the rock.

Imagine what savvy investors your children could become if they learned this simple lesson early in life, and perhaps developed a passion for ownership. Do you want your children to have a house overflowing with possessions, or do you want them to have a portfolio of investments that will secure their future? Be part of the solution, and give them a head start on life and wealth.

As they mature, maximize opportunities to teach your children invaluable lessons about the stock market, mutual funds, IRA accounts, employer-sponsored retirement accounts, and other long-term investments—bonds, houses, and income property, for example—as well as the processes of reinvesting dividends and monitoring growth. Some mutual funds companies offer "young-investor" funds that offer opportunities for children to save, invest, and learn how to handle money and make smart investments.

American Express's IDS New Dimensions, Monetta, USAA First Start Growth, and Stein-Roe's Young Investor are among the mutual funds that invest in child-friendly companies and provide educational opportunities that make learning about money fun . . . and profitable! It's never too early for a mutual fund.

Also snag opportunities to teach your children how to start and run their own businesses. Start with a lemonade stand and have them figure out how much it will cost to buy the lemonade mix, paper cups, and marketing materials, such as magic markers and posters. Then help them decide what they have to sell each cup for to earn a profit. As they grow, you can go more in-depth with the projects and the execution—teaching them about product development, planning, labor and material costs, and how to earn a profit. Making beaded jewelry, stationery, or woven string bracelets that they market through a handcrafted stand parked at the edge of your driveway can result in profit and confidence. Starting a mowing business, taking on a paper route, or conducting garage sales are all jobs that can teach your children useful skills. Grab any opportunity to use real situations to broaden their understanding. And always encourage them to think outside the box—you'll be amazed at how quickly they formulate ideas and get excited about them.

This kind of creativity will foster their development on many levels, giving them an edge in deciding what interests them, what their natural talents are, what needs to be done to earn a living, how they want to spend their days, and what skills they need to develop to succeed at their chosen profession. Guide them, but also allow them to experience the trials and tribulations, the successes and the failures. Teach them the value of seeing money as a commodity that they can use to invest in their own futures, and increasingly hand over the financial reins as they grow.

Why Allowances Must Be Earned

Parents who don't require their children to earn an allowance set up a precedent for feeling entitled that will come back around to bite those lovely, spoiled children when they reach adulthood. When you pay your children an allowance based on the energy they are willing to invest to complete tasks, you teach them lessons that sharpen their thinking. Moreover, you teach them methods of earning, saving, investing, and spending that will enrich them all their lives. Even if you begin allowances in first or second grade, it's good to tie them to the successful completion of simple "jobs" around the house. Obviously, expectations will rise as the child's ability to contribute—and to understand the game—increases. Some valuable lessons include these:

- The number of hours they have to work to afford desired items
- The ability to spend money only when they have it
- To necessity of saving for what they really want

By the time they are nine or ten, transition into budgeting basics. For example, sit down with your children and establish parameters for what you will provide as a parent and what they will now be expected to buy with their allowance. Children need to understand that you will pay for their needs (housing, clothing, food, education, medical care, and so on), but that their wants (such as video games, toys, videos, or branded clothing) should be earned and paid for with their allowance.

ALERT!

Advertisers know their market, how susceptible children can be, and how to play upon your desire to please your children. From 1980 on, advertising directed toward children has increased more than tenfold, jumping from $100 million a year to $10 billion a year.

In addition to matching their savings, you might also agree to pay one-half of the cost of educational toys or hobbies but require them to buy their own recreational video games, toys, DVDs, and CDs. Once you set clear parameters, it's important to adhere to them—doing so teaches your maturing children these important lessons:

- How to connect energy expended with compensation
- How to delay gratification, and why it's wise to do so
- How to distinguish between wants and needs
- How to set priorities and make difficult choices
- How to learn from their mistakes
- How to determine an item's real value
- How to match their expectations to their income
- How to care for expensive investments
- How to put the brakes on when they fall short

Since they are on the brink of being responsible for money management—living without a parent's safety net—teenagers require a sharper learning curve. It's time to teach them how to truly live with within their means and to make wise financial decisions. Use your newly polished skills to help them create both a budget and financial goals, and then allow them to make mistakes (within reason) and to suffer the consequences. Even though you are still paying for their needs, you can allocate a set figure to be spent on clothing and shoes and then give them responsibility for making purchases. Before they begin, help them compose a list of what they need (two pairs of jeans, two pairs of shoes, three blouses, a jacket) and then calculate the costs. When you've arrived at a fair estimate, you could offer to let them keep any savings they generate by comparison shopping, reordering priorities, or lowering their expectations.

They're Never Too Young to Save

As soon as children spot shiny abandoned pennies, it's time to find an inexpensive, unbreakable piggy bank—you can have them paint a plastic bottle, for instance—and encourage them to drop the pennies into it. They will love seeing the pennies accumulate, and when they've filled the bank, you can show them how their savings will buy a treat. This helps them learn a sense of value and the benefits of saving.

Older children will want to enjoy the benefits of cash in their pockets, but urge them to save a minimum of 10 percent and offer to match whatever they save—they might just go for 25 percent. Use a visual chart to build excitement and reinforce good savings habits.

If you really want to wow a preteen, show her how depositing $1,000 in her savings account and adding $50 per month ($25 of her savings matched by $25 of your money) will compound over the next decade, earning her $8,815 for college. This assumes that the account returns 4 percent per year—if you take some risk and invest, making 8 percent per year, that figure would be $11,165.

The Pros and Cons of Credit Cards for Kids

For the sake of convenience, parents sometimes thrust credit cards into their children's hands. However, unless that parent shows the child the credit card bill when it arrives and requires the child to pay all, or a significant portion, the parent is not helping the child learn about fiscal responsibility. If your child is using credit cards, he or she needs to know that when a bill arrives, the inability to pay it in full leads to additional (and substantial) charges, and that someone has to pay real dollars to make it go away. If you don't do this, your children may think the balance magically disappears or that they can continue to run up charges without incurring consequences.

FACT

In 1999, more than 150,000 teenagers filed for bankruptcy—constituting more than one out of fourteen total filings in 1999. Recent studies have shown that more than a third of the nation's college students have four credit cards and average $2,800 in charges. In 2000, a third of all undergraduates had more than four credit cards.

Advantages of Credit Cards for Kids

Although many parents do give their children credit cards, the list of good reasons to do so is actually very short. The only pros to children having credit cards are these:

- They can be used in emergency situations.
- They can be used as a learning tool.

Since your children will be offered credit cards as soon as they are eighteen, teenagers do need to learn the dangers of relying upon credit cards, but it's best done under close parental supervision. If you go this route, assign a credit card with a $1,000 limit for them to use, and then make sure they receive and pay the bills. If they carry a balance, show them how much interest they are paying and illustrate how that can substantially increase their costs. For example, $1,000 at 19.8 percent that is whittled down by minimum payments of 2.5 percent will accumulate $648 in interest over the 5.5 years it takes to pay off. That grows significantly if children continue to use the card during the five years. Instead, show them how to confront their debt and bring their balances down to a far more manageable level.

Ideally, you want your children to know the dangers they face if they accept credit card offers and rack up charges they cannot afford to pay.

Disadvantages of Credit Cards for Kids

The cons of giving your teenagers credit cards that you pay are far greater in number and far more compelling. They include the following:

- Your teenagers don't have a real sense of money being spent.
- They don't realize the real value of a dollar.
- They don't learn responsibility for budgeting resources.
- They develop unrealistic expectations about what they can afford.
- They may become used to overextending, procrastinating, and living in denial.
- They could rack up high bills you can't afford to pay.
- They could start off on the wrong foot in terms of how they use credit.

The most important lesson you can impart to your children is not to spend what you don't have. If your children see you overextending yourself, they will adopt all the unconscious and conscious attitudes and behaviors that go along with it—charging to the hilt, acquiring credit cards to pay other credit cards, incurring massive interest, paying late, and continuing to spend. On the other hand, if you teach your children that they can only spend what they can pay for in cash, they will have a far more solid foundation for building and growing wealth.

What You Can Do

Instead, teach by example. Treat credit cards like emergency safety nets. If you have to use your credit card, show your teenagers how you immediately revise your budget, paring back on nonessential spending and allocating the saved dollars to pay the balance down to zero. Basically, when it comes to credit cards, teach your children the following:

- The benefits of paying in cash
- How quickly charges accumulate
- How much interest adds to the final cost
- How difficult it is to pay down excessive debt
- The consequences of paying late, or failing to pay

Once your children are in college, keep them fiscally responsible by monitoring their credit status and helping them create and adhere to workable budgets. If they have credit cards, make sure they notify all their creditors when they move. If they don't do this, by the time the credit card company tracks them down, they will have incurred late fees and damaged their credit report. Remind them of the consequences, and encourage them to create a checklist to follow whenever they move.

Using the Internet as a Teaching Tool

Like every other topic under the sun, the Internet is a gold mine for educational resources. Your child can use the Internet to research whatever money or investment topic interests them. A wealth of Web sites devoted to financial literacy—making learning about money fun—is available at your fingertips. Some of the best include these:

- The American Bankers Association's Web site (at *www.aba.com*) has a "kidstuff" section that provides educational ideas, calculators, budgeting forms, credit card debt calculation, and guidelines for what's appropriate at what age.
- Kidsbank.com (at *www.kidsbank.com*) explains money and banking basics, including a "millionaire calculator" that allows kids to see how long it would take them acquire wealth through savings. It's kind of dry and doesn't have sound effects, but it offers easily readable educational text aimed at children in the third grade and above.

- ING Direct's Web site (at *www.orangekids.com*) uses cartoon guides to teach fourth- to eighth-grade kids about money, investing, and saving. It's colorful, fun, interactive, and very informative.

Your children need you for many things, and teaching them about money ranks high on the list. You wouldn't dream of crippling your children, but keeping them in fantasy land when it comes to money, investments, budgets, goals, and dream fulfillment does just that. Arm them instead with knowledge, positive role modeling, discipline, and guidance. If you love your children and want them to succeed in life, teach them that when it comes to generating, growing, and maximizing personal finance, responsibility and realistic expectations lead to wealth. Irresponsibility and unrealistic behaviors lead to bankruptcy.

Chapter 19

Living a Frugal Life

One of America's greatest poets and philosophers, Henry David Thoreau said, "Money is not required to buy one necessity of the soul." Thoreau understood that a frugal life is a bountiful life—filled with soul nourishment, dreams coming true, experiences being lived, vibrant, intimate relationships, and unbridled joy. And it's all won by spending less than you earn, saving for the future, and making your money grow. Frugality helps you accomplish your financial goals, and, as such, frugality is a state of mind to be embraced wholeheartedly.

Changing Your Money Attitudes

One of the biggest fears is the bracing fear of scarcity. Many women lie awake at night picturing themselves as homeless vagabonds, victims of financial disaster, fated to live in a makeshift tent, pushing a grocery cart filled with rags, dirty blankets, scraps of food, and their last $20. By focusing on these negative—and most unlikely—images, women are blinded to the beauty and bounty of life.

ALERT!

Desperately rich housewives? The majority of television shows depicting "real life" actually depict upper-class families, and watching them may trigger unconscious urges to overconsume. Harvard professor Juliet Schor found that households that watched the most television tended to have lower-than-average savings. So turn off the television, and start saving toward your own bright future.

Basically, you need to adjust your own attitudes about money and how you will live your life. Unfortunately, women are subconsciously taught that their attitudes and behaviors should be dictated by standards set by society, advertisers, magazines, movies, television, and, increasingly, celebrities. There are two diametrically opposed ways of looking at the world:

- **Out-sightedness:** You feel helplessly reactive to an external locus of control, which means whatever happens is essentially unrelated to your own thoughts and behaviors—everything becomes externalized. This is also called monkey mind, a mind that doesn't retain focus and can be easily manipulated by outside forces.
- **In-sightedness:** You have an inner locus of control. You have solid attention filters that select what's important to your mind. You know that you can choose what you think and for how long you choose to think about it. You develop a laser-like attention.

The other monkey on your back is feeling deprived. An old way of thinking might have equated frugal living with being deprived—and how it hurts to feel deprived when you're working so hard, managing a household by yourself, and raising children. The trick here is to switch tracks, to literally change the way your look at your situation. You're not deprived; you are the master of your fate—you are choosing frugality. Thus, frugal living becomes an enlightened consciousness, a choice.

It's up to you to decide why, for whom, and for what you are living. Once you have made those choices, stand up proudly and pat yourself on the back. Live your philosophy, and in no time you'll be expanding your thoughts, your dreams, and your finances.

You aren't depriving yourself or your children. Instead, you are consciously making choices that nourish your soul and build toward real financial security. Find ways of rewarding yourself that don't have anything to do with money—take a hike in the woods, read a classic novel, take a hot bath, invite friends over for a potluck, or write in your journal.

When You Need to Spend Lavishly

Spending lavishly is, in fact, necessary when the money being spent benefits your and your children's health or when it's being spent on education or skill development. It's also wise to spend lavishly when it comes to paying into their college funds and your retirement funds. It's also okay to spend lavishly on home improvements that will bolster its value. In this case, however, lavishly does not mean casually, or without serious contemplation. The basic concept here is that when you spend money on investments, you are building a stake in something that will offer a return, rather than spending on things that hold no value over time. It's not smart to cut corners on your most basic needs, such as health and dental care, insurance, education, or upkeep of your home. These are investments that will strengthen your finances over the long run.

You may also spend lavishly on quality goods, as long as you spend more but buy less. For instance, buying two high-quality jackets rather than ten cheap jackets will actually save you money. The more expensive jackets will last longer and always look better. But to maximize savings, buy classic shapes and fabrics, and buy sparingly. The genius of buying higher-quality goods is that you don't buy what you don't need, and you buy minimal quantities. If you create a quality test for yourself—Is it a classic shape? Is it a durable, low-maintenance fabric? Can I build a wardrobe around it? Will it still look fashionable three years from now?—and stick to it when you are shopping, you will resist trendy, low-cost items that bulk up your closet and deplete your budget.

When a Bargain Is Not a Bargain

Never buy something because it's a "bargain." If you don't really need an item, it's not a bargain. Advertisers bank on consumers' susceptibility to "bargain consciousness" by posting signs that say "$200 rebate" or "an additional 40 percent off." If you don't need a new television, saving $200 on an $800 television is not a bargain. Instead, you've just wasted $800.

Between the catalogues, Amazon.com, and eBay, we are awash in visual stimulation tempting us to spend. "A wealth of information creates a poverty of attention," Nobel Prize winning economist Herbert Simon noted. "Our busy, busy brains have been on overload for eons, and [they are] still being constantly bombarded with enticements to believe anew that we need more possessions to make us happy."

The only way to benefit from price discounts is to have a list of items you really, really need (new bras, backpacks or sneakers for your children, and so on) and to watch the ads. Then, go to the store with a firm resolution to only buy the items you need. Avoid any temptation to add anything—a sweater, a DVD, a pair of shoes for your daughter, or a new set of towels—no matter how much they are discounted.

Jason Anthony and Karl Gluck, authors of *Debt-Free by Thirty*, say you should always be able to answer the following three questions before you buy anything . . . and that means any*thing*:

1. **Do I need this?** Do you really need this item, or are you desiring it for purely emotional reasons? If it's clothing, jewelry, overpriced shoes, expensive cosmetics, or a new laptop when the old one is working fine, the answer is probably "no."
2. **Can I get this cheaper?** Have you researched on the Internet to find the lowest price? Can you wait until it goes on sale? Can you find a used one online or at a flea market?
3. **How will this affect my debt-reduction plan?** You are living a frugal life so that you can reinforce your emergency fund, your children's college funds, your retirement funds, or to work toward a down payment for a house. So before you plunk down your credit card, ask yourself if you're ready to suffer the consequences.

Remember that a frugal life means fulfilling your real intentions and not placating transitory or impulsive feelings. Instead of buying another *thing*, make the pleasure of knowing you have just taken another step toward your ultimate goal, the real reward.

Having Fun Without Spending Money

Beliefs shape reality more than reality shapes beliefs. If you doubt this, watch one hour of television and snap your fingers every time someone is overtly or covertly selling you on the idea of acquiring objects or status. You'll find that advertisers and television shows are always bombarding you with images of lifestyles you are supposed to desire so deeply that you'll spend your last dime on them. If you doubt their power, think back to the 1980s when mullets, skin-tight leggings covered by blousy tops, and frightfully ostentatious, rhinestone-covered handbags were in vogue. What images are you being urged to desire today?

Purveyors of video games, television, movies, games, and toys bombard your children daily in attempts to convince them that it takes money to buy things to make you happy. It's up to you as a responsible single mother to show them otherwise. All you have to do is survey your local library to find a variety of books to stimulate fabulous, low-cost to zero-cost ideas. Use these ideas for activities that will spare your budget and inspire your children's creativity.

In *101 Things Every Kid Should Do Growing Up*, for example, the author suggests low-budget activities like these:

- Taking a late-night "pajama ride" to get ice cream cones (McDonald's frozen yogurt cones are slightly more than $1 and delicious)
- Spending a sunny day decorating the driveway using colored chalk
- Creating a scrapbook (no fancy books or decorations required, use everyday items or have children write a memory and draw their own picture to illustrate it)
- Camping in the back yard (use a sheet instead of a tent, tell spooky stories, roast hot dogs over a barbeque)
- Spending a night star-gazing (depending upon their age, have your children research constellations; if they're small, thrill them with stories about the sun, the moon, stars, and constellations)

FACT

The American Psychological Association states that people who buy into the consumer culture reported lowered feelings of personal well-being. Individuals who say that goals for money, image, and popularity are "relatively important" to them also reported less satisfaction in life, fewer experiences of pleasant emotions, and more depression and anxiety.

Create a creativity box or basket. Toss in paints, scissors, decoupage paste, buttons, paints, rhinestones, beads, glitter, confetti, pressed leaves or flowers, magazines, ribbons, string, wrapping paper, shells, unwanted promotional CDs, broken toy bits, keys, and other odds and ends. On rainy days—or broke days—and try some of the following activities:

- Buy an inexpensive birdhouse (check your local hobby store) or use a small box to create a birdhouse and then paint or decoupage.
- Decoupage magazine art onto poster board to create personal collages.
- Use old keys to make a wind chime.
- Paint or paste images onto those unwanted promotional CDs and use them to create a mobile.
- Spend the day weaving string friendship bracelets. String a few beads on or weave in ribbons for variety.
- Buy blank note cards or stationery from the hobby store's dirt-cheap bin (or at a dollar store) and teach your children the value and beauty of handmade gifts, note cards, and gift tags by letting them create some for their friends and family.

You can also spend time with your children playing hopscotch, fielding baseballs, creating treasure maps, stacking cards, inventing words, or making finger puppets. In other words, when it comes to entertaining, educating, and enriching your children, use your imagination instead of your wallet.

Concrete Ways to Foster Frugality

J. Paul Getty, once one of the richest men in America, said millionaires pay meticulous attention to even the smallest details and miss no opportunity to reduce costs in their businesses. Well, if J. Paul Getty can do it, why can't you? Running your household is your business, and its profitability depends upon the opportunities you find and the choices you make to minnow costs. Consider yourself the CEO of your household.

Using the Internet

The Internet has opened up vast opportunities to save money. If you're a Web surfer, you can easily find sites that offer coupons, discounts, and bargains. You can establish a free e-mail account at sites like Mail.yahoo.com, Exite.com, Hotmail.com, Gmail.google.com, or Mail.lycos.com and use it exclusively for online bartering. Sample clubs such as Startsampling.com, Olay.com, and Eversave.com will send you free samples of products in exchange for an occasional marketing survey. Other online clubs, including Momdotcom.net, Thefrugalshopper.com, Mycoupons.com, or Justfreestuff .com, offer free samples of a variety of products and often sponsor contests that can win you money or prizes.

You can also use the Internet to comparison shop for goods and services. Web sites such as Bizrate.com, Pricescan.com, or Epinons.com will help you find the lowest price online. Often you can print out the page and use it to bargain at a local store, which means you get what you want at the lowest price, and you save on shipping! Also you can locate coupons at sites like Couponmaker.com, Siteforsavings.com, Couponnet.com, or Valpack .com that you can print and take to a local retailer.

Many online retailers offer codes that you enter to save money or obtain free shipping. Individual retailers usually have information listed on their Web sites, but you can find a variety of codes by visiting code sites (such as Slickdeals.com, Jumpondeals.com, or Edeals.com) or by visiting code forum sites (such as Fatwallet.com or Dealcatcher.com). Many are also offering point programs (such as Mypoints.com, Clubmom.com, or Ebates.com), in which you accumulate points that can add up to savings.

Clipping Coupons the Old-Fashioned Way

You can also use the old-fashioned system of collecting coupons, applying for rebates, actually mailing in mail-in offers, and waiting for sales. All of these offers can save you substantial sums, particularly when used to buy products you love and use repeatedly. You can also write simple fan letters to companies whose products you favor. Frequently, they will respond by sending you a handful of valuable coupons. You can actually score prominent branded makeup, hair products, and expensive skin care creams at 10 to 20 percent discounts by looking for the point-of-sale (POS) tags that are redeemable when you match up your sales receipt with the store's weekly catalogues at drug stores. Occasionally, these rebate services refund 100 percent of the purchase price, which means you get free mascara or hand lotion for the cost of a postage stamp.

Some grocery stores (Albertsons, Ralphs, Fry's, and Food Lion, for example) and drug stores (CVS, Eckerd, and Drugstore.com, for example) offer instant discounts or a point system. If you combine coupons or weekly specials with accumulating points on basic products, you'll rack up savings faster than the blink of an eye. Even if you can't bring yourself to buy fresh vegetables, fish, meat, or fruit from the large chain grocery stores, you can buy all your basics there and save enough to afford gourmet items from your favorite local market or farmer's market.

Yes, You Can Save on Groceries

There are endless resources for trimming costs on groceries and household items, but a few primary ones include these:

- Always shop with, and adhere to, a list.
- Comparison shop, looking for lower unit prices.
- Buy staples like canned goods, salad dressing, or mayonnaise at a discount store that offers sharp discounts such as two for the price of one.
- Purchase generic rather than branded items. This alone could save you 40 percent on groceries.
- Avoid packaged or frozen goods.
- Check your receipts for errors before you leave the store.
- Team up with a friend or two to join a wholesale superstore to bulk buy and share necessities. (Just avoid those impulse buys.)
- Buy cosmetics at discount drug stores, which are cheaper than grocery stores.
- Plant a vegetable garden, or buy at farmer's markets just before they close.
- Never shop hungry—this alone can save you 10 percent a year.
- Shop on Mondays, when prices are usually lower.
- Invite friends over for a potluck rather than meeting at a restaurant.
- Skip beverages when you dine out (that includes soda for the kids).
- Brown bag your lunch at least twice a week.

Most grocery stores report that 50 percent of their income comes from impulse buys. That's why they put the necessities, like eggs, milk, butter, in the back of the store. If you stick to the perimeter of the store (where vegetables and fruits are stocked), you'll sidestep a lot of impulse purchases that blow your budget and your diet.

Other Fun Ways to Live a Fabulously Frugal Life

Vintage clothing stores hold treasures at very affordable prices. Ditto for consignment stores. Flea markets are another way to shop without spending much, or better yet, nothing at all. In fact, why don't you pare down your household by selling your superfluous possessions? Auctions are also fun, but only when you're shopping for affordable treasures—old picture frames, a silver cake knife, a rhinestone broach, or a vintage hat—or using it as a learning experience. Remember, no matter where you shop, there's nothing wrong—and everything right—with just looking.

Viva la musica! Exotic music takes you out of your real life world and into imagination. Leaf through travel books or magazines and fantasize, and expand your horizons. For inspiration, try Brazilian, African, Cuban, Indian, Turkish, Irish, French, or Russian, whatever works.

Visit local museums. Most museums have a free day every month, and many have discounted prices during off-peak hours. Museums are a great way to entertain the entire family.

Pretend you are a tourist in your own town. Check your local paper or go to your local library or bookstore and read through travel books for your area. Ask the kids to find three places that they'd like to check out, and select two or three of your own. Look for quirky places, like a local cupcake factory, or a train museum, or a famous hot dog stand. Take turns picking which one you visit, and take along a picnic basket. It's fun, it's cheap, and it's educational.

Chapter 20

Avoiding Common Financial Mistakes

Now that you've acquired a financial vocabulary and an in-depth understanding of personal finance, you have vastly increased your ability to make decisions that will positively affect your future. You also have specific guidelines for instituting plans that will greatly assist you in managing your current finances and growing your wealth. As a wrap-up and a reminder, it's equally important to know common financial mistakes and how to avoid them.

Face Reality and Make a Plan

If you don't know where you stand, you cannot make decisions to change your reality. Sticking your head in the sand will cost you money. If you ever want to acquire wealth, you have to start by taking stock of where you are financially today, including a full and complete accounting of your income, your expenses, and your debts. Then you have to create a plan that changes your present reality and moves you toward your financial goals.

Even if you, like many women, can't help longing for a valiant man to come galloping to your rescue on his noble steed (or Mustang, Mercedes, or BMW), you have to learn to be on your own and to take complete fiscal responsibility for your household. You owe it to yourself and your children to chart and maintain your financial path.

In order to reach your financial goals, you must take the time to write them out explicitly and then follow your own well-thought-out plan. In terms of your financial life and investments, prepare a list of the major things you want to be able to afford—a reasonable retirement and a vacation every year would be a good start—and then figure out what you have to save and when, and what you will invest in before you spend your savings. Set finite goals that you can readily achieve and build upon your success. Once you learn how to set goals and implement what's necessary to achieve them, you are well on your way to creating the types of goals that will increase your finances and fulfill your dreams.

A savvy investor always computes her net worth and then creates an action plan to increase her assets and decrease her liabilities. Do the work, and the wealth will come.

Establish a Retirement Fund

Admit it—you're older than you were last year. Sadly, this is an irreversible trend. One day you will not be able to work, will have to support a parent who can't take care of herself, or will run into other financial troubles that can only be fixed with two things: love and money. Money is often more difficult to come by on short notice. No matter what your age, today is the best time to start accumulating savings to tide you through the unexpected. At a minimum, set up an IRA and make annual contributions. Hopefully, once your see funds accumulating, you'll find the motivation and the discipline required to bolster them with additional contributions.

FACT

Recent figures show that 52 percent of Americans earn enough to pay their basic expenses, with little to less than zero left over for savings. In fact, Americans used to save 10 percent of their income, but that dropped to 5 percent in the 90s, and since June of 2005, it has fallen below zero, which hasn't happened since the Great Depression.

The government offers opportunities to use pretax dollars, but often it's only the rich who learn how to use them to their advantage. IRA funding that allows you to sock away money before paying taxes and that grow tax-deferred, and health savings or flexible spending plans that use pretax dollars to pay medical expenses are excellent ways to use pre-tax dollars. Find out the plans that are available within your company, and jump on board immediately.

Watch Those Deductions

An astounding number of Americans miss legal deductions that would decrease their taxes. As a single mother, you need to maximize any means of saving. Even if you love the government, you cannot afford to be one of its primary benefactors. You can avoid paying more taxes than necessary by following a few simple rules:

- Stay current on tax laws, use a computer tax program, or consult with a tax advisor annually.

- Put tax-advantaged investments like municipal bonds in taxable accounts, and put taxable investments in your IRA and other tax-advantaged accounts.
- If buying a mutual fund in a taxable account, make sure that the fund's turnover is low. Also, check when the fund makes its next distribution (similar to a dividend payment). Part of the distribution may be taxable, so if you buy just before a distribution you will have to immediately pay taxes on the fund's gains.
- Try to sell stock that you own after at least a year; long-term capital gains rates are much lower than rates on short-term gains.

If you have a gain in one stock and a loss on another stock, it may be worthwhile to sell both stocks so the gain on the first stock cancels out the loss on the second. This will eliminate the need to pay taxes on the gain.

Get in the Game!

Make sure to take the extra step to start saving and then invest those savings. Shying away from the stock market, or failing to buy investment property because you're afraid that you'll screw it up and lose money in the long run, means that you'll never grow beyond your present circumstances.

ALERT!

Women often fail to value themselves or their talents in the workforce. Men, on the other hand, almost always negotiate for a higher salary or benefits when interviewing for new jobs or pushing for promotions. Rather than settling for what's offered, ask for what you know is a reasonable salary, fee, bonus, or raise, and—by all means—feel worthy.

Increasing your knowledge, making concrete plans, and taking some risks are essential steps in gaining financial independence. Even if you make mistakes—and you will—you will grow and you will learn to make better decisions. Trust yourself and get in the game!

Investing Pitfalls

Getting emotional about your investments will usually cost you. On the other hand, it's valuable to make emotion-driven mistakes early in your investing career so that in the future you will realize when you are either too excited about an investment (and tend to invest too much in it) or when you are overly worried about an investment (and tend to sell too early or as the investment is about to rebound).

A number of investing pitfalls arise from getting emotionally wrapped up in your investing decisions. Investors in individual stocks frequently sell winning stocks too early. They also refuse to sell losing stocks because they want to "get back to even" on the loser, despite evidence that the business of the losing company may not turn. Meanwhile, they miss the tax break they could have received by selling the loser to offset other capital gains.

Two sure ways to miss your financial goals are failing to get in the game and giving up too early. Giving up early ensures that you will never realize your plan's potential; it may also condemn you to poverty in your old age. Even when markets dip or emergencies arise, stick to your plan and ride it out.

Investors of all stripes tend to get emotional just at the wrong time, selling when a market has already fallen and everyone believes that it will continue falling, and buying after a big rally, when most people believe that the rally will continue indefinitely, but is actually ending. You can avoid this pitfall by not investing all your funds at the same time. You should also stick to mutual funds and ETFs, where the size of your mistake will be smaller than if you buy into the wrong stock. If you make and stick with your financial plan, you will be able to avoid the emotional side of investing and prosper.

Not Doing Your Homework

Learning the lingo, asking questions, and researching stocks or investment companies are essential steps to your long-term success. You have to be willing to learn a vocabulary of investment options, and their benefits or detriments, so that you can then discuss them with a financial advisor or broker. Failing to learn the basics puts you at the mercy of a broker or financial advisor, who may or may not be making decisions in your best interests. We've given you a basic understanding and a financial vocabulary, but it would behoove you to do in-depth research on specific stocks or mutual funds, and the tax consequences of each. Protect yourself by arming yourself with as much knowledge as possible, and keep expanding that knowledge so that you truly become a savvy investor.

Putting All Your Eggs in One Basket

One of the biggest and most debilitating investment mistakes you can make is not diversifying your portfolio. If you put all your funds into a small number of stocks and bonds, you may make money, but you can also lose a lot of money quickly.

Diversification decreases the risk in your portfolio and makes you better able to meet your financial goals. Keep in mind that to make your portfolio diversified, you need to invest in a few different asset classes that don't move up or down at the same time. Investing in a few different kinds of stocks and bonds, and perhaps adding a couple percent of a diversified commodities fund for variety, isn't a bad place to start.

Appendix A

Resources

Books About Women and Money

Smart Women Finish Rich: Nine Steps to Achieving Financial Security and Funding Your Dreams, by David Bach

Girl, Make Your Money Grow! A Sister's Guide to Protecting Your Future and Enriching Your Life, by Glinda Bridgforth and Gail Perry-Mason

The Ten Commandments of Financial Happiness: Feel Richer with What You've Got, by Jean Chatzky

Your Money or Your Life: Transforming Your Relationship with Money and Achieving Financial Independence, by Joe Dominguez and Vicki Robin

Making Bread: The Ultimate Financial Guide for Women Who Need Dough, by Gail Harlow and Elizabeth Lewin

The Nine Steps to Financial Freedom: Practical and Spiritual Steps So You Can Stop Worrying, by Suze Orman

The Road to Wealth: Everything You Need to Know in Good and Bad Times, by Suze Orman

Money, A Memoir: Women, Emotions, and Cash, by Liz Perle

The Soul of Money: Transforming Your Relationship with Money and Life, by Lynne Twist

Books and Web Sites on Divorce and Remarriage

Financial Custody, You, Your Money, and Divorce, by Joan Coullahan, CDP, CFP, and Sue van der Linden, CFP

Money with Matrimony: The Unmarried Couple's Guide to Financial Security, by Sheryl Garrett, CFP and Debra A. Neiman, CFP, MBA
- *www.divorce-online.com*
- *www.divorce-help.com*
- *www.nolo.com*

Credit Card Debt, FICO Scores, and Identity Theft

Credit Reporting Bureaus

Equifax
P.O. Box 740241
Atlanta, GA 30374-0241
(800) 685-1111
✎ www.equifax.com

TransUnion
P.O. Box 1000
Chester, PA, 19022
(800) 916-8800
✎ www.tuc.com

Experian
P.O. Box 949
Allen, TX, 75013-0949
(888) 397-3742
✎ www.experian.com

Counseling and Information

National Foundation for Consumer Credit (NFCC)
Provides credit counseling
(800) 388-2227
✎ www.nfcc.org

National Association of Consumer Advocates (NACA)
A good resource for finding a reputable law firm to handle credit disputes
✎ www.naca.org

Identity Theft Resource Center
Help with identity theft issues
(858) 693-7935
✎ www.idtheftcenter.org

Privacy Rights Clearinghouse
Help with identity theft issues
(619) 298-3396
✎ www.privacyrights.org

Postal Contact
✎ www.usps.gov/websites/depart/inspect

SEC Office of Investor Education and Assistance
450 Fifth Street, NW
Washington, DC 20549-0213
(202) 942-7040
✎ www.sec.gov/complaints.html

Passport Assistance
✎ www.travel.state.gove/passport_services.html

Federal Communications Commission
Consumer Information Bureau
445 12th Street, SW
Washington, DC 20554
✍ *www.fcc.gov*
(888) CALL-FCC

Tax Fraud Contact
(800) 829-0433 or,
IRA Taxpayer Advocates Office
(877) 777-4778

Books

Debt-Free by Thirty: Practical Advice for the Young, Broke, and Upwardly Mobile, by Jason Anthony and Karl Cluck

Girl, Get Your Money Straight!: A Sister's Guide to Healing Your Bank Account and Funding Your Dreams, by Glinda Bridgforth

Generation Debt: Why Now Is a Terrible Time to Be Young, by Anya Kamenetz

Your Credit Score: How to Fix, Improve, and Protect the Three-Digit Number That Shapes Your Financial Future, by Liz Pulliam Weston

Starting Your Own Business

Contact Information

National Association of Commissions for Women
Provides information and assistance
8630 Fenton St., Suite 934
Silver Spring, MD 20910
(800) 338-9267
✍ *www.nacw.org*

Center for Women's Business Research
Nonprofit agency that researches issues related to women-owned business
1411 K Street, NW, Suite 1350
Washington, D.C. 20005-3407
(202) 638-3060
✍ *www.nfwbo.org*

Small Business Administration (SBA)
1110 Vermont Avenue, NW, Ninth Floor
Washington, D.C. 20005
Provides extensive information on business setup, business plan creation, pricing, finding employees, financing, budgeting, strategic management, and many other topics specific to women-owned business. They frequently offer one-on-one counseling and can also help you acquire low-interest loans to get started. Their Service Corps of Retired Executives (SCORE) are available for consultation.
✍ *www.sba.gov*

Office of Women's Business Ownership SBA
409 Third Street SW, Fourth Floor
Washington, D.C. 20416
(202) 205-6673
✑ *www.owbo.sba.gov*

Publications Services, MS-127, Board of Governors, Federal Reserve System
Will send you a free copy of *A Guide to Business Credit for Women, Minorities, and Small Business*
Washington D.C. 20551
(202) 452-3245
✑ *www.federalreserve.gov*

International Franchise Association
1350 New York Avenue, NW, Suite 900
Washington, D.C. 20005-4709
✑ *www.franchise.org*

Association of Small Business Development Centers
8990 Burke Lake Road
Burke, VA 22015
(703) 764-9850
✑ *www.asbdc-us.org*

American Women's Economic Development Corp.
71 Vanderbilt Avenue, Suite 320
New York, NY 10169
(212) 692-9100
✑ *www.awed.org*

Books

Free Money and Help for Women Entrepreneurs, by Matthew Leske and Marsha Martello. Has federal and state-by-state information on grants, loans, and special programs or resources for entrepreneurs.

Starting on a Shoestring: Building a Business Without a Bankroll, by Arnold S. Goldstein, Ph.D. Excellent information on the SBA and how to finance on a shoestring.

Small Business Guide: Starting Your Own Business, by Peter Hingston. Very concise and thorough information in layman's terms.

101 Best Home-Based Businesses for Women: Everything You Need to Know About Getting Started on the Road to Success, by Priscilla Y. Huff. A great resource for generating ideas and getting some basic tips on starting up.

Business Plans That Work for Your Small Business, Alice H. Magos and Steve Crow. Good resource for seeing exactly how to format a business plan and what needs to be included.

Niche and Grow Rich: Practical Ways to Turn Your Ideas into a Business, by Jennifer Basye and Peter Sander

Making a Living Without a Job: Winning Ways for Creating Work That You Love, by Barbara J. Winter

Saving for College

SEC's 529 plan Web site
✍ *www.sec.gov/investor/pubs/intro529.htm*

Savingforcollege.com
Good information about 529 plans and other means to save for college.
✍ *www.savingforcollege.com*

The Federal Student Aid Web site
The definitive information about FAFSA applications and federal education loans. The Web site also lets you sign up for a FAFSA PIN and submit your FAFSA information online.
✍ *http://studentaid.ed.gov*

Buying/Selling a Home or Car

Bankrate.com
A good source for finding current average money market fund rates, CD rates, and checking account rates. The site also has a mortgage payment calculator that will show you how much your mortgage will cost per month, how much of every payment is interest, and how much pays down the principal balance of your loan.
✍ *www.bankrate.com*

Edmunds.com
A good source for information about buying new and used cars; includes car reviews.
✍ *www.edmunds.com*

Realtor.com
The National Association of Realtors' Multiple Listing Service search engine allows you to search literally millions of homes for sale.
✍ *www.realtor.com*

Yahoo!
This portal site's real estate page provides useful real estate information
✍ *http://realestate.yahoo.com*

LeaseGuide.com
An online guide to leasing a car
✍ *www.leaseguide.com*

The Federal Reserve's guide to vehicle leasing
✍ *www.federalreserve gov/pubs/leasing/resource*

Protecting Your Assets: Insurance and Wills

Life insurance calculators
- *choosetosave.org*
- *tiaa-cref.org*

Life insurance Web sites
- *www.term4sale.com*
- *www.ameritasdirect.com*
- *www.insure.com*

A.M. Best ratings
- *www.ambest.com*

Standard & Poor's ratings
- *www.insure.com*

Insurance quotes
- *www.accuquote.com*
- Termquote (800-444-8376)
- Quotesmith (800-556-9393)

Wills and Trusts
- *www.legaldocs.com*

Free Consumer's Tool Kit for Health Care Decision-Making
- *www.abanet.org/aging*
- *www.practicalbioethics.org*

Child Care

Au pairs
- *www.aupairinamerica.com*
- *www.interchange.org*
- *www.exchanges.state.gov*

Alliance of Professional Nanny Agencies (APNA)
Screens nanny agencies
- *www.theapna.org*

International Nanny Association (INA)
Educates nannies and nanny agencies
- *www.nanny.org*

Day care center licensure and information
Check for licensing at National Resource Center for Health and Safety
- *www.nrs.uchsc.edu*

Parent Savvy: Straight Answers to Your Family's Financial, Legal, and Practical Questions, by Nihara Chodhri, Esq. An excellent resource for many parenting issues.

Taxes

The Internal Revenue Service

You can find a ton of useful information and download tax forms from the IRS Web site. You can also call (800) 829-1040 to speak to an IRS representative, or go to your local IRS office (click on "individuals" and then "contact my local office" to find an office near you, and keep in mind that June through February are the best months to go with a list of questions).

☞ *www.irs.gov*

Regulations for Your State

You can use this site to obtain information about your state's tax breaks.

☞ *www.taxes.yahoo.com/stateforms.html*

Teaching Your Children About Money

Mutual Funds for Children

Stein Roe's mutual fund provides quarterly newsletters with puzzles, contests, and articles aimed at educating children about money.
(800) 338-2550

☞ *www.younginvestor.com*

USAA First Start Growth

(800) 235-8377

Monetta Express

Money-market account and mutual fund investor programs
(800) 666-3882

American Express IDA New Dimensions

Provides kids, parents, and money program with investor programs and educational materials
(800) 437-4332

Kids' Money

Provides inventive tips for teaching children about money

☞ *www.kidsmoney.org*

Resources for Frugal Living

Books

Frugal Living for Dummies: Practical Ideas to Help You Spend Less, Save More, and Live Well, by Deborah Taylor-Hough

The Mom's Guide to Earning and Savings Thousands on the Internet, by Barb Webb and Maureen Heck

The Tightwad Gazette, by Amy Dacyczyn

Web Sites

- www.frugaliving.com
- www.allthingsfrugal.com
- www.thefrugalshopper.com
- www.miserlymoms.com
- www.lowermybills.com
- www.mysimon.com
- www.dealtime.com
- www.ebay.com
- www.ubid.com
- www.priceline.com
- www.travelocity.com
- www.cheaptickets.com

Appendix B
Additional Reading

365 TV-Free Activities You Can Do with Your Child, by Steve and Ruth Bennett

A Girl's Guide to Money, by Laura Brady

The Standard & Poor's Guide to Saving and Investing for College, by David J. Braverman

The Easy Will and Living Will Kit: Three Easy Steps to Complete Your Will, Living Will, and Powers of Attorney, by Joy S. Chambers

Paying for College Without Going Broke, by Kalman A. Chany with Geoff Martz

The Seven Spiritual Laws for Parents: Guiding Your Children to Success and Fulfillment, by Deepak Chopra

Estate Planning Basics: What You Need to Know and Nothing More!, by Denis Clifford

The Women's Wheel of Life: Thirteen Archetypes of Women at Her Fullest Power, by Elizabeth Davis and Carol Leonard

101 Things Every Kid Should Do Growing Up, by Alecia T. Devantier

Magic Trees of the Mind: How to Nurture Your Child's Intelligence, Creativity, and Healthy Emotions from Birth Through Adolescence, by Marian Diamond, Ph.D., and Janet Hopson

Business Owner's Toolkit (Second Edition) Launching Your First Small Business: Make the

Right Decisions During Your First 90 Days, ed. by John L. Duoba and Paul J. Gada, LL.M., MBA

This Is How We Do It: The Working Mothers' Manifesto, by Carol Evans

The 5 Lessons a Millionaire Taught Me About Life and Wealth, by Richard Paul Evans

The Complete Guide to Protecting Your Financial Security When Getting a Divorce, by Alan Feigenbaum, CFP, and Heather Linton, CPA, DFP, DVA, CDFA

Nice Girls Don't Get Rich: 75 Avoidable Mistakes Women Make with Money, by Lois P. Frankel

The Girl's Guide to Being a Boss (Without Being a Bitch): Valuable Lessons, Smart Suggestions, and True Stories for Succeeding as the Chick-in-Charge, by Caitlin Friedman and Kimberly Yorio

Take Yourself to the Top: Success from the Inside Out, by Laura Berman Fortgang

Fifty Simple Things You Can Do to Improve Your Personal Finances: How to Spend Less, Save More, and Make the Most of What You Have, by Ilyce R. Glink

The Complete Idiot's Guide to Managing Your Money, by Robert K. Heady and Christy Heady, with Hugo Ottolenghi

What It Takes: A Modern Woman's Guide to Success in Business, by Amy Henry

Life or Debt, a One-Week Plan for a Lifetime of Financial Freedom, by Stacy Johnson

The Path: Creating Your Own Mission Statement for Work and for Life, by Laurie Beth Jones

The Money Rules: 50 Ways Savvy Women Can Make More, Save More, and Have More!, by Susan Jones

Go It Alone: The Secrets to Building a Successful Business on Your Own, by Bruce Judson

The Complete Guide to Credit Repair, by Bill Kelly Jr.

The Insider's Guide to Buying a New or Used Car, 2nd Edition, by Burke Leon and Stephanie Leon

Smart Women Take Risks: Six Steps for Conquering Your Fears and Making the Leap to Success, by Helene Lerner

Pitch Like a Girl, How a Woman Can Be Herself and Still Succeed, by Ronna Lichtenberg

Getting Divorced Without Ruining Your Life: A Reasoned, Practical Guide to the Legal, Emotional, and Financial Ins and Outs of Negotiating a Divorce Settlement, by Sam Margulies, Ph.D., J.D.

Miserly Moms: Living on One Income in a Two-Income Economy, by Jonni McCoy

Bonnie's Household Budget Book: The Essential Guide for Getting Control of Your Money, by Bonnie Runyan McCullough

The Energy of Money: A Spiritual Guide to Financial and Personal Fulfillment, by Maria Nemeth, Ph.D.

Smart and Simple Financial Strategies for Busy People, by Jane Bryant Quinn

Surviving Separation and Divorce: A Woman's Guide to Regaining Control, Building Strength and Confidence, and Securing a Financial Future, by Loriann Hoff Oberlin

The Wall Street Journal Complete Personal Finance Guidebook, by Jeff D. Opdyke

Toxic Success: How to Stop Striving and Start Thriving, by Paul Pearsall, Ph.D.

Building Wealth in a Paycheck-to-Paycheck World: Ten Steps to Realizing Your Dream No Matter What You Earn, by Paul Petillo

Success, Advice for Achieving Your Goals from Remarkably Accomplished People, ed. by J. Pincott

Second Acts: Creating the Life You Really Want, Building the Career You Truly Desire, by Stephan M. Pollan and Mark Levine

The Total Money Makeover: A Proven Plan for Financial Fitness, by Dave Ramsey

The Small Business Start-Up Guide: A Surefire Blueprint to Successfully Launch Your Own Business, by Hal Root and Steve Koenig

The 250 Personal Finance Questions Everyone Should Ask, by Peter Sander, MBA

The Divorce Organizer and Planner, by Brette Sembler McWhorter, J.D.

What I Know Now: Letters to My Younger Self, by Ellyn Spragins

Millionaire Women Next Door: The Many Journeys of Successful American Businesswomen, by Thomas J. Stanley, Ph.D.

Secrets of Six-Figure Women: Surprising Strategies to Up Your Earnings and Change Your Life, by Barbara Stanny

The Martha Rules: Ten Essentials for Achieving Success as You Start, Build, or Manage a Business, by Martha Stewart

The Unofficial Guide to Starting a Small Business, by Marcia Layton Turner

All Your Worth: The Ultimate Lifetime Money Plan, by Elizabeth Warren and Amelia Warren Tyagi

The Complete Idiot's Guide to Starting an eBay Business, by Barbara Weltman

Not Poorer: The Newlywed's Financial Survival Guide, by Deborah A. Wilburn

The Woman's Book of Money and Spiritual Vision: Putting Your Spiritual Values into Financial Practice, by Rosemary Williams

Feng Shui: Do's and Taboos for Financial Success, by Angi Ma Wong

Index

THE EVERYTHING SERIES!

BUSINESS & PERSONAL FINANCE

Everything® Accounting Book
Everything® Budgeting Book
Everything® Business Planning Book
Everything® Coaching and Mentoring Book
Everything® Fundraising Book
Everything® Get Out of Debt Book
Everything® Grant Writing Book
Everything® Guide to Personal Finance for Single Mothers
Everything® Home-Based Business Book, 2nd Ed.
Everything® Homebuying Book, 2nd Ed.
Everything® Homeselling Book, 2nd Ed.
Everything® Improve Your Credit Book
Everything® Investing Book, 2nd Ed.
Everything® Landlording Book
Everything® Leadership Book
Everything® Managing People Book, 2nd Ed.
Everything® Negotiating Book
Everything® Online Auctions Book
Everything® Online Business Book
Everything® Personal Finance Book
Everything® Personal Finance in Your 20s and 30s Book
Everything® Project Management Book
Everything® Real Estate Investing Book
Everything® Retirement Planning Book
Everything® Robert's Rules Book, $7.95
Everything® Selling Book
Everything® Start Your Own Business Book, 2nd Ed.
Everything® Wills & Estate Planning Book

COOKING

Everything® Barbecue Cookbook
Everything® Bartender's Book, $9.95
Everything® Cheese Book
Everything® Chinese Cookbook
Everything® Classic Recipes Book
Everything® Cocktail Parties and Drinks Book
Everything® College Cookbook
Everything® Cooking for Baby and Toddler Book
Everything® Cooking for Two Cookbook
Everything® Diabetes Cookbook
Everything® Easy Gourmet Cookbook
Everything® Fondue Cookbook
Everything® Fondue Party Book
Everything® Gluten-Free Cookbook
Everything® Glycemic Index Cookbook
Everything® Grilling Cookbook

Everything® Healthy Meals in Minutes Cookbook
Everything® Holiday Cookbook
Everything® Indian Cookbook
Everything® Italian Cookbook
Everything® Low-Carb Cookbook
Everything® Low-Fat High-Flavor Cookbook
Everything® Low-Salt Cookbook
Everything® Meals for a Month Cookbook
Everything® Mediterranean Cookbook
Everything® Mexican Cookbook
Everything® No Trans Fat Cookbook
Everything® One-Pot Cookbook
Everything® Pizza Cookbook
Everything® Quick and Easy 30-Minute, 5-Ingredient Cookbook
Everything® Quick Meals Cookbook
Everything® Slow Cooker Cookbook
Everything® Slow Cooking for a Crowd Cookbook
Everything® Soup Cookbook
Everything® Stir-Fry Cookbook
Everything® Tex-Mex Cookbook
Everything® Thai Cookbook
Everything® Vegetarian Cookbook
Everything® Wild Game Cookbook
Everything® Wine Book, 2nd Ed.

GAMES

Everything® 15-Minute Sudoku Book, $9.95
Everything® 30-Minute Sudoku Book, $9.95
Everything® Blackjack Strategy Book
Everything® Brain Strain Book, $9.95
Everything® Bridge Book
Everything® Card Games Book
Everything® Card Tricks Book, $9.95
Everything® Casino Gambling Book, 2nd Ed.
Everything® Chess Basics Book
Everything® Craps Strategy Book
Everything® Crossword and Puzzle Book
Everything® Crossword Challenge Book
Everything® Crosswords for the Beach Book, $9.95
Everything® Cryptograms Book, $9.95
Everything® Easy Crosswords Book
Everything® Easy Kakuro Book, $9.95
Everything® Easy Large Print Crosswords Book
Everything® Games Book, 2nd Ed.
Everything® Giant Sudoku Book, $9.95
Everything® Kakuro Challenge Book, $9.95
Everything® Large-Print Crossword Challenge Book

Everything® Large-Print Crosswords Book
Everything® Lateral Thinking Puzzles Book, $9.95
Everything® Mazes Book
Everything® Movie Crosswords Book, $9.95
Everything® Online Poker Book, $12.95
Everything® Pencil Puzzles Book, $9.95
Everything® Poker Strategy Book
Everything® Pool & Billiards Book
Everything® Sports Crosswords Book, $9.95
Everything® Test Your IQ Book, $9.95
Everything® Texas Hold 'Em Book, $9.95
Everything® Travel Crosswords Book, $9.95
Everything® Word Games Challenge Book
Everything® Word Scramble Book
Everything® Word Search Book

HEALTH

Everything® Alzheimer's Book
Everything® Diabetes Book
Everything® Health Guide to Adult Bipolar Disorder
Everything® Health Guide to Controlling Anxiety
Everything® Health Guide to Fibromyalgia
Everything® Health Guide to Postpartum Care
Everything® Health Guide to Thyroid Disease
Everything® Hypnosis Book
Everything® Low Cholesterol Book
Everything® Massage Book
Everything® Menopause Book
Everything® Nutrition Book
Everything® Reflexology Book
Everything® Stress Management Book

HISTORY

Everything® American Government Book
Everything® American History Book, 2nd Ed.
Everything® Civil War Book
Everything® Freemasons Book
Everything® Irish History & Heritage Book
Everything® Middle East Book

HOBBIES

Everything® Candlemaking Book
Everything® Cartooning Book
Everything® Coin Collecting Book
Everything® Drawing Book
Everything® Family Tree Book, 2nd Ed.
Everything® Knitting Book
Everything® Knots Book
Everything® Photography Book

Everything® Quilting Book
Everything® Scrapbooking Book
Everything® Sewing Book
Everything® Soapmaking Book, 2nd Ed.
Everything® Woodworking Book

HOME IMPROVEMENT

Everything® Feng Shui Book
Everything® Feng Shui Decluttering Book, $9.95
Everything® Fix-It Book
Everything® Home Decorating Book
Everything® Home Storage Solutions Book
Everything® Homebuilding Book
Everything® Organize Your Home Book

KIDS' BOOKS

All titles are $7.95

Everything® Kids' Animal Puzzle & Activity Book
Everything® Kids' Baseball Book, 4th Ed.
Everything® Kids' Bible Trivia Book
Everything® Kids' Bugs Book
Everything® Kids' Cars and Trucks Puzzle
    & Activity Book
Everything® Kids' Christmas Puzzle
    & Activity Book
Everything® Kids' Cookbook
Everything® Kids' Crazy Puzzles Book
Everything® Kids' Dinosaurs Book
Everything® Kids' First Spanish Puzzle and
    Activity Book
Everything® Kids' Gross Cookbook
Everything® Kids' Gross Hidden Pictures Book
Everything® Kids' Gross Jokes Book
Everything® Kids' Gross Mazes Book
Everything® Kids' Gross Puzzle and
    Activity Book
Everything® Kids' Halloween Puzzle
    & Activity Book
Everything® Kids' Hidden Pictures Book
Everything® Kids' Horses Book
Everything® Kids' Joke Book
Everything® Kids' Knock Knock Book
Everything® Kids' Learning Spanish Book
Everything® Kids' Math Puzzles Book
Everything® Kids' Mazes Book
Everything® Kids' Money Book
Everything® Kids' Nature Book
Everything® Kids' Pirates Puzzle and Activity Book
Everything® Kids' Presidents Book
Everything® Kids' Princess Puzzle and Activity Book
Everything® Kids' Puzzle Book
Everything® Kids' Riddles & Brain Teasers Book
Everything® Kids' Science Experiments Book
Everything® Kids' Sharks Book
Everything® Kids' Soccer Book
Everything® Kids' States Book
Everything® Kids' Travel Activity Book

KIDS' STORY BOOKS

Everything® Fairy Tales Book

LANGUAGE

Everything® Conversational Japanese Book with
    CD, $19.95
Everything® French Grammar Book
Everything® French Phrase Book, $9.95
Everything® French Verb Book, $9.95
Everything® German Practice Book with CD,
    $19.95
Everything® Inglés Book
**Everything® Intermediate Spanish Book with
    CD, $19.95**
**Everything® Learning Brazilian Portuguese
    Book with CD, $19.95**
Everything® Learning French Book
Everything® Learning German Book
Everything® Learning Italian Book
Everything® Learning Latin Book
**Everything® Learning Spanish Book with
    CD, 2nd Edition, $19.95**
Everything® Russian Practice Book with CD, $19.95
Everything® Sign Language Book
Everything® Spanish Grammar Book
Everything® Spanish Phrase Book, $9.95
Everything® Spanish Practice Book
    with CD, $19.95
Everything® Spanish Verb Book, $9.95
Everything® Speaking Mandarin Chinese Book
    with CD, $19.95

MUSIC

Everything® Drums Book with CD, $19.95
**Everything® Guitar Book with CD, 2nd
    Edition, $19.95**
Everything® Guitar Chords Book with CD, $19.95
Everything® Home Recording Book
Everything® Music Theory Book with CD, $19.95
Everything® Reading Music Book with CD, $19.95
Everything® Rock & Blues Guitar Book
    with CD, $19.95
**Everything® Rock and Blues Piano Book
    with CD, $19.95**
Everything® Songwriting Book

NEW AGE

Everything® Astrology Book, 2nd Ed.
Everything® Birthday Personology Book
Everything® Dreams Book, 2nd Ed.
Everything® Love Signs Book, $9.95
Everything® Numerology Book
Everything® Paganism Book
Everything® Palmistry Book
Everything® Psychic Book
Everything® Reiki Book

Everything® Sex Signs Book, $9.95
Everything® Tarot Book, 2nd Ed.
Everything® Toltec Wisdom Book
Everything® Wicca and Witchcraft Book

PARENTING

Everything® Baby Names Book, 2nd Ed.
Everything® Baby Shower Book
Everything® Baby's First Year Book
Everything® Birthing Book
Everything® Breastfeeding Book
Everything® Father-to-Be Book
Everything® Father's First Year Book
Everything® Get Ready for Baby Book
Everything® Get Your Baby to Sleep Book, $9.95
Everything® Getting Pregnant Book
Everything® Guide to Raising a One-Year-Old
Everything® Guide to Raising a Two-Year-Old
Everything® Homeschooling Book
Everything® Mother's First Year Book
**Everything® Parent's Guide to Childhood
    Illnesses**
Everything® Parent's Guide to Children
    and Divorce
Everything® Parent's Guide to Children
    with ADD/ADHD
Everything® Parent's Guide to Children
    with Asperger's Syndrome
Everything® Parent's Guide to Children
    with Autism
Everything® Parent's Guide to Children with
    Bipolar Disorder
**Everything® Parent's Guide to Children with
    Depression**
Everything® Parent's Guide to Children
    with Dyslexia
**Everything® Parent's Guide to Children with
    Juvenile Diabetes**
Everything® Parent's Guide to Positive Discipline
Everything® Parent's Guide to Raising a
    Successful Child
Everything® Parent's Guide to Raising Boys
Everything® Parent's Guide to Raising Girls
Everything® Parent's Guide to Raising Siblings
Everything® Parent's Guide to Sensory
    Integration Disorder
Everything® Parent's Guide to Tantrums
Everything® Parent's Guide to the Strong-Willed
    Child
Everything® Parenting a Teenager Book
Everything® Potty Training Book, $9.95
Everything® Pregnancy Book, 3rd Ed.
Everything® Pregnancy Fitness Book
Everything® Pregnancy Nutrition Book
Everything® Pregnancy Organizer, 2nd Ed., $16.95
Everything® Toddler Activities Book
Everything® Toddler Book

Everything® Tween Book
Everything® Twins, Triplets, and More Book

PETS

Everything® Aquarium Book
Everything® Boxer Book
Everything® Cat Book, 2nd Ed.
Everything® Chihuahua Book
Everything® Dachshund Book
Everything® Dog Book
Everything® Dog Health Book
Everything® Dog Obedience Book
Everything® Dog Owner's Organizer, $16.95
Everything® Dog Training and Tricks Book
Everything® German Shepherd Book
Everything® Golden Retriever Book
Everything® Horse Book
Everything® Horse Care Book
Everything® Horseback Riding Book
Everything® Labrador Retriever Book
Everything® Poodle Book
Everything® Pug Book
Everything® Puppy Book
Everything® Rottweiler Book
Everything® Small Dogs Book
Everything® Tropical Fish Book
Everything® Yorkshire Terrier Book

REFERENCE

Everything® American Presidents Book
Everything® Blogging Book
Everything® Build Your Vocabulary Book
Everything® Car Care Book
Everything® Classical Mythology Book
Everything® Da Vinci Book
Everything® Divorce Book
Everything® Einstein Book
Everything® Enneagram Book
Everything® Etiquette Book, 2nd Ed.
Everything® Inventions and Patents Book
Everything® Mafia Book
Everything® Philosophy Book
Everything® Pirates Book
Everything® Psychology Book

RELIGION

Everything® Angels Book
Everything® Bible Book
Everything® Buddhism Book
Everything® Catholicism Book
Everything® Christianity Book
Everything® Gnostic Gospels Book
Everything® History of the Bible Book
Everything® Jesus Book

Everything® Jewish History & Heritage Book
Everything® Judaism Book
Everything® Kabbalah Book
Everything® Koran Book
Everything® Mary Book
Everything® Mary Magdalene Book
Everything® Prayer Book
Everything® Saints Book, 2nd Ed.
Everything® Torah Book
Everything® Understanding Islam Book
Everything® World's Religions Book
Everything® Zen Book

SCHOOL & CAREERS

Everything® Alternative Careers Book
Everything® Career Tests Book
Everything® College Major Test Book
Everything® College Survival Book, 2nd Ed.
Everything® Cover Letter Book, 2nd Ed.
Everything® Filmmaking Book
Everything® Get-a-Job Book, 2nd Ed.
Everything® Guide to Being a Paralegal
Everything® Guide to Being a Personal Trainer
Everything® Guide to Being a Real Estate Agent
Everything® Guide to Being a Sales Rep
Everything® Guide to Careers in Health Care
Everything® Guide to Careers in Law Enforcement
Everything® Guide to Government Jobs
Everything® Guide to Starting and Running a Restaurant
Everything® Job Interview Book
Everything® New Nurse Book
Everything® New Teacher Book
Everything® Paying for College Book
Everything® Practice Interview Book
Everything® Resume Book, 2nd Ed.
Everything® Study Book

SELF-HELP

Everything® Dating Book, 2nd Ed.
Everything® Great Sex Book
Everything® Self-Esteem Book
Everything® Tantric Sex Book

SPORTS & FITNESS

Everything® Easy Fitness Book
Everything® Running Book
Everything® Weight Training Book

TRAVEL

Everything® Family Guide to Cruise Vacations
Everything® Family Guide to Hawaii
Everything® Family Guide to Las Vegas, 2nd Ed.
Everything® Family Guide to Mexico
Everything® Family Guide to New York City, 2nd Ed.
Everything® Family Guide to RV Travel & Campgrounds
Everything® Family Guide to the Caribbean
Everything® Family Guide to the Walt Disney World Resort®, Universal Studios®, and Greater Orlando, 4th Ed.
Everything® Family Guide to Timeshares
Everything® Family Guide to Washington D.C., 2nd Ed.

WEDDINGS

Everything® Bachelorette Party Book, $9.95
Everything® Bridesmaid Book, $9.95
Everything® Destination Wedding Book
Everything® Elopement Book, $9.95
Everything® Father of the Bride Book, $9.95
Everything® Groom Book, $9.95
Everything® Mother of the Bride Book, $9.95
Everything® Outdoor Wedding Book
Everything® Wedding Book, 3rd Ed.
Everything® Wedding Checklist, $9.95
Everything® Wedding Etiquette Book, $9.95
Everything® Wedding Organizer, 2nd Ed., $16.95
Everything® Wedding Shower Book, $9.95
Everything® Wedding Vows Book, $9.95
Everything® Wedding Workout Book
Everything® Weddings on a Budget Book, $9.95

WRITING

Everything® Creative Writing Book
Everything® Get Published Book, 2nd Ed.
Everything® Grammar and Style Book
Everything® Guide to Magazine Writing
Everything® Guide to Writing a Book Proposal
Everything® Guide to Writing a Novel
Everything® Guide to Writing Children's Books
Everything® Guide to Writing Copy
Everything® Guide to Writing Research Papers
Everything® Screenwriting Book
Everything® Writing Poetry Book
Everything® Writing Well Book